James Sta

UNDISTINGUISHED SERVICE

COMPILED BY STUART STARK

Design, typesetting and publishing by UK Book Publishing

www.ukbookpublishing.com

ISBN: 978-1-915338-31-0

UNDISTINGUISHED SERVICE

MY PART IN WORLD WAR
TWO AND OTHER MEMORIES

JAMES STARK

CONTENTS

CONTENTS

INTRODUCTION

In 1993 I received a phone call from my Father to tell me that he would no longer be able to drive, and more importantly never be able play golf again. His eyesight had been failing for some time and he had been diagnosed with macular degeneration. Unbeknown to me or my older sister my Father had decided at this juncture in his life to commit his personal memories, particularly those of his time spent in the army during the Second World War, to paper. He started writing his memoir in 1989, with only my Mother being aware of his decision to do so. Towards the end of his story his writing starts to falter as his eyesight begins to deteriorate quite badly and the book is sadly left unfinished.*

It wasn't until after my Father passed away in April 2004, aged 83, that I stumbled upon an old brief case with three handwritten blue binders inside, which at the time, I took little notice of. Fast forward a few years and I came across the binders again, but this time I sat down and started to take more interest. Fortunately, my Fathers handwriting was very legible and as I started to read each page a fascinating and almost unreal story unfolded. Like so many others who had served their country during the war, he would very rarely mention or even talk about this period in his life. When I had completed reading his memoire, I just felt so grateful that he had taken the time and effort, even though his sight had been failing, to write down his war time memories.

He had elected to hand write the original manuscript in pencil, which after such a long time, the pages were slowly starting to fade. I spent almost 180 hours over a six-month period carefully copying his 321 handwritten pages and approximately 90,000 words, word for word and paragraph by paragraph which I saved to my computer at home. I then started to think about the possibility of publishing his incredible story. To complement my Fathers text, I have collated and added some photographs from his personal collection that relate directly to this period in his life.

I am so pleased he took the time and trouble to produce such a fascinating and personal account of his moment in history.

Thank you, Dad

Stuart Stark
Middleton-in-Teesdale
County Durham

---

* Chapter Twenty - New Arrivals and MTB's, this paragraph appears:

"I was just very lucky to be in the right place at that particular time. However, becoming classified as a Specialist was to come home to roost with me seven years later in the most amazing circumstances. More of that later."

At the end of the book I have copied in two forms dated 1st January 1952 and 25th April 1952 that relate to this paragraph and due to his memoir being unfinished I cannot find anything else regarding this intriguing statement. The book finishes with no further reference to this event and there is no record of how this was concluded.

FOREWORD

It was four years ago. Norah was doing her annual spring cleaning. As usual she would dust and polish like mad but also carry out a yearly ritual of sitting on our back bedroom chair and surrounding herself with opened boxes of family memorabilia. She would then have a wonderful time remembering fond memories of bygone days, then carefully box, dust and then put them away in the cupboard for another year.

During her memorising with the past that year she discovered an old large manilla envelope which contained my Army Service Pay book, Officers Passbook and Release from Military Duty book, along with other documents relating to my war service. I knew I had kept them, along with all my medals. However, included in the envelope was a book I had completely forgotten about. It was a well-worn bright red hard covered 6" x 4" Cash Book - my Red Book - which had been with me all through my war service, issued as a sort of diary. I am looking at it now. It contains a monthly balance sheet in detail of my pay and allowances from the day I was enlisted until the day of my release. It mentions grades and promotion records and many other details. But what fascinated me most of all was that I had recorded all my postings and the dates they took place.

The discovery of my old Red Book made me start to think back about my days in uniform (all be it 50 years ago). It was the posting of information that enabled me to recall my movements in the correct sequences and I soon realised that my recollections were quite clear. I could remember names of many individuals and places being confident they were correct. Anecdotes, incidents and happenings came easily to mind, and I started taking notes. It was then I began to realise that maybe I had a rather unusual army career just a bit different from what one would expect. By no means spectacular but just out of the ordinary. I talked about it with Norah, and it was she that encouraged me to put my story down on paper. I had no difficulty in thinking about a title as "Undistinguished Service" came easily to mind.

The early part of my story is not connected with the red book as the first chapter is about my spell in the Home Guard. I remember it well as it turned out to be of vital consequence to me and my future. The dates I mention throughout my tale are accurate. The same applies to names and individuals mentioned as I am sure they are correct if not I say I cannot remember. I often remember rank but not name. I have taken the liberty on quite a few occasions to digress from my main theme by introducing details of my upbringing, family background and history, school days and other titbits. I feel they are relevant to my story in trying to describe myself as I was at that particular time of my life and mainly the six years in the history of our country when we were fighting for our survival.

It is a true story. I have tried not to embellish by adding fanciful details. I have endeavoured, maybe not successfully, to relate my feelings and emotions in particular instances as I recall them. Statistics, technical details, battle orders and information and the like I obtained from books and papers available to anyone, copies of which I have in my possession. I am fortunate to have a photograph album with pictures many of which coincide with my story and the family history side also in particular, my tour of army duties overseas.

Looking for a reason why I have gone to all this bother? That statement is not for myself as I have really enjoyed doing it. Maybe it's because one day my grandchildren will ask "What did you do during the Second World War Granddad?" It would take some explaining!

James Stark
Springfield
Elwick Road
Hartlepool
1993

MEMORABLE DATES

3rd August 1939	War declared
11th July 1940	Joined Home Guard
22nd April 1941	Enlisted at Edinburgh into Royal Army Pay Corps. Reported to Command Pay Office, Unit Accountants branch.
25th April 1941	Posted to DCRE (Deputy Commander Royal Engineers) Perth as Unit Accountant.
12th November 1941	Posted from DCRE Perth to DCRE Stirling.
25th March 1942	Promoted Corporal.
18th June 1942	Posted from DCRE Stirling to CRE (Command Royal Engineers) Glasgow.
24th June1942	Became engaged.
17th June 1943	Married.
3rd December 1943	Posted from CRE Glasgow to CE (Chief Engineers) Scottish Command HQ Edinburgh.
30th December 1943	Grade A1
21st March 1944	Posted from CE to Regimental Paymasters 31st Battalion Edinburgh.
9th May 1944	Transferred to Field Cashier Section of the Corps and appointed to Active Service Field Cashier Unit (No3). Posted to RAPC Command HQ London for special duties. Promoted Acting Sergeant.
10 May 1944	After briefing at Command HQ taken by road to Camp J7 near Uckfield, Sussex being in the assembly area for the invasion of Europe - code named Overlord.
6th June 1944	D Day.
10th July 1944	Transferred from Camp J7 to Camp J3 south of Lewes close to Newhaven - an important embarkation port.
19th August 1944	Posted back to Regimental Pay Office 31 Battalion, Edinburgh.

7th May 1945	Germany surrender.
13th May 1945	Following embarkation leave, reported to RAPC Depot, London. Then to War Office. Seconded to the Royal West African Field Forces Regiment, for Field Cashier duties.
22 May 1945	By train to Glasgow, embarked on the Queen of Bermuda bound for India.
13th June 1945	Disembarked at Bombay and sent to Kalyan Transit Camp to await further orders.
12th July 1945	By train from Bombay to New Delhi and on to Meerut.
15th July 1945	Arrived Meerut and started Field Cashier duties at the forward base pay office RWAFFR.
6th August 1945	News that Norah was pregnant. Atomic bomb dropped on Hiroshima.
14th August 1945	Japan's unconditional surrender.
15th August 1945	VJ Day.
28th August 1945	Promoted to full Sergeant.
12th September 1945	Japanese surrender accepted and signed in Singapore by Lord Mountbatten.
1st November 1945	Commissioned 2nd Lieutenant Field Cashier and Paymaster and transferred to No 11 Command - Pay Office, 83rd Battalion RAPC and posting to Southeast Asia Command (SEAC) HQ Singapore.
5th November 1945	Departed by troop train from Meerut.
8th November 1945	Arrived Calcutta.
15th November 1945	Embarked troop ship from Calcutta.
18th November 1945	Arrived Chittagong.
19th November 1945	Departed Chittagong.
25th November 1945	Disembarked Singapore.
20th January 1946	Moira born.
22 April 1946	Promoted Lieutenant and Paymaster.
17th July 1946	Embarked Singapore on the troop ship the RMS Mauretania.
3rd August 1946	Disembarked Liverpool and to York for demobilisation.
April 1952	Reserve and Auxiliary Forces (Training) Act, 1951 - enforced

Total service:	5 years 3 months 12 days
Overseas service:	1 year 2 months 12 days
Singapore – Liverpool:	9,176 nautical miles

CHAPTER ONE:
WAR IS DECLARED

War was declared at 11am on Sunday 3rd September 1939 just two days before my 19th birthday. I remember exactly where I was and what I was doing, playing golf at Turnhouse Golf Club on the outskirts of Edinburgh. I had been playing for twelve years having become a member of the Falkirk Club when I was seven and my handicap was two.

That fateful day I was playing with my great pals Ian McDonald, Gordon Shannon and another friend. We were on the 10th hole having played my second shot and we were walking our way up the hill to the green.

In those days the main road from Edinburgh to the north of Scotland ran past the clubhouse along the west side of the course. Further along on the other side of the road was the RAF Turnhouse Air Station, now Edinburgh Airport. It was a very important RAF base for fighter planes. The national emergency had been on for many months, and it was at full strength and on continual maximum alert. They had very special responsibilities namely the defence of the famous Forth Bridge and the huge Rosyth Naval base which were only a few miles away. They were two of the main enemy targets in the whole of Scotland.

From the hilly part of the course, which included the 10th green, you looked down on the airfield. I could see the runways and the parked aircraft including movements of air crews, it was that close. When the wind was from the east, we were used to the planes taking off and roaring above our heads on the hill and taking very little notice of them. Suddenly the airport sirens rang out. That was nothing unusual to us as they practiced alerts and scrambles regularly. RAF Turnhouse had been friendly with the golf course for many years. We got to know their routines, as many of the lads who were golfers frequented the club and had a round with the members. Consequently, we were always aware of any unusual "goings on". After some minutes the sirens stopped and there was a deadly silence. Suddenly the intermittent blare of hooters, a rasping roar, sent a chill down our spines as we knew that was the aircraft scramble sound - for real. Sure enough in seconds the Avro Anson fighters were roaring over our heads going east. We then had confirmation of our worst fears as we could hear in the distance the Edinburgh city sirens screaming their warning - the war was on.

Like everyone on the course we returned to the clubhouse. I recall quiet discussions taking place. We all listened to the wireless which dear old Bill Turnbull the professional brought in from his house. We heard the declaration of war by Neville Chamberlin and the news information that followed. The announcer said we had to wait for a special announcement and when it came, we all received an awful shock. German bombers had attempted to drop bombs on the Forth Bridge and nearby naval base but without any success as our fighter planes had intercepted and chased them off. Some bombs had landed in the area around Edinburgh but there were no reports of civilian causalities or damage to property.

Everyone at the Golf Course had only one thing in mind, to make for home immediately which we all did with very little being said as we all had our own private thoughts to contend with. It transpired that the local scare was not quite so serious as it had sounded. Two or three German bombers had made rather an inept attempt to have a go at the bridge and the naval base but at the sight of our fighters had jettisoned their bombs and scrambled for home. However, the incident goes down in history as the first bombs dropped on the UK of the Second World War. That single incident happening as it did immediately after war was declared had a tremendous impact on the people of the UK. It made everyone realise we really were at war and any complacency or doubts could be dispelled. We knew then we had a fight on our hands and ranks were closed and sleeves rolled up ready for the battles ahead to defeat Hitler.

When war broke out in September 1939, I was in digs at Belgrave Terrace, it was a suburb on the north side of Edinburgh, three miles from Turnhouse. My mother and I had lived in Corstorphine at 11 St Johns Avenue from early 1936 to late 1938. My father was in the Merchant Navy all his working life with the Ellerman Lines as an engineer officer at sea. He had survived the First World War although by the skin of his teeth at times! The Ellerman Lines in those days were recognised as the largest shipping company in Britain with hundreds of vessels trading all over the world. He became the youngest Chief Engineer in the company and rose to Senior Chief Engineer.

It was a tough life at sea then and father, like all other sailors, only ever got home on short leaves and therefore never really knew what home life was like. Fortunately, wives of Chiefs and Captains could join their husbands and sail with them round the European and UK coasts. Dad was promoted to Superintendent Engineer during the late half of 1938 which meant he was ashore for good at the company HQ in Liverpool.

Mum and Dad then became resident at 10 Sedbergh Road, Wallasey which was just across the river Mersey in the Wirral, Cheshire. That house was their first real home. It is quite unbelievable to contemplate nowadays that until then during twenty-one years of marriage it was the first time, they had spent more than a month together in a home of their own. Thinking about it I doubt if I was ever with them both together for more than a month at a time from the day I was born until the day Dad died. The first time he saw me I was two years and seven months old. Such was life in the Merchant Navy in the old days. Our lives always seemed to be made of the sorrow of parting and then the long and patient wait for the joy of a safe home coming. I remember it as a continual cycle all my young life. I was mad on ships from my earliest years and when asked what I wanted to be, the answer was obvious. However, Dad always discouraged me and also mother was never very enthusiastic either. I have never regretted taking that advice.

When they moved to Wallasey from Edinburgh it was arranged, I should go into digs. As I was halfway through my five year staff apprenticeship with Waddies learning the printing and stationery trade which included attending the Herriot Watt College three nights per week. Mrs McGavin was highly recommended, and I can say that again it was home from home for me. Not only that, destiny, fate, call it what you like, certainly took a hand! Mrs Mac had a daughter called Norah with an "H" and when the war started, I had already fallen in love with her.

It was a very worrying time for every family. Men were being called up into all three services by age groups and thousands were volunteers. Many had fought and survived the bloodiest war only twenty years previously 1914-1918 when over one million of our young men in their prime were slaughtered in the trenches on the Western front. Those who survived many with grown up children, yet they were ready, willing and proud to fight for their country again. They had the worry of their sons also being enlisted to fight and at a later date, their daughters being in uniform, doing dangerous duties. No wonder mothers had to be brave, full of courage and with nerves of steel.

From early 1940 we lived in expectation of an attempted German invasion. A strict blackout was imposed after dark, as air raid shelters were built, and food rationing put into being. During May of that year the Local Defence Volunteers (LDV) was formed. The name did not fit and very soon it was changed to the Home Guard. An appeal was made for men of all ages between 17 and 60 who could handle a rifle to join.

The primary objective of the force was to oppose possible landings on British soil by German parachute troops. The Home Guard was therefore made up of young men who had some time to go before their call up was due and men in reserved occupations and older men beyond call up age. The last group mentioned were very definitely in the majority being over 50's - yes and the over 60's and 70's! They had been involved in the 1914/18 war and were raring to go and could not wait to get back into uniform. It is on record that in only a few weeks over one million men had volunteered. It is true that in the very early days of the Home Guard members armed themselves with shot guns and any type of personal weapons they could find, including swords, pikes, homemade ball and chains, anything they could attack a German with.

The Home Guard was formed and developed on the proper regular army principles, with down the line command from general officers to privates. Also, from division to battalion to company with officers and noncommissioned officers, who had the previous war experience. It was not long before the battalions were equipped with rifles, automatic weapons, heavy machine guns, mortars and grenades etc. and weekend training was instituted by regular army training staff. Battledress uniform including all ammunition, greatcoats, caps, gaiters and boots were supplied - all as given to the fighting troops - and a .303 rifle. Service was unpaid but certain out of pocket expenses could be recovered.

The objective of the Home Guard was quite clear. The defence of your own locality and in no time at all every inch of the British Isles was defended. The greatest accolade they received was that within eighteen months of formation the existence of this large part time national army enabled the military authorities to liberate regular forces from the defence duties for training for overseas theatres of war.

The modern generation knows the Home Guard thanks to television, as Dad's Army but make no mistake it was a truly great army and played a vital part in winning the war in particular the victory in Europe.

CHAPTER TWO:
ENLISTMENT

Early in 1940 the national call-up was going in such a way that I knew my turn would come towards the end of the year. I was hoping my enlistment papers would be delayed enabling me to complete my apprenticeships in January 1941 but that is another story. I was going to have some months to spare, so on the 11th of July 1940 I joined the Home Guard, Edinburgh (West) Battalion, Corstorphine Company "B" Section at Gogarburn Sanatorium for mental defective patients. The company orders were to guard the southern perimeter of the RAF Turnhouse Airfield from 10.00pm to 6.00am every night for the duration of the war. I signed application forms, was accepted and reported for duty. Without delay I was kitted out and supplied with a .303 rifle and was ready for action.

There were sixteen of us in B section. I was the youngest. A few were in the 30/40 age group knowing they might eventually be called up if the war went on a few years. The reminder were veterans of the 1914/18 war. One or two had seen action in the Navy and Air Force but the others had experienced the horrors of the trenches at Flanders and the battles of Passchendaele, the Somme etc. in the army and had medal ribbons on their uniforms to prove it.

Our section was commanded by a Staff Sergeant, and he had two Sergeants under him the remainder being like myself, Privates. Those who had been in the previous war retained their rank as officers or Non-Commissioned Officers (with equivalent rank if they had been in the Navy or Air Force). The whole command structure of the Home Guard was therefore ready made from top to bottom and it followed that their experience was invaluable. That was the secret of The Home Guard's initial speed of readiness and contributed to their tremendous success.

All my colleagues in B section, like all other sections, were from Corstorphine and the surrounding area. I knew some of them when I arrived, a wonderful cross section of people, bankers, train drivers, butchers, insurance managers a headmaster of the local school all come to mind as they are in my album of photographs.

We had five sections in our Company and each section was on duty every 5th night. The Company was commanded by a Captain assisted by two Lieutenants. They visited sections regularly and would turn up at any time during the night. Rank was always respected, and we maintained discipline of a very standard. That was another reason the Home Guard was so efficient. Duties were taken very seriously as it must be remembered we really expected the Germans to land by parachute and at the same time invade us from the sea. Britain was very vulnerable in those early days and we in the local Home Guard were worried at having the Forth Bridge, Rosyth Naval Base and an RAF fighter station, well known enemy targets and right in our own back yard.

There were of course guardsmen on day duty, and they were usually men who were retired or who could fit in time during the day. The day duty HQ was not at Gogarburn but at a large farm a few miles away where they also had very good facilities. I was a member of one of the Corstorphine Company night duty sections made up of men who worked during the day.

Every fifth night, if it was during the week, I would arrive home from Waddies about 6.30 having had a fifteen-minute walk and same time train ride from our factory which was in the Stockbridge area of Edinburgh. After a meal it was not long before I had to do a bit of spit and polish, change into uniform and be ready for the army transport which arrived at the end of the road sharp 9.30. It collected and transported us to Gogarburn about four miles away. At 10.00pm promptly our section would be on parade for inspection by the staff sergeant and then we would be allotted our duties for the night.

Gogarburn Sanatorium was a large hospital for the mentally ill and the grounds covered many acres. There were several large ward buildings taking care of many patients, most of them in permanent residence, with a large staff to look after them. The main Edinburgh to Glasgow Road ran along the north side of the grounds and across the road not far away and separated by some fields was the aerodrome. We were able to keep an eye on things from our side of the main road. Our orders were to patrol within the boundary of the Sanatorium grounds as we had a good view of the road and the surrounds. On the aerodrome side the RAF regiment lads who were specially trained to guard airfields were continually on patrol and had regular liaisons with us.

Our guard duties were in four shifts 10-12, 12-2, 2-4 and 4-6 in pairs. We did the job properly walking up and down the perimeter with our loaded rifles in sling position on our shoulders in all weathers in the pitch dark for two hours, reporting each half hour to the Guard room. During each two hours there was another man on duty. He was in the Guard Room beside the telephones. We had outside lines, also field telephones connecting us with the RAF and a whole series of routines to go through. His most important duty however was to have a hot mug of tea ready for the sentries when they reported in the middle part of their watch. It was therefore routine that 12 men had specific duties between 10.00pm and 6.00am. Those not on duty always had plenty to do between 10 and 12 usually instruction. It was important we got to know all about the .303 rifle as it had just been stuck in our hands to get on with. We also received instruction about automatic rifles such as the Sten and Bren guns, hand grenades, mortars and stick bombs etc. If we were lucky and not on sentry duty that night, it was bed around 12.30 until 5.30 in the morning. we had comfortable camp beds with plenty of blankets, but we had to sleep in what I think in army jargon was called "emergency awareness" meaning everything on! It was disturbed sleep with guards changing every two hours.

We had excellent accommodation and facilities. we had the use of the Sanatorium's large concert hall from 9.30pm to 6.30am. Our sleeping quarters were on the stage with plenty of room. We could use the main part of the hall for parading, drilling and army instruction. We had the use of the kitchen with all mod cons and always had food left for us by the nursing staff. In fact, we guardsmen were spoilt rotten! The outhouses had been given over to us permanently and were ideal for use as a guard room and armoury. I recall the day duty guardsmen came over and checked them out every day. I soon got used to being on duty every 5th night. On one or two occasions we were taken on a Saturday night to Redford Barracks outside Edinburgh for Army instruction by the famous Royal Scots Regimental instructors. I also remember being with them at the firing butts in the Pentland Hills using live ammunition. We were ready for the Germans if they tried to land near us!

I was in a great squad at Gogarburn although all the others were older than myself. We had many a laugh and a few frights. A few stick out in my memory. I think it was on the 4th shift, 4-6 one night when two of us were on sentry duty in the quiet pitch black. suddenly and without any warning one of the inmates jumped out from behind some bushes and trees right in front of us, yelling his head off! We got one hell of a fright and he was wearing only a white night shirt. It turned out he had escaped from a ward with the intention of giving us a fright. We had a problem taking him back to the ward as we had been warned to be careful how we handled patients as they could be awkward.

The RAF boys often tried to scare us and one night set off a yellow (stand by) alarm, pandemonium broke out all over the place. An official enquiry was held, and they got a real ticking off, luckily our section was not on duty. Our armoury was, I suppose, 10 - 12 feet square with no windows just air vents. One night a sergeant and myself were testing rifles and inserting dummy rounds I think to check firing pins. How it happened we never got to know but a live round somehow had found its way in amongst the dummies! In a flash yours truly and a sergeant were on the floor with a bullet ricocheting from wall to wall above our heads. One of us could quite easily have been killed. We of course had to report the incident.

An official enquiry was held but fortunately no further action was taken against us. The sergeant I was with had the presence of mind to call the staff sergeant immediately and ask him to check the ammunition stock, which he found correct. It was an unsolved mystery, but it made us realise we were taking part in times that could be dangerous and not just playing war games. It was for real, and we always had to realise that fact.

I have the most vivid recollection of what happened at 5.30am every morning. One of the inmates became a great pal of the Home Guard. He was deformed and had a hunch back and a limp and really was like the Hunchback of Notre Dame in the film and he had a very loud rough voice. The Sanatorium awoke at 5.30am but our pal was up at 5.00 and made for the concert hall. He then proceeded to brew up a gallon or more of strong black tea. At about 5.30 he would then - I can see him now - stand in the middle of the stage and bellow "Wake up, wake up, wake up, you bastards!" and howl with raucous laughter. He would then proceed to shove into your hand a thick hospital pint mug of his scalding hot black tea. You were awake and sitting up immediately you heard his voice, and he had a habit of sloshing the tea around and we were all scared of being scalded for life! He was a simpleton but would do anything for us and in fact became a sort of mascot to the Home Guard and loved by everyone and devoted to us all. He received many a present of cigarettes and pocket money. We gave him a fancy name which he adored but I cannot remember it!

I have mentioned that many of my Home Guard colleagues were 1914/18 war veterans. I was a young lad of twenty about to take part in another bloody war but much greater than the previous one. I wanted to know what I was in for and asked questions and obtained answers. I am sure they opened up and talked more freely to me about their experiences than they had done to anyone else. In 1914 they had been my age. Come Armistice Day they were twenty-four to twenty-five and many of them were lucky indeed to be alive. The very last thing they expected was to be involved in another war aged between forty-seven and fifty. Not only that, most of them had sons and daughters who could also become involved. So here they were in battle dress uniform again, on guard duty again, carrying over their shoulders a .303 rifle again, with live ammunition up the spout again, and orders to shoot and kill Germans again! No wonder they were anxious to talk about their experiences and give advice and warnings to a young lad like me. I listened and took part in numerous discussions during my many hours on duty with them and what they said sunk into me and was to be of tremendous value in the future. I reached the conclusion that one single piece of advice was a common factor. It was, never but never volunteer for any duty but take things as they come and accept them. Your destiny is then in the hands of the Good Lord! I can say with all honesty and truth that from the day I was enlisted I never once volunteered but accepted what came my way without question. Maybe as my story unfolds that is the reason why the Good Lord did look over me during my five and half years in the army.

During the second half of 1940 the British Army had been badly beaten in Europe by the Germans. They had however fought a wonderful rear guard action culminating in the evacuation at Dunkirk. It was a bad blow to the country's morale, but we had Churchill to give us confidence. Nevertheless, a young man of my age looked ahead with some apprehension and worried for themselves and their loved ones as the future was uncertain, but the Home Guard had given me a lot of confidence and stimulation which was to see me through the war.

During 1940 the Armed Forces Compulsory Enlistment act was geared to accept all young men as soon as they reached their 20th birthday and for me that was the 5th of September. My five-year apprenticeship with Waddies was due to end on the 14th of January 1941. I realised and so did my boss that those four and a half months were crucial to me. The reason being that if I did not complete my full time, I would be compelled to complete an extra year on my return after the war. That was the rule laid down by the Scottish Master Printers for anyone taking diploma exams as I was.

The war office was very strict about delaying call-up dates and usually only considered exempting the likes of university students studying for their finals. Nothing daunted my superiors at Waddies, namely Mr. Ward the Chairman and Managing Director, Miss McDonald the Company Secretary and Mr. Thomson the Works Manager between them they wrote a letter to the War Office and sent it off. I have no idea what they said but it must have been convincing because some time later an official OHMS letter arrived saying my call-up was deferred until after the 31st of January 1941.

Being in the 5th year of my apprenticeship at Waddies I had been through all the departments including factory and office and was then in the most important one of the lot for me, namely Costing and Estimating. Because of war time staff difficulties, I was assisting Mr. J A Thomson the Works Manager (JAT as he was affectionately known). He was one of the old school, kind, considerate and so keen to pass on his knowledge of the printing trade which was second to none. In many ways I have him to thank for any success I had with the company. When I was demobbed and returned to the company, I was fortunate enough to be taken under his wing in the works department. I was twenty-six and became his assistant works manager. Bob McKie who took over from JAT as Works Manager when he retired was a great friend and eventually became Production Director and sat on the main board with me. (In 1948 I was transferred from Production to Sales Manager at our London Office)

It is interesting to recall my return in 1946. It is so easy to forget the many problems caused by the war, when peace arrived and just how serious and awkward, they could be. The Emergency Electrical Power Act was one of them. The reason being that many power stations throughout the UK had been bombed and were being rebuilt. Therefore, not enough electricity was being generated to cover the daily demand and to avoid overloading, which could be serious, electricity had to be rationed in the winter months. The problem was overcome by all factories producing 50% of their goods during the day and 50% during the night. I was given the responsibility of sharing with Bob McKie the night shift working. We did it through the two long winters of 1947/48. We each worked one week on days and one week on nights 10pm to 8am. When Bob was on days I was on nights and vice-versa changing over at weekends. We really took terrific punishment during those winters as our body systems became disorientated as time went on.

Bob was about three years older than me and had a lot more production experience. I was thrown in at the deep end as it was all lithographic and letterpress departments running during the night. They were big departments with a lot of machines of all sizes going full bore and having tough old department foreman to deal with. Somehow, I survived and the learning and experience I gained in these two years was tremendous. I got to know all about the technical side of printing production and the cost of doing so and coupled with my paper warehouse training I could cost and estimate jobs with reasonable accuracy.

I was later to discover that the Directors had noted the experience I had gained during the two winters of production responsibility and thought that I might be worth a trial "on the road". It happened that I found myself, quite suddenly, transferred to the Sales Department on trial on the 1st of July 1948. On the 4th of October that year I was on my way to London and never looked back. When I retired at the end of 1980, I had clocked up forty-five years with the company and had been a main board member for twenty-one years.

CHAPTER THREE:
7680868 PRIVATE
STARK J. RAPC

The 21st of January passed and so did March in 1941 but in early April the OHMS envelope arrived containing many forms for completion and a request that I attend the Army Medical Centre, Assembly Rooms, George Street, Edinburgh for a medical examination. It was only then that I knew for certain it was the Army for me and not the Navy as Mother and Father expected it to be.

I duly reported and a surprise was awaiting me. The doctor said my heart had an overbeat and I was given medical grade B1 which meant non-active service. He said I would be called for another medical in six months. It was a shock to me as I fully expected to be A1 and I had always felt fit having played golf regularly since I was seven.

Thousands of young men were being called up for service and you were either very fit, fairly fit or not so fit and I happened to be in the second category. There was never any animosity between pals, friends and families. The whole country was in a serious and determined mood with everyone pulling their weight. Along the way they were accepting and coping with good luck and bad, happiness and sorrow, courage and fear, to beat any grudges. At that time everyone realised that the risk of being killed or maimed for life was about 50/50 either in or out of uniform due to the destruction being done throughout the country by German bombers.

Unknown to me then my B1 grading was the first significant factor which guided me on my career along an amazing path of good fortune.

My enlistment papers duly arrived saying I had to report for my military service with The Royal Army Pay Corps, Command Pay Office, Scottish Command, Unit Accountants Branch, Randolph Crescent, Edinburgh at 9.00am on 22nd April 1941. I remember thinking that this request sounded a bit peculiar and odd. It was only a twenty minute tram ride away into the West End and a few minutes' walk down to Randolph Crescent which contained very posh and elegant houses of great architectural quality.

I now refer to the many forms received for completion, some via me and others from my employers. One of them which had to be completed and signed by Waddies asked what my specific job was at the time within the Company. W Thomson entered correctly "Cost Accountant". That simple entry without any doubt turned out to be a significant factor for me.

I duly reported in good time and discovered that many of the houses in Randolph Crescent had been requisitioned. I found myself in a large very pleasant office with Army, ATS and civilian personnel hustling about. In no time I was in a large private office in front of a big desk behind which sat a rather austere rotund officer certainly in his 50's called Captain Scott who was the Chief Unit Accountant of Scottish Command. He had a file in front of him which obviously contained the forms and reports relating to one James Stark. He did not say much. I was a cost accountant - yes - the very man he was looking for as cost accountants were very hard to come by. He made me feel I was a very highly qualified one at that - not just an apprentice in the printing trade. He had answered yes, not me, in fact I said nothing except "Good morning!" He was not interested in anything else about me and shunted me off to another office where a sergeant was awaiting my arrival. I completed many documents, one which said I would receive the standard rate of pay for a soldier joining namely, 2/6 per day (£0.125p).

Everyone was very nice and friendly, and I was eventually told to report at the RAPC Quartermasters Stores to be kitted out in uniform and then go home! I really thought they were joking and playing a rookie trick on me. The kind they played on first day lads in the factory - "Go upstairs to Jock Brown and ask for a long stand" routine.

Every soldier when enlisted no matter what medical grade had to commence immediately six to eight weeks weekly basic training at an appropriate training camp. That was well known standard procedure. I had phoned my mother and father the night before, kissed Norah and her mother goodbye in the expectation of being on my way to or at a Training Camp somewhere that night. I eventually realised that they were not pulling my leg and went off to the Quartermasters Stores.

I was kitted out from top to bottom with all the standard gear inside and outside. With the exception of the greatcoat, it was all put in a huge kit bag, and I remember struggling home on the tramcar during the afternoon to the surprise of Mrs Mac and Norah when she arrived home from work.

The following morning 23 April 1941 I was a soldier of the King, 7680868 Private Stark. J. RAPVC reporting for duty at Randolph Crescent. Thank goodness for the Home Guard, at least I knew how to wear a uniform and most important had the know how about wearing new army boots, as it was obvious no one was going to bother telling me. In no time at all I was again in front of Captain Scott, on this occasion having given a salute of sorts, stood to attention and called him Sir. I remember he handed me a sheet of paper which was headed Scottish

Command Orders of the Day, which had many paragraphs, but one had red pencil lines on either side which immediately caught my eye. I cannot recall the exact wording, but it said to the effect - 7680868 Private Stark. J. RAPC to be posted on 25th April 1941 to DCRE Perth as a Unit Accountant. The Captain said something like "Good luck Stark, I'll see you in Perth when on my rounds and the Sergeant will get you up today and tomorrow, dismissed!". I was absolutely bewildered. DCRE, unit accountant, what the hell did all that mean? I spent the next two days, as the Captain said, receiving lots of information, and there was plenty of it to receive.

I feel at this point in my story it will be easier to understand if I explain the meaning of DCRE namely - Deputy Commander Royal Engineers. The mention of Royal Engineers to most people including military personnel conjured up of bridge building over rivers and ravines, the dangerous job of mine laying or mine defusing, bomb defusing and disposal, building and making new roads through the jungle etc. They were always up front in the battles where the going was toughest doing the specialised work with tremendous courage and bravery. It was maybe forgotten they had very important duties at home on a large scale which were not generally known about but very essential to the war effort. Come to think about it my story is about drawing attention to certain aspects of what went on behind the scenes during the war and that was generally not known about.

By April 1941 the call-up of our men and women had been in full swing for eighteen months. Thousands of fighting men into Britain from the Colonial Empire and many Europeans had come in at Dunkirk. (An awful lot more were to come as the Americans were not yet in the war.) Accommodation had to be found for everyone. Barracks had to be extended and new ones built. Hospitals extended and new ones built. All sorts of military establishments were necessary including training camps and prisoner of war camps, all had to be built. The list was endless. These requirements made it necessary to requisition estates, including stately homes, to be used as hospitals, headquarters, communication centres etc. Also requisitioned were office blocks, warehouses, hotels and sometimes ordinary homes, football grounds, golf courses and so on. It was a huge undertaking and commitment costing millions of pounds in contracts and had to be handled and accounted for by professional experts in civilian life now in or seconded to the Army. They all came under the jurisdiction and command of their professional counterparts in the regular army namely The Royal Engineers.

They had a huge and most efficient organisation that covered every square foot of the United Kingdom.

The senior officers were: -

CE Chief Engineer - Colonel
CRE Commander Royal Engineers - Lieutenant Colonel
DCRE Deputy Commander Royal Engineers - Major
In Scotland the command structure was: -
CE at Scottish Command HQ - Edinburgh
CRE Glasgow / CRE Edinburgh
DCRE's Glasgow / DCRE's Edinburgh

From memory Scotland was divided up into 12 areas with a DCRE responsible for each area. Their officers were in strategic towns and cities such as - Inverness, Aberdeen, Perth, Stirling, Dumfries and others. More officers were concentrated in and around the huge conurbations of Glasgow and Edinburgh. Each DCRE was responsible to one of the CRE's who in turn answered to "The Chief" at HQ. The CE and CRE's were regular soldiers highly qualified in Civil Engineering, Architecture and Surveying. The DCRE's were similarly qualified some being regular others enlisted into the army from the large building and construction companies.

Each DCRE had his own office and staff which included a few army personnel usually ATS who were drivers as transport was a priority. The majority were civilian's male and female. Drawing office draughtsmen, surveyors, clerks of work, office managers, contracts finance clerks, typists etc. Staff one would find in any large building or construction company. It was an exempt occupation. Almost all the work was contracted out. Huge monetary contracts were issued regularly. The army had a very strict code of practice and regulations which had stood the test of time for keeping a tight central control on all works, administration and costs. Each area command throughout the UK had similar RE set-ups to that of Scottish Command. It is also worth keeping in mind that the Royal Navy and RAF looked after themselves and had their own similar organisations.

So it came to pass that on the 25th April 1941 on only my fourth day in the army and still not a word about training. I said goodbye to Norah and her Mum again. I must have felt a bit apprehensive, and no doubt looked a real rookie in my brand new uniform and kit. I had been issued with a train warrant and was soon on my way to Perth all on my own into the unknown world of the RAPC, DCRE, CRE, CE, RE and hundreds of other abbreviations I was about to discover!

Transport was awaiting me at Perth station, and I was taken to the DCRE office. It was situated in what had been a beautiful big house standing in its own grounds at the top of a hill in the residential part of town. I reported to the Unit Accountant, who was a Staff Sergeant named David Pountney and his Corporal assistant. They had a very pleasant office which had been a large bedroom overlooking the gardens.

Staff Pountney was a cockney, a regular soldier, had enlisted as a boy, been most of his service in the Pay Corps and a long time in the Unit Accountants branch. He had also been on many tours of duties overseas. He knew army regulations relating to RAPC/RE backwards, word for word, could hardly speak the Kings English, talked in army jargon and like many cockneys was a wizard with figures. I discovered later that he was the reason I was sent to Perth. Great urgency was required, and it was well known that he was the man who would stuff my head with Unit Accountants duties and regulations in such a way that I would need ever forget them. I can defiantly vouch for that fact!

I was given a desk, chair and cupboard space so to be ready for action the following day. There was still no word about my initial army training. In fact, Staff Pountney was horrified and just could not believe that I had been posted without army training. His language reaction startled me. It was something like "Good God Almighty and you have been attached to the Black Watch for F and L", (which I discovered stood for food and lodgings). I was soon to realise why he reacted with such venom.

The Black Watch was one of the oldest and most famous of the Scottish regiments. Notorious for their discipline and producing fearless fighting men in their kilts and Tam O'Shanter head gear with the proud red hackle. They had put the town of Perth on the map as it had always been their headquarters and their large barracks was a landmark. It was stone walled round its boundary not unlike a prison and entered through massive iron gates. Inside the main feature was an enormous tarmacadamed parading square the size of a football pitch. The square was surrounded on each side by a three-storey black stoned tenement style barrack block which housed hundreds of men in spartan conditions to say the least. There were many additional blocks for officers, officers mess, sick bay, weapon training, transport and offices etc. It was in effect a self-contained regimental headquarters with everything running like clockwork and buzzing with action day and night as I was about to discover.

The DCRE transport took me down to the barracks and through the main gate and dumped me and my kit outside the Orderly Room where I waited for quite some time. An RAPC private, obviously a rookie, suddenly arriving on their doorstep with his kit was a most unusual occurrence. It took the Orderly Room Sergeant time and trouble to find an order saying I was to be with them on attachment for food and lodgings. I can remember my first impressions of the barracks. They were certainly ancient but everything about them was so clean, scrubbed, painted, polished and with white edging lines painted along every road which were swept at regular intervals. Every soldier in sight and there were many, was immaculate with an army haircut, scrubbed face, sharp crease in trouser or kilt pleats, boots spit and polished to shine and everyone walking at marching pace.

The Orderly Room Sergeant left me in no doubt that immediately I put a foot in the barracks I was subject to their rules, regulations and discipline. I would always walk at marching pace except when on or around the perimeter of the square when I would march to attention. I would always give eyes right or left and perfect salute to all officers and not only call him "Sir" but also the Regimental Sergeant Major and the Company Sergeant Majors. Also, when addressing a Sergeant, I would shout "Sergeant". I was escorted to one of the buildings and into a ground floor barn of a place known as the Disposal Unit. I was given a few square feet in a flat corner of the stone floor which had three heavy wooden timbers 6' x 1' wide, placed on two trestles, one at each end of the floor. I was issued with a straw filled pillowcase and two heavy army blankets. There was a wooden locker, which had seen better days, for my gear. That was my lot and my living quarters. I was petrified. Here I was amid one of the roughest, toughest regiments in the British Army at their headquarters where discipline could only be described as fierce. I had only been in the army four days and did not even know how to salute correctly. My effort was alright for the Home Guard but certainly not to the standard expected by the Black Watch. Worse still was that I did not then know a word of jargon and often just did not understand what was being said to me.

In the Disposal Unit there were rows upon rows of similar beds to mine. There were continual comings and goings day and night maybe one or two lads, or maybe a hundred or so lads, with all their kit bags leaving to join various battalions or regiments. Not too far away there were huge wash houses with basins, showers and latrines, all old fashioned but very clean. There was always plenty of hot water and like every inch of the barracks thoroughly inspected for cleanliness by orderly officers every day.

The same applied to the cookhouses and mess. It was a huge place with long wooden tables and bench seats. There were three serving areas and we queued up with our Billy cans in each hand. Right for main course and everything in together and left for pudding. Separately they had huge churns with hot strong tea for your tin mug. The food was basic but very well cooked and plenty of it and under the circumstances, enjoyable. The Cookhouse Orderly Officer was always doing the rounds and any complaint was always listened to and if necessary, received instant attention.

Fear made me learn all the routines with great urgency and the only way I could do so was by copying other soldiers. Always being ultra-smart, sleeping on my carefully folded trousers to keep them creased, cleaning badges and buttons, making boots shine and doing it all every night before lights out. The eagle eye of the Sergeant and Sergeant Majors were on you immediately after breakfast and I always had to pass a few of them on my way out. The gutter language they used appalled me until I got used to it and came to understand what they were saying.

The Black Watch had one of the famous Regimental Sergeant Majors who was certainly a magnificent specimen and knew it, of at least 6' 4" in his kilt with his rank stick always under his left arm. He had a voice that made the old buildings and everyone in them shudder and could be heard a good distance away from the barracks. The Company Sergeant Majors and the Drill Sergeants were all members of the same tribe in other words they treated all lower ranks like muck and to put it mildly were unmitigated bastards. I came under their wrath on a few occasions usually when I had to cross or be on the surrounds of the Holy Ground namely, The Square. I had never been taught in the Home Guard how to march to attention which I found very difficult but tried my best by watching others. I would suddenly receive a great expletive bellow from a distance but when they realised it was me, just dirt, they would ask me to proceed - in the politest way! I stood out a mile in ordinary army headgear and no doubt in other ways as well.

With the complete change of environment, atmosphere, lifestyle call it what you may, I was always ready for bed and slept quite well considering the strange bed and movements and noise which often took place. There was however one event which happened every single morning which took some getting used to. At precisely 6.00am a bugler marched into the centre of the barrack room and sounded reveille at full blast which also wakened the dead! Ablutions were at 6.30, breakfast at 7.00, roll call 7.45, inspection parade 8.00. I was excused the later as being on duty myself at 8.00 and having twenty minutes' walk to the office. Like lunch, breakfast was good. I recall one billy-can being filled with porridge and the other with a huge grill of everything plus of bread, butter and tea.

Another incident comes to mind about the barracks. It concerned the special pass I had. It must have been waiting for me the day I arrived as it did cause something of a stir. It said I had freedom of movement in or out of the barracks at any time of day or night. It was signed by the DCRE and countersigned by the Black Watch Adjutant. Keeping in mind that during war time a serviceman could not move away from his allotted place of duty without a pass, it was essential I had one. It was right that it was nigh impossible to get either in or out of the barracks without a pass. There were guards on round the clock duty and every person had to pass through the Orderly Room where an officer and Sergeant were always on duty. They changed regularly and a new face would often confront me. I soon realised an awkward situation was arising which I had the feeling was a jealous complex especially from the Sergeants. They just did not like the wording on my pass. They would make me wait a long time saying the officer was not available and think up some sort of excuse. Eventually their attitude came to the surface when one of the Sergeants made me wait ages and became very objectionable and said something like "Who the hell are you a Pay Corps Private who has a day and night open ended pass!" Summing up courage I shouted "Sergeant, I am the Unit Accountant to the Deputy Commander of the Royal Engineers in Perth. Please let me through without any further delay or I shall report you to him and your Adjutant!" He had just no answer to that grand sounding speech which took him (and me) completely by surprise and he let me through. I was learning fast and gaining confidence. The word soon got around, and I had no more further bother during the rest of my stay at the barracks.

CHAPTER FOUR:
PERTH

The day after I arrived in Perth and reported for duty Staff Pountney set about stuffing me with Unit Accountant rules and regulations and how to carry them out and the authority I had in doing so. He also explained the very important working relationship I would have with the Royal Engineers. I discovered every DCRE had at least one RAPC Unit Accountant and the CRE's three or four. We worked flat out for about a week, working until night, culminating in a meeting with the DCRE himself. He confirmed what staff Pountey had anticipated that with the agreement of Captain Scott I was being appointed Unit Accountant for Hutting Dumps, under his control and situated near St. Andrews and Falkirk. (I was quick to discover that a Dump was an army terminology for storage place i.e., petrol dump, ammunition dumps etc.)

The DCRE explained about what I have already mentioned being the terrific urgency about expanding existing establishments and building new ones especially training camps. It was now red alert orders from the War Office and Churchill which caused Hutting to become a number one priority. With all this in mind he said how delighted he was that a "Cost Accountant" had been posted to him. It is a wonder I wasn't a nervous wreck!

Both the DCRE and Staff admitted that the accounting for the stock at the Dumps was in a shambles and months behind. The position was that the Army Audit Branch was on the backs of the CE and CRE's requesting very definitive action. Even in war time, heads could roll, and regular officers' careers be in jeopardy. But that as it may it was not going to be long before I discovered the real cause of the trouble. Hutting Dumps had only come into existence with the war. In peace time when Hutting was required it just went through the system like any other item and holding in stock was not necessary because of low demand. When war started the request for Hutting increased tremendously and eventually to such an extent that it developed into a huge business project for the Royal Engineers. Large Dumps had to be prepared and located in strategic positions throughout the UK. They had to be staffed, administered and accounted for and many DCRE's were given this additional responsibility adding to the already very heavy workload and the DCRE was one of them.

What had happened was that Hutting had become a bit of a nuisance. It was not mentioned in any of the manuals and therefore there was no finger pointing and quite specifically to where or to whom the responsibility lay. This was most unusual as "who carried the can" has always been quite clear and never in any doubt in all three British Services. A "nobody's baby" situation had developed and in no time the baby had grown into a giant which had become out of hand all along the line. That was when and why I came on the scene. My orders from the DCRE were that I had a free hand to sort things out at the three Dumps. I would have to use public transport but would be issued with bus and train travel warrants, lodging and food allowance, also a special duty ration book when I was staying away which would be often. I would also be given a special pass which would cover me with Military Police and other authorities on all my travels.

I must have thought to myself that all this was amazing and ridiculous. Here I am the lowest of the low, Private pay 17/6 (0.87p) per week, all in! Only in the army five minutes about to check, record and price stock valued at many thousands of pounds which are the responsibility of a Captain (the rank of all Dumps commanding Officers) and I have direct access to his boss. However, I was to discover the Army often worked in mysterious ways at times and more often than not - certainly with the Royal Engineers - with great efficiency and few loopholes as their systems were always fairly watertight.

All DCRE's and their staff were responsible for placing contracts. Regarding Hutting, the contract orders were given in the main to timber mills who manufactured them in sections which could easily be joined together. Contracts also had to be awarded for the ancillary items such as glass, down pipes, roof insulation, stoves for heating etc. It was in fact the birth of the famous Nissen Hut which still can be seen around today. From memory I can give a good example of what might happen.

Following all the preliminary work and the discussions made by the appropriate top brass, a site being chosen, and agreement reached with landowner and local authority etc. a training camp and barracks would be required. It could be to house the one to two thousand or more troops and built and completed from start to finish in a month. A typical kind of war time request as so much would depend on it being completed on time. That included an awful lot of timbered sections, also beds, tables, chairs, cupboards and shelves, heating and so on. Keeping in mind also the building of the foundations, drawing office work, contracts, a place for every single item, all the administration and above all, not forgetting - people. On site workshops, erecting teams, foremen, clerk of works and others often working 24-hour shifts. Night working in black-out conditions using very restricted lighting. I have illustrated one order from hundreds a Dump would receive to give an idea what the overall situation was like at the time, and it was easy to understand it could soon get out of hand.

When the DCRE informed me and said I had access to him and his staff I detected a great sense of relief coming over Staff Pountney, just as if a load had been taken of his shoulders. He had been shouting, as best he could, for help from Captain Scott which had fallen on deaf ears until the captain himself had received a kick up the pants from the Audit Branch which made him grab the first Cost Accountant - so called - who appeared on the scene! Staff admitting knowing next to nothing about Hutting, which I soon discovered as was the case with all the regular army fellows having only come to life since war started. He was therefore only too pleased to leave everything in my good hands, to deal with the DCRE and his staff and leave him out of it. The nuisance value was showing and being a regular he did not want a black mark on his all-important record file.

I could not have been full of confidence when I got myself ready for my first tour of duty was to Oldmeldrum some thirty miles north of Aberdeen. My Red Book tells me I travelled by train and bus on the 6th of May 1941 and was away for six days. I discovered all Hutting Dumps were similar in layout and personnel. In control was the Commanding Officer, a Captain with an assistant always a senior NCO usually a CSM(Q) Company Sergeant Major Quartermaster. All other staff were civilians headed by a Chief Clerk. Some were for office work but the majority handling and loading etc. which was heavy work. The Dumps took up a lot of ground and always had at least one large hanger like building and other smaller ones for all their stocks. There was continual movement of goods in and out. I received a warm welcome at Oldmeldrum as it was obvious from the C.O. that a permanent link was essential between them and DCRE. I was soon deeply immersed in CRV's and CIV's namely Certified Receipt Vouchers and Certified Issue Vouchers which were to become part of my daily life for the next three years although I did not know it then. They were the key that controlled all transactions, and their importance was just absolute as far as I was concerned and right from the start made that known and built my system around them.

I cannot remember who I lodged with at Oldmeldrum for the six days and during any of my other visits. I am certain it would be with the family of one of the staff at the Dump which was usual. I was always made welcome and very well looked after and always asked if I would come again next time. There was good reason for all the fuss. They received ration allowance for me 3s 3d per day plus lodging allowance of 1s 3d per day making 4s 6d (0.22p) per day. Sounds nothing nowadays but there was an important bonus my special ration book which entitled them to generous extra rations. Manna from Heaven and worth its weight in gold.

There was a huge backlog of paperwork at Oldmeldrum but with the help of the C.O. and other office staff I must have developed a system which was to stand the test of time because I used it from then on. I have very happy memories of my Hutting Dump days. I must have been able to overcome rank problems and any animosity which could have developed because of my rather awkward position. I am sure right from the start I made it my aim to be trusted and to play the game fairly and gain and retain their confidence especially that of the C.O.

A wonderful piece of news was awaiting me on my return from Oldmeldrum. I was leaving the barracks and going into a private billet. I had been told it would happen as it had been agreed at HQ that Unit Accountants should be in private billets as freedom of movement was essential for them to carry out their duties. It might be necessary to attach them to a local barracks until billets could be found as was in my case. The point had been proved as I was a dammed nuisance to the Black Watch in every respect especially the freedom of movement bit. We came to understand each other's problems, but they were glad to see the back of me and I of them. It had made me realise what the infantry was like, and I was not impressed.

I was lucky with my billet. It was a council house on quite a new estate about twenty minutes' walk from the office. Mr. and Mrs. MacDonald were a wonderful couple and did everything possible to make me comfortable. Their only son who was about my age was in the Royal Artillery had just recently been married and was stationed down south. I sort of took his place and they made it home from home for me. In a very short time, I had met their neighbours and friends and was often invited into their homes. Norah came up to Perth on a couple of occasions and they made her so welcome.

Mr. MacDonald was a wonderful character, in fact they both were. He worked for the local authority highways section which included being a grave digger and always had plenty of stories to tell. In those days I doubt if he would earn much more than three pounds a week so the 34s/5d (£1.72p) per week they received for me was more than welcome. But the extra rations they were entitled to as well was really something special.

I have a story to tell about Mr. MacDonald and his pipe smoking. I've often told it to fellow pipe smokers who considered it unique. As it happens, I can speak with a great deal of experience as I stopped smoking in 1987 when I realised a pipe had been in my mouth every day for 50 years. I was one of the very few who started smoking a pipe at 17 and not cigarettes and continued to do so. Mr. MacDonald smoked large bore Louie Pipes, a famous make and expensive even in those days. On the fireplace hearth in the sitting room a bowl of rum was permanently in place which he kept topped up. After his evening meal sitting up in his fireside chair, he would take a pipe from the bowl which had been steeping in the rum from the previous evening. Then with a clean rag he would tenderly wipe the pipe with great care and place it on the mantelpiece. It would be ready for smoking the next day. He would then take the pipe he was smoking that day bring from his pocket Bogey Roll Tobacco which was jet black and manufactured and sold in continuous small roles, dreadful looking stuff. He would carefully peel away with his sharp penknife small pieces from the end of the roll, rub them down between the palms of his hands then take out from the bowl what remained of his previous pipeful and mix it with his freshly rubbed down tobacco put the mixture back in his pipe and light up. The Bogey Roll and rum mixture must have been the most pungent ever to come out of any pipe. He tried hard to make me smoke a pipeful, but I had some respect for my lungs as it must have been like smoking hell fire. This ritual went on every day and a rum steeped pipe was always ready for him every evening. Mrs. Macdonald smoked cigarettes like a chimney and my pipe was seldom out of my mouth. When we were all together during an evening the whole house must have had a blue/ black smokescreen. I wonder what Mr. MacDonald's inner tubes were like. He would likely live until a hundred!

After returning from Oldmeldrum I spent some time linking my systems to the DCRE routine and in particular with their established costing and accounting set-up. The contract arrangements, prices, costs etc. were their province, mine was the Dump stock but the two had to be finally linked together and recorded. That was the accountant's job.

I soon had to visit the Dumps at St. Andrews and Falkirk and put them on the same stock accounting footing. I stayed a few days at each place until I cleared the backlog. Like at Oldmeldrum I found everyone very cooperative, and I got on well with the C.O. and his staff and again found excellent lodgings. My luck again was quite amazing because my aunt and uncle lived in Falkirk and only a mile or so from the Dump. They had a room for me, and I therefore had ready-made digs any time I was there. In fact, I could see in the distance from their house where I was born, so I really was on my home ground, but more of that later.

As time went on at Perth, I found myself becoming more involved with the DCRE and his technical and contract staff than with my RAPC colleagues. Staff Pountney never bothered me as he and his Corporal were loaded with the other accounting work for DCRE. Captain Scott was very happy the way things were going, and, on his inspection visit, made it clear I was to carry on working with DCRE in other words to continue doing my own thing. I did not realise it at the time, and it certainly was not intentional, but I was gradually building up a little empire for myself. My record system was such that when a Hutting request or problem arose within the DCRE office it was realised that Starky should be contacted as he could give the answer. It must be remembered that everything was urgent at that time and usually legitimately so. It followed that the planners, clerks of works, site managers were often in contact with me, and I would be asked to sit in at a meeting with my books handy.

It was a time when there was urgency and determination about the whole country which had closed ranks to beat the Germans. A working day was twenty-four hours and there was as much work and activity going on during the night as there was during the day. Every person was under some sort of pressure and kept going and morale never flagged. I was working long hours but the only night duties I recall were either fire watching or invasion emergencies which were usually false alarms or rehearsals which could happen frequently. I was always officially on call if in Perth and made sure I knew exactly where to go and what to do when the sirens sounded. In a local emergency every person in army uniform was under the command of the Black Watch and knew it and would not dream of stepping out of line. I keep repeating how I welcomed my Home Guard training because I still had not received any initial training. There was always a feel at the back of my mind that this situation would be discovered, and I would be whisked off for six weeks to the Black Watch Training Centre, perish the thought!

I was enjoying the army. I was in effect my own boss, I had a cosy private billet, could see Norah regularly, could travel the countryside with freedom and comfort by bus and train, my job was interesting and really quite important, I was only a Private but so what, I was just accepting what came along and being paid every week. My Red Book shows I was able to fit in my first leave from the 17th to 24th September 1941 when I travelled to Wallasey to see my mother and father. I also noticed my grade and pay had increased from Private C111B to C111 was worth an extra 3s 3d (0.16p) per day - and don't forget, all in - my finances were on the increase!

It must have been early in November I was told to attend a meeting in the Major's office with Captain Scott and was surprised to find also the DCRE Stirling and two officers from the CRE in Glasgow also present. It had been obvious to me, and all others involved that in Scotland site positions where Hutting was required were changing territorially. The DCRE's in the Midlands, West of Scotland, Glasgow and in particular the Highlands and Islands right up the West Coast for training grounds were becoming very busy with troops arriving. A tremendous amount of accommodation was required where Hutting was the answer.

The decision taken at the meeting was that therefore the control of Hutting should be transferred from the DCRE Perth to the DCRE Stirling for geographical reasons which was common sense. Just before the meeting finished, I must have thought I was hearing things when told that my appointment as Unit Accountant (Hutting Dumps) would be through Command Orders in a few days. Another surprise was when told I would be responsible direct to Captain Scott as I was being posted to Stirling on my own and a transfer from Perth was being arranged.

I had been in Perth nearly seven months and apart from the Black Watch experience I had really enjoyed myself. I had gained a lot of knowledge about the army and Hutting and had devised a system which seemed to work, having visited all three Dumps and on several occasions and the powers that be were happy. There was something I could not quite understand and always had an uneasy feeling about. If this was the real army it was certainly not what I had expected. No training, no drill, no parades and forgetting about the Black Watch, really no discipline. I was only a rookie Private but had been given a lot of responsibility, freedom and direct access without question to the most senior officers. It was all a bit frightening, and I was certain the bubble I was in would severely burst - but where would it blow me to when it did? There was only one thing to do - just keep soldering on.

I will remember the party laid on for me the night before I left the MacDonald's. Although it was November it was Hogmanay routine visiting all the neighbours' houses and having a drink. I had got to know them all and they were a wonderful friendly crowd. There were hugs and kisses all round and tears from Mrs. MacDonald when I said goodbye the following morning. It was the 12th of November 1941 and that day I was on my way from Perth to Stirling.

CHAPTER FIVE:
STIRLING, WALLASEY, FALKIRK AND THE CARRON COMPANY

I knew Stirling well having been born and brought up ten miles away. Many of my pals had been educated at the High School. The DCRE office was in the nicest part of town, Kings Park and in one of the many elegant houses just across the road from the golf course opposite the first tee. I had played the course often.

On arrival the DCRE gave me some bad news. It would be ten days before I could be accommodated in a private billet and had been attached to the local Royal Army Ordinance Corps depot in town for food and lodgings. Like all Ordinance Depots it was a huge place with heavy guns, artillery, mortars, machine guns and all sorts of equipment all over the place. All the RAOC lads were technicians, and it was their job to keep the army fire power in working order. There was the same standard of discipline and the same urgent atmosphere and concentration abounding as in the Black Watch but that is where the similarity ended. Instead of spit and polish and creases in trousers and kilts it was oily faces, grease-stained overalls and mucky messy roads with lots of noise, diesel oil and petrol fumes.

I remember being quite thrilled to find myself being accommodated in one of "my" huts. It was one of the bigger ones taking forty men. It had two of the coal fired cast iron stoves with the upright flue and outlet through the roof. Perhaps the simplest and best heating system ever made. I would know all the specifications off by heart and no doubt checked the code number buried into one of the roof timbers which would tell me which Dump it came from. There were many rows of similar huts as a lot of men were being housed in the Depot. There were also a few old stone buildings which were officers' quarters also officers and senior NCO's messes. The food would be good and plenty, it always was.

When I think about the RAOC Stirling, it always brings to my mind a small ruddy faced Cornishman who was a Lance Corporal in the Pioneer Corps. He was an odd job man about the place, there was one in every barracks and one of their important duties being to keep the latrines clean and disinfected. They were affectionately known as the "shithouse wallah!" He was in the hut, and I had noticed him with the evening paper spread out on the table beside the stove running his fingers along the type very slowly and mouthing the words. He was wearing an old pair of glasses which I thought required renewal and officer's help. I was astonished to discover that he did not know how to read and was flabbergasted when he told me he could not write either. Just how did he get accepted for the army? Surely there was only one answer. He was such a nice wee bloke and would do anything for anybody. He was the friend of every person in the Depot from the Commanding Officer down and no one would dare say a bad word against him. Whoever had helped him must have been on leave as I well remember reading letters to him, he had received and writing letters to his wife and family. He dictated them to me best he could in a broad Cornish accent, and I had great difficulty in understanding. I just now remember he was always washing and scrubbing himself with red Lifebuoy soap because duties. (He deserved a medal along with his stripe.) He used to make my hair stand on end when he would rub his shaving brush into the Lifebuoy soap and proceed to brush his face thick with lather then take an old fashioned 'cutthroat' open razor and shave. He was a one off and my army education was being extended!

I soon settled in at Stirling. I had been a bit worried about being responsible directly to Captain Scott thinking my style might be cramped not so much by him but maybe by others at Command HQ discovering the amount of freedom I had. However, that never happened. The captain was only too pleased for me to carry on as usual and just keep him up to date from time to time. For all I know he may have been receiving regular reports from the DCRE's about me. On my arrival the DCRE's gave me information which confirmed the priority of Hutting. The schedule for the intake of troops into Scotland was terrific.

My records show that I was visiting the Dumps at St. Andrews and Falkirk every week. I was also in continual liaison with the DCRE staff as the centralised Hutting system I had built up was working well and saving time which was at a premium.

Reverting back to the RAOC depot. I was only there ten days, but they were full of interest. The experience was quite the opposite of the Black Watch. The depot had tight security and routine discipline but caused me no hassle as they understood the position I was in right from the start and in fact made me welcome. My private billet was a fine old stone-built house halfway up a steep cobbled hill leading to Stirling Castle. I found myself with a very nice married couple well on in years and I just cannot remember their names. I had quite a large bed-sit room always cosy from a good fire with meals of good and plentiful food served in my room. Every part of the house was neat, tidy and polished just like the owners. They had no family, and it was the first time they had taken in a 'lodger" I had a feeling they did so as being their part of the war effort.

As my time went on at Stirling `and with the Americans entering the war Hutting priority became even greater because even at that early-stage preparations were being made for the arrival of thousands of their fighting men. All the Hutting requisitions were being filtered through me as I had become the accepted link between the DCRE departments and the Dumps. I found myself being involved at meetings at all levels as my records could often supply answers to very urgent questions. I was really in a crazy situation as it was not unknown for senior Command and Staff Officers to be in deep conversation with "Starky" and calling me by my nick name. I was often out and about on sites with clerks of works and technical staff.

Captain Scott continued to pay me regular visits and always appeared happy with the way things were going. On one such occasion and quite out of the blue he told me I had been promoted substantive Corporal. I see my promotion date was 25th March 1942 and my pay increased to 6/3d per day (£2.19p per week with all clothing, food and lodgings supplied - I could put money in my Post Office savings account!) With two stripes on my arms, I was on my way up the British Army ladder.

I have mentioned that the DCRE office was adjacent to the first tee of the Kings Park Golf Centre. Soon after my arrival I was asked by one of the staff if I had been a member of the Falkirk Tryst Club? The questioner turned out to be Nan Wilson who was a Stirlingshire County player and remembered me being on the Tryst junior team. She was a very good golfer as was her husband who was also with the DCRE being a Chartered Surveyor. They got me a set of clubs and I played once or twice in the evenings with them. I recall Nan getting me involved with a Red Cross competition for the war effort which included some professionals stationed in the area. During my whole army service of over five years, I doubt I played more than a dozen rounds of golf.

During my seven months at Stirling, I managed to see Norah about once per month to six weeks or at weekends. If I recall correctly my routine was to be at the Falkirk Dump on a Friday, then go by train to Edinburgh in the evening. Then return on a very early train to Stirling on the Monday morning. On the odd occasion she would come to Falkirk where we would meet up at my aunt and uncles. I was very lucky to have my special travelling pass which could take me as far as Edinburgh if necessary to see Captain Scott. I do not recall ever doing so but I certainly told him about every visit as he could easily have spotted me in town. One of our weekends together was never to be forgotten as we became engaged. We were quite certain that we wanted to live our lives together and prayed we would survive to do so. We had made up our minds to marry as soon as we could. It was at a time when we really feared for the survival of not only ourselves but our country.

The future looked dark and bleak as the Germans were on our doorstep just across the Channel ready to invade - or so we thought - and in the Far East the Japanese had captured Singapore which was a devastating blow to the whole country. As I write, and looking back, it is difficult to comprehend just what our thoughts were, not only about the future but the present as it was. Everyone was living from day to day knowing that it was possible we might not live to see the next day. However, as a country, as a people, we had two tremendous assets working in our favour. First, we were working as one by having a togetherness which gave us the will to win and the determination and courage to do so. Second, we had Winston Churchill to lead us. I had one eight day leave from Stirling and travelled down to Wallasey to see my mother and father and I am not likely ever to forget it.

Liverpool was being bombed to hell every night by hundreds of German planes. The city was circled by batteries of anti-aircraft guns placed on the outskirts with the purpose of making a shell barrage around the city to keep the enemy bombers from hitting the docks which was one of the main targets in Britain. Wallasey, just across the Mersey, was on the outskirts and just down the road from our house near to the golf course. Beside the river were lines of batteries and goodness knows how many guns. The noise they made was shattering.

When the war started Father did not fancy an Anderson shelter dug into the garden. What he did was order a very large dining room table - constructed of heavy sheet steel - used when building a ship's hull. It was a major operation to make it fit our dining room as it weighed quite a few tons, but he was confident if the house fell on top of it, those underneath would survive. I spent every night of my leave along with Mother and our tame budgie under that table and was frightened to death!

Father was either over in Liverpool attending to his ships or out in Sedbergh Road and around doing air raid warden duty like all the other men who were not in service being over age. So many did not survive the ordeal. Dad made me promise I would stay in the shelter with Mother until the all-clear, as her nerves were almost in tatters. I knew what he meant as I soon realised the chances of survival were 50/50. The nights were awful. The continual bombardment from our guns. The 'screecher" bombs, when the screeching got louder you knew they were going to be close. The eerie noise of the "whiners" the incendiary firebombs. The previous week one had come through our roof but fortunately Dad, his neighbour Mr Johnson, and those helping got it out before serious damage was caused.

Worst of all were the silent land mines which came down by parachute from the bombers. They were devastating, exploding with such terrible noise which could be heard for miles. They caused awful damage and could wipe out a whole street at a time. One night a bomb exploded down the street. Dad and Mr. Johnson were together, heard it coming and knew it was going to be very close. Dad flattened himself behind a front garden wall, but Mr. Johnson was a fraction late in taking such action. A small piece of shrapnel entered his open mouth and went straight through his right cheek. It left him with a bad scar for the rest of his life. Luck had been with him as he could have killed on the spot.

I remember Dad coming in covered in blood from helping Mr. Johnson who had fortunately received quick attention from the Doctor. The sight of Dad did not do Mother's nerves any good, or mine either! I am sure Dad had become immune to the danger being all part of the day's work like thousands of other civilians, male and female in London, Southampton, Coventry and all the other cities being bombed every night. God knows how they carried on seldom getting a decent night's sleep and in continual danger. They must never be forgotten.

At the end of my leave, I was shattered and very worried about them and said so. Sometime after they moved temporarily to Ormskirk, which was outside the target area, until the bombing almost stopped, and they then returned home. They just could not continue to take the nightly strain at Wallasey especially Mother. Looking back, she was never quite the same person again but they were lucky and thousands were killed by the bombing of Liverpool.

The horrors of the Blitz over Wallasey and Liverpool as witnessed by my Mother and Father in three letters written to me in December 1940:

10 Sedberge Road
Wallasey
Cheshire
Saturday night 9.30 pm, 21st December 1940.

My Dear Jim

Of all the nights we have had this one beats the lot. Your Pa is one of the fire fighting squad tonight.

The raid started at 6.30 pm again, and has never given up for a minute. About 8.30 pm, half a dozen incendiaries fell here at the top of the road, fifty yards away. There are two fire brigades at St. Hilary's Church. One fell through the roof of the house next to Mrs Lunday on the opposite side of the road and Dad was round the corner with Mr Johnson putting it out up in a bedroom.

Five minutes ago the barrage balloon at the foot of the road broke away and we ran out to see what was happening and believe me it was sitting in the middle of the road, and off it went again. Dad was scared it would go on fire. God knows where it is now. They have just put out another incendiary at Broadley's.

The City of Pittsburg, the large Ellerman cargo ship, was lying alongside a blazing shed today. The funnel was all blistered with the heat from the fire. The City of Corinth (Ellerman Cargo Ship) was hit, a bomb fell right on her and went through two decks, there was a lot of damage done. Dad says at Tate & Lyle's place the hot sugar was running down the walls like treacle. A bomb fell in the churchyard at St. Hilary's last night by the old tower and one fell in the park at the foot of the road again. So we were fifty yards either side from each. It is absolute hell just now, dear knows when it will ease up, you could read a paper with the light of bursting shells. Our sand bags are coming in handy. They are filling their buckets from them. I am sitting in the shelter just now with Billy (the tame budgie) beside me. I was out when the incendiaries were all blazing. Mr Robinson was pumping away at his pump, Mrs Robinson helping. I wonder where Helen and the other visitors are, they were to arrive tonight. A whistle has just gone. It is getting terrible tonight. Dad has his tin hat and needs it, believe me.

12.15 am. Still in the shelter but this is our first lull. Mr Johnson, our next door neighbour, says the General Hospital is full of casualties and they are taking them now to Leasowe Hospital. He says St. George's Hall in Liverpool is burning, you know the big hall at Lime Street. 2.00 am. Still it goes on and just now we thought our end had come. All the back windows are blown out. A house in the next street, Claremont Road, has been hit. It was a terrific bang. What a night this has been and it is going on as if it had newly started. Mr Johnson was out calling on Bill (neighbours) and their windows are out too and I expect Miss Wilson will be. We are just perished with cold. I sincerely hope we do not have colds after it. 3.00 am. Still thundering away. Dad says the whole skyline is red. There must be many fires. They certainly have left their mark on Merseyside. I have *been in here since 6.45 last night. 5.00 am. All clear.*

Sunday 7.15pm. Jim my dear this terrible business started tonight again half an hour ago, after last night it is frightening. Last night a bomb dropped in Uppingham Road at the back of us, in front of the house next to Mrs Lunday and burst a water main and a gas main. We had no gas this morning but it is all right now but poor pressure, but precious. Every house in Claremont Road is damaged between the Church and the top of The Break. The house hit is absolutely no more. It is very sad and when we saw them this morning could only breathe a prayer of thankfulness for being alive. We have the kitchen window covered with linoleum and have left the others until we get them covered, and oh the breezes! We both feel the effect of last night. Dad is away out helping with the incendiaries again. Mr Wilson, our neighbour, got one right through his roof last night and was in a stew getting it out. I think I see them, thank goodness Grandma is not here. Helen Robinson arrived at Lime Street Station last night at 9 o'clock and was in a shelter until 6.00 am this morning and did not get across home until 8.00am. 12.00 Midnight. We have had an easy night of it, touch wood. They started off with a bang but lately have been coming in one by one. We are going now to risk bed as we could do with some sleep.

Hope to hear from you soon with loving thoughts and embraces

Your loving Mother

10 Sedberge Road
Wallasey
Cheshire
Sunday 22nd December 1940.

Dear Jim

It is now midnight and we are going to risk bed. Tonight has been nothing compared to the last two and I am thankful. Apart from a bomb in the distance and two incendiaries in the street it has been fairly quiet.

I have had many varied experiences in my life and had some narrow escapes but I have never experienced anything like last night. It was simply a horror and we are frankly glad to be alive in the morning. Three bombs within a hundred yards, and this is no exaggeration, in one night makes one review life from a serious angle. Your mother got a bad shaking but stood up well to it. Around two in the morning there were two terrific thuds, the house rocked and bits of Uppingham Road fell on us and I thought we had got it. Strange to say I was quite cool and the thought passed through my mind that anyhow we live together and you know what that means to your mother and also to me. I was scared earlier by those incendiaries, they do more damage than bombs, but once I left the house to do a man's job, I was very proud of your mother for not holding me back. I forgot all about fear.

The Church and street were lit up in a most amazing way, the worst one was the Pellings, three doors up in his front garden, what a blaze it was. Mrs Robinson, brave soul that she is, was pumping like hell at her stirrup pumps, but no water was coming out, as she had forgotten to put the suction pipe into the bucket, so I put it right. While we were doing this three or four incendiaries were blazing wildly in the street in front of the Church and the guns and *bombs were making an awful din. We were a fine target as waves of flames were overhead all the time. We got them out but a fire was going good and strong from a window in the next street, so Johnson, Robinson and myself were off to it dropping in the street alongside the wall when we heard the swish of a bomb! The incendiaries had come through the roof of the house into the top bedroom. The man in the house was scared useless and the place was black with smoke, so we got the stirrup pumps to work with no assistance, we were lucky to get the fire out. This happened around eight o'clock and was only one of many incidents.*

When I go to Liverpool tomorrow I will see the damage, I am sure it must be great as the whole sky was alight last night and the fires are not out yet.

So Jim you missed it by one week and I don't think we can have these experiences again.

Excuse the scribble

Best of luck from

Your Father

10 Sedberge Road
Wallasey
Cheshire
Monday - Liverpool - 23rd December 1940

My Dear Jim

The damage is appalling. All Church Street, Bold Street, Bon Marche, The Market, Central Station. Over here it is terrible. We certainly have been left battered and bleeding.

I have got my windows boarded up with asbestos felting so the cold is kept out at last and Winnie has cleared up the glass etc.

The all clear did not go until 6.00 am this morning from twenty minutes to seven last night and we had another warning at 7.00 am and have had several more today.

Thinking of you all the time.

With fondest love

Your Mother

When back at Stirling I managed to visit my old friends the Taylors at Larbut which was only a few miles away by bus and tram. I was in effect going home to my roots as I was born nearby at Carron. The sprawling industrial town of Falkirk included in its suburbs Carron, Stenhousemuir, Bainsford, Camelon and Larbert. It had always been a most important heavy industrial town famous for iron foundering and engineering.

Scotland has always been famous the world over for producing highly skilled engineers and many came from the Falkirk district. The reason being that in its heyday it had ten large iron and steel works each with huge foundries and employing thousands of men and women.

During the two World Wars of 1914/18 and 1939/45 - they were all on twenty-four hour nonstop production vital to the war effort making guns, tanks, shells and all types of ships engines and boilers. In other words, anything and everything made from iron and steel. Falkirk was known as the town where night could be like day. Maybe because of black-out restrictions, blast furnacing was controlled during the 1939/45 war but in peace time night could be like day when the furnaces lit up the night sky. I remember that taking place. I remember awaking in the morning and seeing the red-hot ash glowing on the tips which would become shale as it cooled down during the day. I can still "feel" the smell of the acrid smoke which wafted from the tips. I was born - along with my brother - and I lived until I was almost eight certainly no longer than six or seven hundred yards from the huge tips. I could see them from my bedroom window. How did that come about?

Where I lived, was within the grounds and boundary of the huge complex, which covered between two- and three-square miles and belonged to the oldest, largest and most famous iron and steel works in Scotland namely Carron Company. The company was established in 1760. It was Scotland's first factory. Made Carronade guns used by Nelson and Wellington. James Watt carried out experiments there when inventing the steam engine. John Adam became a partner in 1769 and the company produced the Adam Fireplaces. It had its own fleet of ships, made the famous GPO pillar boxes, manhole covers, the old cast iron then pressed steel sinks and baths but to mention a few of the Carron products.

My Father being in the Merchant Navy was away from home such a lot that my mother and I lived with her parents, my grandfather and grandmother Mercer also Aunt Margaret my Mothers sister. As it happened there was plenty of room for us all. My Grandfather, John Mercer, joined Carron Company from school at the age of fourteen in 1880. He served a five-year apprenticeship studied and worked hard and became a brilliant engineer with many patents to his name. He worked his way right up the ladder to number two position of the whole organisation which was Engineering Manager. He also became involved with many engineering, iron, steel and shipping associations and company boards throughout Great Britain.

He died with unbelievable sadness when talking to me and my grandmother at the age of sixty-four when I was ten. How I wished he had lived longer until I was able to appreciate what a great man he was. I think every inhabitant of Carron, there would be many thousands, were either employed or owed their living to the company. Most of the foundry workers lived with their families in long rows of terraced houses in dingy streets which were close by the works. It was said that all the houses were built within the sound of the works hooter. They were steam hooters which gave mighty piercing blasts which could be heard for miles around. One hoot was five minutes before a shift change and two hoots was change time on the dot as being late meant pay docked. The whole population of the Falkirk area was time controlled by factory hooters. I so well remember my mother saying, "hurry up that's the 8 o'clock hooter". There would then be the mid-day at 12 noon and the back shift at 4pm. "You should be fast asleep the night shift hooter has gone". All these little memories come flooding back to me quite clearly.

Continuing the answer to my question - "How did that come about?"

With my Grandfathers important executive position with the company went an estate called Mount Carron. I have mentioned about seeing the shale tips from my bedroom window, so it will be realised it was close to the works but nevertheless it was a beautiful place. We lived in a large and spacious mansion house with many rooms, standing in an area of ground. There was a kitchen garden, flower garden, two grass tennis courts, large eighteen hole putting green with combined pavilion situated on a stepped lawn going down to a third step being lawn in front of the house.

On one side of the house were kennels for the dogs, a laundry and outhouses. Near at hand was a large hen house with a huge enclosed, wire netted run for the Rhode Island Reds. At the back of the house there was a large lawn with borders and cut out beds full of flowers. At the foot there were lovely trees with seats under them. Some were shaped to make an archway which led to a footpath to a white arched bridge with a gate at each end which crossed a canal that ran along the border of the estate. The pathway along the other side of the canal lead to the works and offices. I can see my Grandfather opening the first gate and turning round waving to me at my bedroom window as he did every morning at quarter to eight precisely. I recall the time without any doubt as he always "went in with the men" at the eight o' clock hooter.

It was a large house to run but we had a maid called Nellie who was treated as one of the family and had her own little apartment with a private stair down to the massive kitchen. Her mother who did not live in was laundry maid on a part time basis. My Grandmother and Mother helped by my Aunt did all the cooking.

There was a similar size estate next door for the managing director George Pate. It was a large house and again with beautiful gardens also a lake. Between the two estates beyond our tennis courts, were several cottages where the chauffeurs, gardeners and handymen were housed with their families. There were quite a few of them as they looked after both estates.

How lucky I was to be born and brought up during my early years in such an environment. By what I have written it could be taken for granted that John and Janet Mercer were very rich, maybe even country class and came from blue blooded money and stock. Nothing could be further from the truth. John Mercer's father was a miner. John was born and raised in a row of cottages at Carronshore - part of Carron - called Blackmill. He went to the local school and as previously mentioned left at fourteen.

His father died when he was young, and his mother continued living at Blackmill until she died. I can just remember being taken by my Mother to see her when she was very aged, and bed ridden. Janet Mercer my Grandmother, was a wonderful person and was one of a family of fourteen, seven boys and seven girls. All her brothers and sisters' husbands and wives if they had them were all regular visitors to Mount Carron and all "Aunties and Uncles" to me. I was involved in a very large but close-knit family. They were real nice down to earth and good living folk some of them often struggling to make ends meet when times were bad which could be often during the 1920's and 30's.

John Mercer made it to the very top and no doubt was one of the highest paid men of the engineering trade in Scotland as would be expected in his position with Carron Company. My Grandparents were obviously "well off" but never in the very rich upper strata class. They were just not made that way and knew it, but they had been well brought up and gained experience along the way. They could cope alright and became involved at the highest level but never made any pretensions about status. Mother and Father used to talk to me about them as when I grew up, I became curious. They explained about the frightening thoughts in their minds especially of my Grandmother when her husband was promoted knowing they would have to occupy and run the huge house and estate and also be responsible for the staff. Granted it was provided for by the company including the houses and wages of the staff with the exception of inside help, furniture and food. It was an extraordinary situation to be in and quite an incredible undertaking but that is the way it was working at the top for Carron Company in those days. They must have been a courageous pair as prior to that they had lived in just a nice comfortable four-bedroom house in Russell Street, Falkirk. It was only when John Mercer died that it became known he had a been a benefactor not only to members of the family who had financial struggles at times but others outside the large circle who were in need. Fortunately, he left Grandmother without any financial worries.

I made a nostalgic visit to Carron in 1985 and discovered the house had been demolished and what had been the beautiful lawns and gardens were like a jungle no doubt all being made ready for a modern development. Also, the once great company with a worldwide reputation had been fragmented into many minor establishments. The huge complex had been split up into bits and pieces. It made me feel very sad. However, I was delighted to see that what had been George Pate's house was still standing and looked in very good condition as did the estate and I noticed the lake was still there. The house was being used as a training college. How I wished they had found some similar use for Mount Carron.

Around the Falkirk area were many prosperous engineering companies whose founders had originally started work straight from school with one of the iron and steel companies. One such person was Robert Taylor who had been an apprentice to my Grandfather as a fitter. During his days with Carron Company, he was developing in his mind the design of a domestic boiler which could heat houses. He saved every penny, obtained some financial help and left the company and purchased a derelict foundry at Larbut. He had confidence in his design, patented it in his own name and started manufacturing them. In a few years his foundry had expanded and with a hundred or more employees working for him he was making his fortune. It was the famous "Tayco Boiler" the up-market way to heat a house in the years between the wars and long before central heating became part of our lives.

Bob and Mary Taylor were a super pair who had four sons and a daughter. They were friends of our family and two of the sons were my best pals. They all played golf, Bob being captain of Falkirk Tryst. We young ones counted the days until we became 7 years old because we could then become junior members of the club. From the late 1920's to the mid 1930's golfing records show that Falkirk Tryst had perhaps the finest junior golfers in Scotland. In 1929 and 1930 Jimmy Lindsay won the British Boys Open Championship. The only time it has been successfully defended to this day. I was a member of Tryst from 1927 to 1936 i.e., from age 7 to 15. I was one of the gang of lads during those years who were shown how to play and taught etiquette by our elders. During summer school holidays all our spare time was spent on the golf course, and we all became low handicap players with a special love of the great game.

Early in 1928 my Grandparents moved from Mount Carron to "Duncoumbe" Larbert. We had a nice four-bedroom house with a small garden quite the opposite to Mount Carron. Mother and I moved to

Falkirk, Aunt Margaret had married and lived with her dentist husband David. Age was catching up with my Grandparents. Grandfather was preparing for retirement and Grandmother was finding Mount Carron difficult to cope with. My father had bought a new house in Falkirk town hoping he would be able to take the odd voyage off and be home with Mother and me. The opposite happened as he was promoted to Senior Chief Engineer and was responsible for the engineering of all the new Ellerman Hall and City Lines ships being built and taking them on their trials and first voyages. The result was we were only at Falkirk for just over two years as with the sudden death of my Grandfather we returned to Larbert to be with Grandmother as Duncoumbe had plenty of room.

It was at Falkirk High School and come 1930 when I was ten a major change took place in my life. I passed the entrance exam to one of the famous Scottish schools, Daniel Stewart's College in Edinburgh and for the next five years during term, travelled every day of the week except Sundays to and from Edinburgh by train. I left home in the mornings at 7.30 and returned about 5.00pm, maybe a bit earlier on Saturdays. I have to say that one of the greatest and most important assets of my life is being a "Daniel."

I have transgressed somewhat in recent chapters away from my army story and have taken the opportunity of including some details about my personal background relative to my upbringing. I feel this is necessary and not out of place as it seems appropriate to do so with Stirling being close to my original home ground. It was in mid-June 1942 when the DCRE suddenly told me I was moving on to higher places. The Command Royal Engineers (CRE) Glasgow wanted me as his Unit Accountant (Hutting Dumps) at his HQ and Captain Scott had agreed. I was very sorry to leave Stirling as it had been a great posting for me. An excellent billet and I felt they were genuinely sorry to see me go. I discovered later that the DCRE had wanted to keep me, but a Major would not stand much chance against his boss who was Lieutenant Colonel. So, on the 18th of June 1942 I was sent off on my own by train to Glasgow.

CHAPTER SIX:
1942 - 1943

The CRE offices in Glasgow were situated in a very nice part of the city near the University and Kelvingrove Park. Park Terrace was one side of a beautiful circle of elegant four-story stone-built terrace houses the kind you see to this day in Edinburgh and Bath. They were and had been grand homes occupied by wealthy people. The CRE had requisitioned a few houses next door to each other as its headquarters. There would be a hundred and more personnel, army and civilian working from Park Terrace. They included many top brass both army and civilian. Civilian and mechanical engineers, architects, surveyors, audit branch accountants etc., i.e., all the people who would make the final decisions relating to work and projects from all of the DCRE's. They were backed up by office staff, typists, clerks and a transport section which was run by the ATS. There was a good NAAFI canteen. Discipline was not strict, but it was there as the place had to be guarded day and night and time keeping was important. There were many DCRE's in the huge conurbation of Glasgow, the surrounding districts and areas. Glasgow was the main port in Britain for troops intake from overseas.

The CRE Glasgow also had within its jurisdiction perhaps the most important area in Britain at the time namely the Highlands and Islands of the west coast of Scotland. It was a TSA (top secret area). All during the war it had great naval significance as our submarines and warships could hide in many of the deep-water sea locks for repairs, servicing and preparation for further action.

When I was at Glasgow the west coast and lochs with mountains coming right down to the water's edge were being prepared for men in flat bottomed boats training to scale up the mountains. Within a year thousands of troops our own and allied would be training day and night to be ready for the invasion of Europe. They all had to be accommodated in hutted camps.

The CRE had on his staff the usual RAPC Unit Accountants. Building and maintenance contracts of all sorts were going through his organisation at a hectic pace, many of them very large and they all had to be recorded and accounted. When I arrived, there were five under the command of Company Sergeant Major McQuade of the regular army. He had two Sergeants and two Corporals which made up the RAPC unit. I remember so well my first meeting with the Sergeant Major as I took an immediate dislike to him as he made sure I understood his rank and that he was a regular soldier and knew his job and his duties to the letter. He then informed me, in a rough voice spitting out each word with a cutting edge, that my reputation had come to his notice. He went on something like this - " I have heard about a Corporal named Stark who has only been in the bloody army just over a year and had changed the whole bloody Hutting procedure to suit himself and low and behold here he is and believe it or not at the request of CRE himself!" - I just had to stand there to attention take the stick and hopefully let him get his feelings out of his system. I certainly realised I would have to tread very warily with him.

Our offices were on the top floor. McQuade was in a large room with his two Sergeants, and he gave me a desk in a smaller room with the two Corporals. They too were conscripts and I immediately got on well with them both. They had suffered with McQuade but said he was not so bad when you got to know him, they advised he was not very popular in the CRE HQ as he threw his weight around - a usual habit with CSM's - but he did know his job. I discovered he had been in a spot of bother with the CRE staff because of delays with Hutting documentation which was causing delivery backlog at the Dumps. The Corporal's opinion was that he didn't appreciate the urgency of Hutting requirements. Things had come to a head when the real upper echelons ordered Captain Scott to do something about it, which resulted in my quick departure from Stirling to Glasgow - hence my non popularity with McQuade!

What happened in the next few days in an odd sort of way helped the CSM and myself to understand each other about the Hutting problem. He got to the stage when he could not say anything but was just open mouthed and shook his head in bewilderment. I was regularly being called downstairs with my record books to meetings with the Lieutenant Colonel (the CRE) and his senior military and civilian staff. Majors (DCRE's) and Captains (Dump CO's) were climbing the stairs to see me and my records and some of them were calling me Starkey. My Corporal pals were complaining they could get no work done and it was all a bit much for McQuade who was on the telephone to Captain Scott in Edinburgh and our boss was with us early next day. It was decided I should have a room of my own with a telephone on the ground floor and have complete freedom of movement exactly as I had at Perth and Stirling. I was to be given the necessary documents of authority again to cope with all contingencies of travel, board and lodgings etc. I was to keep McQuade always in the picture and obtain the help of the other members of our staff if necessary. Captain Scott said he would pay me weekly visits.

What an amazing situation I was in again. I wonder just what was said - and deservedly so behind my back by everyone. It must have been good. A Corporal with a room of his own and a telephone with direct access to all the top brass in the office and outside and them to him. I was walking a tightrope and it was necessary that McQuade and I really got on together and sorted ourselves out and I did not expect that to be easy.

It was easier than I thought. I had not "changed the bloody system" but adapted the procedure routine to fit wartime requirements. In other words, from some huts being required occasionally, to hundreds of them wanted every week always with a war time top priority red stamp on the order. The difference was such that to cope I had proved that an RAPC Unit Accountant was necessary working full time on Hutting only having complete freedom of movement to cooperate with DCRE, CRE and Dump staff at all levels wherever they may be. By doing so my stock records could be kept up to date and answers always be available to all who required them. I promised McQuade he would always be kept in the picture, and I would also explain the system to my RAPC colleagues so they could keep things going if I was off sick or on leave. After all I was part of this team. The air was cleared, he accepted the situation. I am sure he realised that with my (to him) very surprising high "connections" his best policy was to leave me alone to get on with it as if things turned out well the credit could go his way.

In all big towns during the war hotels were taken over to provide accommodation i.e., board and lodgings in particular for Officers and Warrant Officers. NCO's and other ranks usually found themselves in schools and large halls and maybe barracks. I think from memory the majority of the uniformed lads and lasses in the CRE office were in military accommodation as mentioned except Corporal Stark J. He maintained his strict rule, said nothing, and was ready to accept whatever came along and that was a private billet.

The Glasgow District Accommodation Office when he heard about me from the CRE realised I would be just a bloody nuisance to him, and others having permission to come and go as I pleased to fulfil my duties, so he had no hesitation in arguing a private billet order for me. About ten minutes' walk from the CRE HQ lived Miss Lothian. She had a large, terraced stone house not unlike the CRE in Park Terrace but it was not such a posh area although I am sure it had been in years gone by. It had a distinctive old-fashioned style with the servants/trade entrance at the front along with the main front door entrance. The servants and tradesmen had gone through an iron gate, down steep stone steps to a door in the basement. At front ground level there was a wide entrance up a few steps between large heavy wrought iron railings leading to a huge magnificent wooden carved front door. Above were another two storeys making four floors in all. It was a big house which had seen better days, but I can recall a charm and elegance about the place. I have just remembered that all iron railings were taken out during the war to be melted down except those which protected the basement area. I had to get used to Miss Lothian. I can see her now. How can I describe her? She was big but not fat, strongly built, a bit blousy and gave the impression because she possessed large breasts which I think she was proud of as she tended to show them off wearing low cut and tight-fitting clothes. She was a bit raucous, talked men's language, full of fun and laughter, loved a joke and could tell them, a real man's women. She had a heart of gold, cared for everyone, would do anything for you and was a great cook. She had a happy place, I was lucky again. Nowadays I suppose the best way to describe her house is to say it had been typically Upstairs Downstairs style. There was a huge basement dominated by a very large kitchen, big table in the centre which could seat many. There was an old black leaded range, always with a glowing fire, pots and pans, as food seemed to be always on the go. She had her own private quarters throughout the basement which included a large cosy and comfortable sitting room. In the evening sometimes and well into the night she would hold court. A chat and a cup of tea or a drink was always on offer. She liked to keep up to date with all the news and gossip. It was sort of a ritual that everyone reported to her when they came in. She was genuinely concerned and caring. If the sirens went off, she would be up and about making sure we were all ok and brewing up tea for the fire watchers as none of us had to be asked to go up on the roof. She would ply us with mugs of hot tea laced with whisky.

The house had many rooms most of them being occupied. I don't know how she coped as all her lodgers seemed to be on shift work many of them at the shipyards. I think I was the only one in the services and had a small but comfortable bed-sit room on the ground floor. She brought me all my meals and she did likewise for all the others on the ground floor. Those on the two floors above had meals in the kitchen the reason being it was quite a climb up the huge staircase from the basement. I have only a vague recollection of the others in the house. It was an all-male gang although she had a couple of ladies who helped her, and I think they were relations. I knew we all got on well together. If anyone did not fit in, he was out on his ear in no time, Miss Lothian saw to that! We were all coming and going at different times. In a big industrial city like Glasgow in war time it was as busy and noisy during the blacked-out night as it was during the day. Norah and her Mother were made welcome on more than one occasion and they realised I was in good hands as one of her boys.

I was eighteen months in Glasgow from June 1942 to December 1943. Continually on the move and working all hours. With the influx and involvement of troops on the West Coast of Scotland many required accommodation and Hutting was in continual demand. I was involved with two Dumps. Still Falkirk, plus the addition of Stonehouse, which was near Strathaven about twenty miles south of Glasgow, which was the largest Dump of them all. My Red Book tells me I was at Stonehouse twice per week staying overnight and Falkirk once per week. I notice details of rail and bus warrants, but I remember also getting lifts from the CRE transport section.

When not at the Dumps I was visiting some of the dozen or more DCRE offices in and around Glasgow which came under the jurisdiction of the CRE. The DCRE East and West Kilbride, Renfrew East and West, Paisley, Greenock, Dumbarton all come to mind and there were many more. My routine was travelling most days and writing up my stock books at night either in the office or at the billet seven days a week. I also kept being involved in meetings. The only specific duty I performed, apart from collecting my pay on a Friday, was to be a night sentry fire watch, which I think was about once every two weeks. I made sure I played my part in this respect as everyone did including civilian staff. The dock area of Glasgow was a major target. The sirens often blared away, and we had visits from German bombers usually attacking the River Clyde which was always busy with shipping. I suppose we had scary moments on the CRE roof, but I do not recall any real emergencies.

When I arrived in Glasgow in June 1942 it was a time when the result of the war was in the balance. Hitler had brought Britain to its knees and was in control of most of Europe. We had received tremendous setbacks in the Western Desert where Rommel's Panzer Army Divisions had defeated the 8th Army in Libya. The fall of Singapore to the Japanese had been a devastating blow and the mighty strength of the Japs was a considerable worry. It was conceivable at the time that they could conquer the whole of Southeast Asia including our own jewel in the crown - India. Which they very nearly did.

All our large cities were being bombed to hell and the possibility of Hitler's German Army invading our shores was very real. We had lost many thousands of our brave Navy, Army and Air Force lads and bombing had taken a heavy toll of our civilian workers in factories, offices and at home. The future looked very bleak indeed. There were however two spots of light at the end of a very dark foreboding tunnel. First spot - The Americans were in the war with us and we with them, leading to the formation of a colossal, combined effort against Germany and Japan. Also, our "cousins" from our great colonial empire countries were flocking in their multitudes to the Union Jack to fight for us. Second spot - In adversity our will to win was never wavering. It was perhaps one of the greatest times in our history. Surely there has never been such a togetherness. Everyone working, sharing and helping each other with one objective in mind which was the beating of Hitler and his Nazi Germans and the Japanese scum and all they stood for right into the ground forever.

During those uncertain and worrying times Norah and I like so many other young couples became engaged and a year later were married. Looking back, I am sure our feelings at the time were the same as all the others like us namely, every single minute together was so precious. The future was a fog of uncertainty. The life expectancy of anyone in uniform had a question mark over his or her head. The same applied in many instances to the man or woman in the street, but the two of us had confidence and courage in ourselves and our country to face the future knowing that we could have a fight for our very survival on our hands. As the days passed in 1942 a revitalised highly trained to super efficiency 8th Army was being made ready for battle by our new Commander named Montgomery who will go down in history as one of the great, maybe the greatest British soldier. On the 23rd of October he suddenly attacked Rommel's army at El Alamein and won a tremendous battle, pushed on fighting all the way until on the 12th of May 1943 all German forces in North Africa surrendered to him. This was to be the turning point of the war.

I remember a very interesting occurrence during my Glasgow days. The CRE called me into his office and said he wanted me to accompany one of his surveyors along with a Clerk of Works, who were both present, to a site which was located by map reference. This indicated to us that this was a secret establishment, and we would not be told the reference until we were ready to go. We were told to take kit for two nights. The transport section, I think with some surprise to us, allocated an ATS driver and we set off into the unknown a few days later in a small four-seater canvas topped camouflaged Austin. It transpired our destination was somewhere in the mountains and valleys beyond the town of Inveraray, Argyllshire.

My memory about this trip is rather vague but I do recall we had a terrible journey getting there. We were going into a Top-Secret area with, like all the country at war time, no signposts and no village names. We were stopped at check points by Military Police and although we had special passes, they would escort us for miles to the next check point. The countryside was alive with troops and landing craft in the lochs. We were in the training area for the invasion of Europe. I do recall our destination being a Command Unit at the back of beyond and I think they wanted to know if wooden blockhouses could be built halfway up the mountains for training purposes or some such idea. My memory is fairly blank in places about this experience. I always had the misty memory of passing through the town of Inveraray on that war time expedition.

There is a sequel to this bit of my story. In 1989 forty-five years later, Norah and I decided to have a holiday in Argyll and tour around that beautiful part of Scotland in the car. We made our base Inveraray and booked in for a few days at the Loch Fyne Hotel. On entering the Hotel, the first thing that caught my eye was a large picture on the wall of the reception area. It showed the King (George VI) in uniform with a small group of army generals and high-ranking officers photographed in 1943 standing outside the Hotel which had been a private house but was then the Army HQ for the area. He had been on an inspection tour near Inveraray of a commando movement to commemorate all the commandos who trained in that part of Scotland and did not survive the war. We travelled all the country and loch side roads during our excellent holiday, but I was disappointed as nothing jogged my memory relating to my adventure all those years ago.

I have mentioned about Norah and her mother coming through to Glasgow and being well looked after by Miss Lothian. They came on two important occasions as it was to discuss wedding plans. We were so lucky not being far apart at the time as wartime weddings were not easy to organise due to food and clothes rationing and coupons needed for everything and not much money about. However, we managed as all our family and friends rallied round as was the spirit generated by everyone across the land - the "togetherness" again. Despite the non-stop hectic time I was having in Glasgow, compassionate and special leave was only being granted. At the time my Red Book confirms I obtained eight days special leave from 16th - 22nd June. The greatest thing that ever happened to me was on the 17th of June 1943 when I married Norah Alice McGavin at Corstorphine, Edinburgh. Our great happiness is still shared all those years on and with our devoted family.

I am not likely to forget the previous week, despite the intense duty and pressures as a wedding approaches whilst serving in H.M. Forces. This was the number one reason for having a party. It must be remembered that in those difficult days when a sense of fear and anxiety was always in the forefront of all person's mind, a few hours of freedom from such thoughts could make a party, a party, a party! Four such goings on come to mind. In the CRE NAAFI canteen, in a pub near the Stonehouse Dump, in a hut at the Falkirk Dump and finally at Miss Lothians. Fortunately, I survived to tell the tale and be on parade on the great day. Such great kindness was shown to Norah and me by so many people in and out of uniform during those eventful days.

It is interesting to note our financial state of affairs when we married:

My gross pay per day:	£0 6s 9d = £0.34p
I had to give Norah a compulsory allotted amount per day:	£0 1s 6d = £0.07p
I could afford to give Norah a voluntary allotted amount per day:	£0 1s 6d = £0.07p
My net pay per day:	£0 3s 9d = £0.19p
Norah received mortgage allowance p/w:	£0 1s 6d = £1.12p
Add allotments to my pay:	£1 1s 0d = £1.05p
Norah's salary at Scottish Insurance:	£2 5s 0d = £2.25p
Our total combined income per week:	£5 14s 9d = £5.74p

I was being fed and clothed and could manage on my £1.31p per week and maybe save just a little. Norah, bless her, was starting to put small amounts in our newly opened joint bank account, determined we would have our own house when I was demobbed. She continued to do so all the time I was in the army, and we had our own house immediately I was demobbed and for three of us!

During 1943 slowly but surely preparations were being made all over Britain for the invasion of Europe. Everyone knew that if we were going to defeat Hitler we just had to invade, there was no alternative - but where and when? Such information had to be at the very top of all top secrets. Our island had been prepared in such a way that it could accommodate and make ready for battle, over a million Army, Navy and Air Force fighting men with all their ships, machine guns, equipment and supplies - the greatest battle force ever. British, American, Canadian all our Empire Countries and our Allies from Europe including the French and Poles who had escaped from the Nazi regime.

I did not realise it at the time but every day in Glasgow I must have been involved playing my very tiny part. As my duty in Glasgow was coming to an end there was a hustle and a bustle, movement and excitement developing coupled with a great seriousness and intensity. Something really big was on the go and we all had a feeling our lives could depend on it. Later we were to discover we were right. During my eighteen months with the CRE I had accounted for thousands of huts. They were required all over the area and especially in Argyll. Thousands of troops came into Glasgow from America and elsewhere and many came from all parts of the UK for training in the mountains, valleys, lochs and West Coast of Scotland coastline and beaches. The huts came from Stonehouse and Falkirk and between visiting them and the many DCRE offices each week I was seldom static if so for only the odd day. I really got to know the city and all the surrounding towns and out of the way places.

Miss Lothian was a godsend, an angel, as I seldom had any time schedule and no idea what was ahead of me, I could return at any time of day or night. Food was always available for her 'boys' as we were all in effect on shift work, if mine could be called such. No wonder we kept her supplied with cigarettes - she smoked like a chimney and the odd bottle of whisky as we could get them cheap. I remember, if we did not let her pay, she would not accept.

CHAPTER SEVEN: SCOTTISH COMMAND HEADQUARTERS AND MEDICAL REVIEW

Towards the end of 1943 requisitions for Hutting began to dry up as accommodation for troops and their training was found to be more than adequate for requirements. I had the feeling my Hutting days were numbered and I was not sure what was in store for me. I thought the logical answer would be to keep me in the Unit Accountants Branch and be posted to a DCRE or CRE somewhere. I knew it was unlikely I would be kept with Sergeant Major McQuade as I discovered he would not be allowed another Corporal because my posting had been extra to his establishment on special duties. Sticking to my rule I would just accept whatever came along.

I think I visited all the DCRE offices and the Hutting Dumps and made arrangements about integrating the special systems we had developed into the normal routine. One day Captain Scott arrived and gave me a copy of a posting order just issued which I must have read a few times to believe it. I was to report to the office of the Chief Engineer, Scottish Command, Edinburgh on the 13th of December. My extraordinary army career continued. I had started near the top and was now reaching the summit. From DCRE (Major) to CRE (Lieutenant Colonel) to CE (Colonel) my two stripes would look even more insignificant than before beside his red tabs!

It is about time I mentioned Sergeant Major McQuade again. After our original problems we sorted out and I had to travel about so much and seldom be in my office for any length of time. The routine agreed was that I would report to him personally every Friday. It was parade day and I just had to be there. I would spend a couple of hours or so with him keeping him up to date with my goings on. He had soon realised the only way for the Hutting job to be done with any success under the circumstances of total wartime urgency, was for me to have personal contact at all levels, no matter what rank, often the higher the better. I appreciate it was not easy for a peace time Sergeant Major to come to terms with that situation. It turns out he was very happy as things kept going well and he left me to do my own thing and didn't interfere. Everything considered I was part of his unit and any kudos obtained would be a plus on his personal file! After a while we overcame our differences and became quite good friends and often had a drink together and it got to the stage where I could call him "Mac" which really was tremendous progress.

His assistants, the two Sergeants and the two Corporals became good pals of mine as I was in contact with one or other of them every day as they were involved with my work on the inside. If it was possible, I looked into my office every day or night, but I always knew they were keeping an eye on it for me. They were very important to me in another way. I relied on them to keep me informed about current Army, Pay Corps, Royal Engineers, local CRE etc. orders which could be vital as far as I was concerned. Very often they had to explain them to me as my level of experience could just about get me through a pay parade and give a salute!

The time came when I had to say goodbye to Glasgow. The eighteen months had been a great experience for me. I had been involved with so many interesting people that often I thought I was in the building, construction and timber trade and found it hard to believe I was in the Army. My goodbyes at the Dumps were tinged on both sides with a touch of sadness. It was being said quite openly by the staff "Starkey's going that means we'll be going". I found it very difficult to respond because I knew it was true. I had developed a great affinity with them all, right from my first visit and without realising it, I had become the missing link between them and the DCRE's which prior to me appearing on the scene had not existed, causing an out-of-control gap in the system. To me the Dumps people were very special. The reason being that apart from the Commanding Officer and his number one, both army, all the other employees were local civilians apart from Falkirk, they were all typical Scottish small town community. Each had developed by the hard work and enthusiasm of their own people huge Army Hutting Dumps in their midst. Earning decent wages they had helped with the economy and prosperity of their town during very difficult days of war.

It must always be kept in mind that in such circumstances it was the 'oldies' who held the fort and kept things going as the young ones were away fighting. I was always aware of the fantastic job they were doing. It was a great privilege for me to have been associated with them.

My main goodbye was to Miss Lothian. She was a one off, a character in her own right. I hope my memory is not playing tricks on me, but I think I presented her with an RE and RAPC cap badge mounted together on a base of polished wood which one of the Dump lads made for me. I seem to recall she was very overcome being such a sensitive and caring person. My Red Book shows that I left for Glasgow by train on the 12th of December 1943 for home in Edinburgh. I would be ready the following morning to report to the office of the Chief Engineer.

The Scottish Command Headquarters of the Chief Engineer were at what had been before requisition, John Watson's School (not to be confused with the famous John Watson's College). I knew it well having passed it every day on my way to Daniel Stewart's College, my old school, which was situated little more than shouting distance along the road. I think John Watson's was a school for pupils requiring special education and like so many of the well-known Edinburgh schools and colleges it was a huge, elegant stone-built building standing in acres of land.

When I reported on the morning of the 13th of December, I was in for quite a shock as I suddenly realised I was back in the real army again. I know for sure the feeling of Black Watch apprehension came over me simply due to lack of experience. Fortunately, one thing I did learn when at the Perth barracks and never forgot was - always be spit and polished - and I did always try to maintain that piece of advice given to me in such dignified language by a certain Regimental Sergeant Major. Anyway, on that day in December 1943 I could at least look the part of a Corporal with experience who had been in the army two years and eight months!

There were sentries marching inside and outside the grounds. and Military Police prowling everywhere. Once I did get passed the Orderly Room at the main gate, I set off up the long drive marching to attention as best I could. Cars kept passing me many of them with flags on the wing which made it an even longer salute, fortunately I knew to do that. In the main building high ranking and senior officers, also senior NCO's such as Regimental and Sergeant Majors seemed to be in profusion. I was to get used to it. After all I was part of the Command HQ for the whole of Scotland where the mighty staff officers and great chaps they were, sent out orders to the Regiments and Corps stationed in the country. It was one of the most important military places in the land and comings and goings went on continually day and night as I was to discover.

I reported to the Chief Engineers office and was given the news that I had been seconded to his staff for three months. I was to coordinate all the Scottish Hutting Dump stocks and costing's ready for them being gradually closed. The Commanding Officers at the Dumps had been informed and when meetings were necessary, they would come to me.

I could not believe that, but it was time. I was disappointed as I would have looked forward to my travels again. I discovered I was the only RAPC Unit Accountant there. Captain Scott's office and staff might need a hand and I could visit them when necessary.

The Captain, I was to discover, left me to my own devices because yet again I was placed in a very odd situation. Being seconded to the CE's office I was under his jurisdiction and in effect was a "Royal Engineer" for three months and took my orders from them. Captain Scott realised this and had agreed my secondment which as it turned out was the obvious thing to do due to the financial implications involved. I was given a desk in a large well-equipped office along with another three NCO's and found myself under the control of a Major, who was a real decent type. My luck was in again as one of the first things I was told was that I would be billeted at home.

As one would expect being at Command HQ everything about the place was very regimented and discipline was strict but fair. I remember on arrival receiving a lecture about taking care about what I said and very definitely keep mum outside. You could not avoid at times being aware of what was going on. I noticed during the first few days I was allowed to visit the CRE Glasgow. It must have been important because that was the only time I was away from Edinburgh during my stay. I worked my way through the costing job and had regular visits from the Dump CO's. I would just inform the Major and arrangements would be made for them to come, and they would turn up on the dot. I hate to think what they thought about being asked to come to see me. They knew it was certainly not my doing as they were good friends to the end. There was a very good atmosphere, a real camaraderie between all the ranks at the HQ. A Brigadier, Colonel, or maybe even Sergeant Major would pass the time of day and chat to a Corporal, and they were all very approachable. I was to enjoy my stay there.

I was only a week in Edinburgh when I was told to report for a medical examination at the Command Medical Centre on 30th December 1943.

So, they had caught up with me. I had been in the Army two years and nine months and my previous medical was before I was called up when they told me I was B1. However, what I had ensured was that I attended for inoculations and vaccinations when they were due. That was a standing order and one thing I did learn early on was always comply with a standing order come what may. An interesting point to mention now is that during my whole army service I must have received dozens of inoculations and vaccinations for all sorts of illness and diseases especially when overseas and not one "took". I was always called back by medical officers for a special and sometimes third shot without success. The vast majority of lads felt some discomfort, and many were out for the count at times for a couple of days, but I never felt a thing.

Two Doctors gave me a thorough going over and I have a vague recollection of running and jumping round a gymnasium - maybe giving my heart a good test - and at the finish being told I was in excellent physical condition, and they had no hesitation in grading me A1, the top classification. As I write I am reading from my tattered Army Pay Book which says: - 30/12/43 medical grade A1 signed Mr. J Kerr, officer in charge, Medical Centre, Edinburgh. The statement confirmed what I thought then and ever since. The diagnosis relating to my heart made by the doctor who examined me prior to my enlisting was wrong. I should have been graded A1 and not B1. Be that as it may, what a significance the lower grading had made not only on my army career but more than just likely, my whole life. Had I been A1 the odds were such then that it is possible I would be a bit lucky to be here now telling my tale. Now is over fifty years on. A couple of years ago I was wired up to the very latest computerised cardiograph equipment at the local hospital and my heart result was still, A1.

I was convinced a transfer posting would come my way following discussions with various colleagues at HQ. They were of the opinion, and I could not have received advice from higher or a more appropriate authority. They all thought that being at HQ it was unlikely anything would happen until my three months were up and I was available. In the passing it was mentioned by someone that the Pay Corps had a tiny elite section for grade A1 personnel but as I had no experience at all about pay matters there was no need to give it another thought. I just had to leave it to fate to take me by the hand and into the future.

Being A1 and not having been in a technical trade in civvy street suitable for the army it was definitely on the cards it would be the infantry for me. It was the general opinion, and I did not relish the prospect because my two choices which would be open to me, namely The Royal Scots or the Kings Own Scottish Borders. They were Highland Division regiments and had been and were to continue to be in all the big battles because Montgomery would not move an inch without his "Highlanders". Norah and I and both our families were obviously a bit concerned and apprehensive about the future, but we realised it was only very mild concern compared to others. Thousands of husbands and wives, Mums and Dads, girlfriends and sweethearts were going through the hell of worry for their loved ones as many would never return and the worst of the war was still to come.

I think I worked what could be termed normal hours at HQ and do not recall ever having any special duties and was so lucky to be living at home. I knew my three months would be up on the 13th of March so had to organise myself accordingly and have the Hutting costed and completed by then for the Audit Branch. I only encountered the Chief Engineer himself on one or two occasions. I cannot remember his name. He was quite small for the army but very popular. What I would term the old school regular army officer. I met a few of that type and always liked them. Typical of him he did something for me which was to be of tremendous personal value later. He must have requested from Captain Scott my personal file and asked the CRE Glasgow and the DCRE's Perth and Stirling for a report about me.

At a much later date in India, I was being interviewed by four senior officers for a commission and they were curious to know how it came about that a then Corporal had impressive reports from a Colonel, a Lieutenant Colonel and two Major's of the Royal Engineers. The question took me completely by surprise as I was not aware it had happened. It was a wonderful thing for the old boy to do. I had obviously been appreciated.

As the 13th of March approached, every day I was looking at the Part 2 orders notice board with some trepidation scanning the column headed - Postings. Sure enough on the 14th my name was there. 7680868 Stark J Corporal Unit Accountant from Chief Engineering Staff RE Secondment to Regimental Paymasters 31st Battalion RAPC Edinburgh on 21st March 1944. My reaction - amazement, what a relief, for the time being anyway. I had a week to tidy up and say my goodbyes and in particular to Captain Scott. He was the one that had realised right from the start that the only way to tackle the Hutting Dump accounting job was to give someone complete freedom of movement to the Dumps and liaison with the DCRE's. He was under pressure from above and he just had to find a Cost Accountant. He noticed Cost Accountant on a form which landed on his desk, a chap named Stark who was rushed in to get the once over by him and the rest is history. He was a surprising character and most unlike a regular army officer. Always relaxed and easy going, certainly with me. Ready to give advice when it was required and always backed me up when necessary. He always seemed satisfied with the way I did things and the simple system I developed and just left me alone to get on with it - for three years.

Writing about them and thinking back they really were from my point of view quite incredible, and I was surely in a one-off situation. One day I was working at Waddies the next I was in the army supposedly as a qualified Cost Accountant which I certainly was not, said so and did not pretend to be but they paid no attention. Within three days I was in Perth in uniform and told to devise a stock and accounting control system for four Hutting Dumps. Given, except for two few spells, private accommodation, freedom to travel all over Scotland, if necessary, all expenses paid and special ration book. Given complete freedom to do my own thing in my own time. Had direct access to senior and high-ranking officers, military and civilian and attended meetings with them. All as a Private Corporal and during the three years had not one hour of army training. In that respect the Home Guard would have been proud of me!

In peacetime Hutting had just been another small item going through the Royal Engineers system. When war was imminent arrangements were made for small Dumps to be set up in strategic spots all over Britain (the same CRE/DCRE organisations were in all areas of the UK similar to that in Scotland). It was never envisaged that so much accommodation for troops would be required and on such a scale. Hutting was the answer and tremendous volume was required. Dumps had to be doubled and trebled in size, the peacetime system could not cope in Scotland which was taking the brunt of the requirements. The situation was becoming serious, and it was at that time I appeared on the scene. I had not a clue about accounting for Hutting. As part of my staff apprenticeships training at Waddies I had spent a year in the paper warehouse and had visited paper mills. I had been shown how to keep and handle stocks of paper and how to keep stock books of the reams of all the various qualities and sizes. I was following the simple system used at Waddies as it was the only one, I knew. All I did was substitute paper for huts and hoped for the best and it worked. I had just been in the right place at the right time.

As I came to the end of a phase in my service career, the army had definitely not been at all what I had expected. I had only glimpsed it in the passing. I must have felt a bit of a fraud having had such an easy and enjoyable time. However, I had followed to the letter advice given to me by my Home Guard colleagues - Never Volunteer! (I could have done so for the RE and stood a good chance of acceptance) take things as they come and accept them. So, I left behind me the CE, CRE's, DCRE's, Hutting, Dumps, Unit Accountant, Captain Scott and all who had been part of my life for the three years on the 20th March 1944, and in no time they would be forgotten.

CHAPTER EIGHT:
REFLECTIONS

I feel this is an appropriate time to again link my army story to biographical details of my own, the link on this occasion being my old school Daniel Stewart's College. I think I can say that it had been accepted in many educational circles that the finest "day" schools, as distinct from "boarding" schools, in Great Britain and just maybe around the world are situated in Scotland with many of the oldest and best known in Edinburgh. They are still "top of the class" today with long waiting lists with difficult entrance exams. The boys and girls who are successful having very proud parents ready and willing to pay expensive fees for their education.

Mr Daniel Stewart was a bachelor and a wealthy industrialist who lived from 1741 to 1814 and left all his money in trust for the designing and building of Daniel Stewart's Hospital for Boys. It took over thirty years for the trustees to accumulate enough money from investments for the project to begin and the foundation stone was laid in 1849. In 1854 (quote) "One of the finest and most elegant buildings in Edinburgh and of Elizabethan style and architecture was complete". It still stands today in all its glory and now as a great school of education.

Following the buildings completion in 1854 the Company of Edinburgh Merchants (later The Merchant Company) took over from the trustees the complete management and in 1870 the hospital became a school and

Daniel Stewart's College came into being. About the same time another three colleges came within the jurisdiction of the Company of Merchants - and still are today. George Watson's College, George Watson's Ladies College and Edinburgh Ladies College, where Norah was educated and later to be renamed The Mary Erskine School for Girls, after the founder.

The two pairs were known locally as the brother and sister schools and remain a famous four throughout the land and beyond. Norah and I will always be grateful and proud to have been pupils at two of those great schools. I can honestly say that my school day memories are happy ones. They must have been hectic at times during the five years I travelled the one and a quarter hour journey from Larbert to Edinburgh by train each day during terms. I had a twenty-minute wait and change for the Glasgow - Edinburgh express at Polmont Station which was halfway. On arrival I had a twenty-minute walk to the school and of course the reverse journey in the afternoon after school. That routine was carried out six days a week as every Saturday morning in the winter I played rugby for one of the teams against other Edinburgh Schools. In the summertime it was golf. We were given the courtesy of all the well-known Edinburgh and Lothian courses but had to be at the first tee before 9.00am. To do that I had to catch the 7.00am train from Larbert.

Each day was very long from the early start to arrival back home, then evening meal, homework, off to bed, then up with the lark next morning and start again. I made many friends on my daily travels collected at station stops along the way at Falkirk, Polmont and Livingstone, some going to Stewart's, some going to the other Edinburgh schools. We all became pals, we had fun, they were exciting times. I wonder if parents today would allow their ten-year-old sons - the age I started - take a similar daily travelling programme to and from school. I doubt it.

I enjoyed school but I was not much good at it, very average. The amazing thing was that from the start I was put in the "A" stream, which was classical, French, Latin, Greek, Science, English Lit, Math and all that.

They would not let me out of it, and I was always floundering and out of my depth. I always maintained that the reason was that I got on very well with the class masters was because they were all golfers and I happened to be a very useful partner when they required one!

As my time went on at Stewart's, Mother was my guide and influence and as I grew up, I realised just what a wonderful job she did on my behalf. She really had most to do with my upbringing because father was away at sea for long spells and home for short spells. That is not to say he did not take the same interest because he did. I do remember him telling me to take Mother's advice as she was always on the spot and had great vision and foresight, which she had. This was proved when I left school and joined Waddies & Company Limited when I was fifteen years plus four months old to be exact.

My Uncle Hugh (Dad's brother) was a headmaster of quite a large school and thought he knew best about my future, namely university and a profession, especially from a school with the standing of Daniel Stewart's College. But Mother just knew I could not make university standard as my results were there to prove it and no extra tuition would do the trick - and I knew it too. This caused quite a family bust up at the time, but Mother stood her ground as she could recognise I was "made for a trade". She really never forgave Hugh for the way he went on at that time. I well remember when I was appointed a Director of Waddies in 1959 how thrilled she was - and would make sure Hugh would receive the news without delay!

Just how did I come to join Waddies? They were requiring a young lad to begin a five-year Printing and Stationery Trade Staff Apprenticeship with them. It was their custom to approach Stewart's College first. The owners of Waddies and by then the in-law side of the family, the Wards, had on the male side all been educated at Stewart's. Mother heard about this and made enquiries. Without telling any of the family she arranged an interview for me having given me great encouragement and confidence to go. I was interviewed by the Company Secretary, Miss McDonald and also by Marcus Ward the Managing Director who, like his two brothers Kenneth and Harry were of course "Daniels". I later discovered Mr Marcus had contacted the Headmaster and my Form Master whom he knew and had all the relevant information about me.

I have two letters which I have kept safely all these years which I feel are worth quoting in detail. The first is dated the 11th of January 1936 from Waddie and Company Limited, Manufacturing Stationers and Printers.

James Stark Esq.

Dear Sir,

Further to the interview which we had with you yesterday we shall be glad if you will arrange to start work on Tuesday the 14th instant on one month's trial to be trained as an apprentice Stationer and Printer.

If suitable we would confirm your appointment for five years at a salary of £15 per annum rising by £5 per annum to £35 in the last year of your apprenticeship and which can only be broken by one months' notice on either side.

The hours are Monday to Thursday inclusive 9am to 6pm, Friday 9am to 5pm and Saturday 9am to 12am but during the first year of your apprenticeship you will require to stay a little later to post the mail. We give fourteen days holiday in the summer plus certain statutory holidays.

Yours faithfully

J. McDonald

Cashier and Secretary

The second letter is dated 19th February 1936

Dear Sir,

As you have now completed one month's trial as apprentice Stationer and Printer, we confirm your appointment for five years at the terms detailed in our letter of the 11th of January but while you are still resident in Larbert and have heavy travelling expenses we are prepared to increase your salary by £5 per annum and your rate will know be at £20 per annum.

Please note this apprenticeship can only be broken by one months' notice on either side.

Yours faithfully

J. McDonald

Cashier and Secretary

Those were the days when to join a firm of recognised prestige or a profession to be trained, parents had to pay for that privilege as salaries were a pittance. Waddies were that type of company. It makes me feel proud to look at the beautiful die-stamped headings the above letters are typed on. Waddies were specialists in die-stamping and supplied their printing and stationery throughout the Empire. Included on the letter heading is the die-stamped wording: - Offices and Agencies at - Plummer House, 5-6 Fancy Lane, Calcutta (little did I know then I was to visit that address later - in uniform). Exchange Buildings, Hong Kong. Also at Bangkok, Batavia, Bombay, Columbo, British West Indies, Rangoon, Shanghai and Singapore. I mention these details as it reminds me about Waddies when I joined them. They were so well known and well established throughout Great Britain and overseas. Harry Ward the export Sales Director spent all his time visiting our colonial countries collecting business and developing Waddies export trade. Very few printing companies had permanent salesmen and overseas offices in those days.

When I left school, I immediately joined the Former Pupils Club and have been an active member ever since. In those days there was only the Parent Club in Edinburgh and the London Club both being long established. As time went on after the war several clubs were formed and most of them are active today. All the well-known Scottish schools have Former Pupil Clubs in their hometown and usually one in London. In my time the school remained part of our life. The FPC kept us in touch about what was going on at school and also with our school pals and friends we had made from other schools through sport and in my case rugby and golf. I am not so sure if boys when they leave nowadays have the same depth of feeling as we had for their schools. Stewarts College was certainly a great influence on me and helped me tremendously along life's way, particularly in business.

Saying so brings to my mind something I shall never forget. I feel it is worth mentioning in detail as maybe it is a reflection of the business attitude during the period just after the war in the late 1940's. For six long years the only business for companies had been war connected. The war was over, and it was time for re-establishment of business. What may be termed "old fashioned" and prewar the 1930's outlook was still with us, but everyone knew the "modern" future was on the horizon. We did not know what it was going to be like but every company worth their salt had to prepare for it. It is the advice given to me by Mr Marcus Ward, the Chairman and Managing Director of Waddies, before being sent to the London office in 1948 to represent the company on the sales side.

"Jim - You will always be smartly dressed in a good quality suit. With it you will wear a white shirt and a stiff white collar. You will always wear a hat preferably Anthony Eden style. You will always wear your Daniel Stewart's College FPC tie when representing the company. You will be supplied with a company car of British manufacture. You will never drive a car of foreign make. We will pay your entrance fee and subscription for joining a first-class golf course of your choice in the London area (which turned out to be South Herts). When travelling by train you will always travel first class including overnight sleeper. If need be, we will help you buy a house in a nice London suburb. We are confident you have the necessary knowledge about our products and how they are produced and the pricing structure. You will never "tout" for business. You will sell yourself to the customer. They must have confidence in you to have confidence in us and our products. We will never let you down and we are sure you will not let us down."

Even in this "ultra-modern" day and age, I think that takes some beating for starters as they were also paying me a decent salary. It is no wonder I gave of my best to Waddies for forty-five years. I don't think I ever let them down. They certainly never let me down. I know Norah will confirm all the points mentioned above and also since that day in 1948 until I retired in 1980, I wore my FPC tie every day I was on company business whether for Waddies or their subsidiary, Barlows. I still wear it regularly, the red rampant lion on the old gold and black background is still noticed and very often mentioned.

Arriving in London at the time I did in October 1948 my initiation as a salesman was into the biggest sales market ever and it turned out to be very difficult and complicated. Because of the terrific bombing most companies had cleared out of London into the provinces and countryside, anywhere to be out of range. When I arrived on the scene a few firms were gradually filtering back if they had premises or accommodation repaired enough to occupy. I discovered many of our customers were still miles and hours away by car in all sorts of odd places and difficult to find. The result was I had a huge amount of travelling to do. Paper was severely rationed, and my work was not finding the customers but how to keep customers happy sharing out what I had available to sell them. I had my quota of paper at Edinburgh for printing, but I discovered

I could supplement it by scrounging from paper mill warehouses in London, loading my car and taking it to a small trade printer I found in Clerkenwell not far from our office called Bluett. He would do the printing and I would deliver to my customers. I kept Bluett going for years. Edinburgh did not mind as I could find plenty of the big jobs for them and I always made a reasonable profit for Waddies from Bluett's processing.

When I arrived in London the famous square mile of the City had still not been cleaned up, being a monumental task. It had been flattened by the continual bombing and burned out by the incendiaries. I can recall standing outside the office we shared in Moorgate - everybody shared premises, telephones and all services as it was the only way to function - and being able to see what was left of Kings Cross Station - two miles away and in between was just rubble. You could look down outside Moorgate Station and "see" the Underground trains running through sections of tunnel which were open to the sky. Looking back, it was quite an experience to be involved in London at that time. Chaos and frustration of some sort was a daily occurrence, but everyone took it in their stride as they still had the wartime determination and spirit to win through against all sorts of odds. It was the early 1950s before business life really returned to something like normal when a buyers' market arrived again. In many ways it was a lot easier to cope with it then than having a print buyer down on his hands and knees pleading with you to accept his order!

I joined the Former Pupils Club not long after my arrival in London and immediately found myself among friends. I think a few that had been at school in my time, but many members were a lot older. They were all well established with years of experience in the big city and in executive business and professional positions. My interest developed as time went on and I was asked to be a member of the committee on which I served for many years until for the club years 1961/1962, I had the honour of being selected President. The highlight of my term in office was being

Chairman at the Annual Dinner which by tradition was held at The Royal Automobile Club in Pall Mall. It was Friday 16th February 1962 with sixty-five members and guests present. It was a proud night for me in more ways than one, because my Father was my special guest.

The position I held then caused me to be at quite a few dinners of other London clubs of other Scottish schools. I was also a principal guest at the Parent Club Dinner in Edinburgh which was always held in the magnificent Merchant Company Hall. I was at the School Founders Day and found myself on a committee at the school dealing with matters which required the advice of former pupils. The other members included The Headmaster, The Vice Governor, representing the Merchant Company, the President of the Parent Club and others. It was a most interesting and stimulating time for me.

I was very fortunate indeed to be able to organise my school meeting dates with my monthly visits to Edinburgh for Waddies main board meetings - or was it the other way round? I seem to recall Mr Ward arranging board meetings to suit me! Maybe it was because I happened to be one of the few Stewartonians on the Board and I had a vote!

When quite suddenly in mid-1963 I was transferred from London to (then) West Hartlepool to become Managing Director of William Barlow & Sons and Alma Press Limited, little did I realise that my closeness to the school would continue. I did not know a FPC was being formed in Manchester and I was only in Hartlepool for five minutes when contacted by an old school rugby player pal of mine by the name of Bill Ralph, who was one of the many Stewarts FP's who had played for Scotland, informed me, not asking, that I was on the committee of the new club. The reason being because of my FPC experience gained in London. I made it clear I would only take a back seat as Manchester was a long way and I had not the time. I attended their Dinner each year and helped when I could doing a short spell as treasurer. After twelve years I succumbed to pressure and was appointed President which was a two-year stint. Our

Annual Dinner was held at the Midland Hotel, Manchester and I was Chairman in October 1976 and 1977. The Manchester Dinners were more informal than London and Edinburgh so enjoyed more by the Headmaster and other dignitaries as they could let their hair down! So, I had to go through all the previous routine twice in Edinburgh but not nearly as demanding as when in London. A bit of a fuss was made however as I was only the third former pupil in history to have been President of two clubs. I know the London Club started in 1906 and Edinburgh a lot further back but I cannot trace the date. Unfortunately, the North of England Club folded in 1984 after twenty-one years due to travel distance combined with cost as it had an overnight stay in the hotel for many.

In the early 1970's another famous Edinburgh school but a smaller one, called Melville College, approached the Merchant Company about a merger with Stewart's and in 1973 the two schools joined forces in the most amicable way and became known as Daniel Stewart's and Melville College. (As a committee member of the North of England Club I was involved with the merger arrangements relating to the FPC's of both schools.) The FPC's joined forces and continued with great enthusiasm. I am still a member and always will be, but I am not involved nowadays but I look forward to receiving their excellent magazine, The Collegian.

I must also mention Norah's school. I have to say that in every way it was and still is, as good a school as Stewart's and in fact is quite a lot older. In our day Edinburgh Ladies College was situated in elegant Queen Street but there was no room for expansion. So, some years ago the Merchant Company built a magnificent new modern school at Ravelstone a lovely part of Edinburgh and only a mile from Stewart's. That was when it was renamed The Mary Erskine School for Girls and like Stewart's is very much in the upper echelon of education in Scotland. It was always known as our sister school and nowadays although apart both co-ed in many respects. Like myself Norah has always taken a great interest as a former pupil and in fact is a lifelong member of the Merchant Maidens Guild.

As former pupils they are called Merchant Maidens. Now that conjures up all sorts of thoughts in one's mind! I would love to attend a meeting of the Maidens but have never been asked! Many moons ago I played in the Stewart's FPC golf team against a whole team of Maidens but that is a far-off memory.

It is now time to revert back to the main theme of my story. However, I hope the reflections I have related will serve to give an understanding of just how significant my school and Waddies have been to me.

CHAPTER NINE:
THE 31ST BATTALION, CAMP J7 AND OPERATION OVERLORD

The 31st Battalion of the RAPC was situated in a series of huge single storey buildings which had been the home of Strang Coupons before the war. They were the original football pools company, established in 1922, who were eventually bought out by Littlewoods. It is interesting to note that the first Strang football coupons were printed by Waddies.

The many buildings covered a huge area on the way to Leith and next door to the Hibernian Football Club ground. Inside and from memory there were I think five or six hundred RAPC personnel of all ranks including civilians. It was the pay office for all the Scottish Regiments. There were others of similar size throughout the UK plus two dealing with only officers pay which were a separate branch of the Corps. A Regimental Pay Office was made up of many different sections which each had twenty to thirty-five staff. The section officer in charge was a Lieutenant who had as a number two a Sergeant. A number of sections would become a Wing with a Captain and a Staff Sergeant as his NCO. Two or three Wings would be a Group with a Major and a Sergeant Major as his NCO. ATS and civilians were also in senior ranking positions but not at top level. The Commanding Officer was a Lieutenant Colonel. That was the general command structure of a Pay Office Battalion. There were of course the other usual officers and NCO's dealing with administration, training, transport, security etc. I was to discover the Pay Corps was a very well organised, efficient and very important part of the British Army.

I can remember reporting to the Adjutant because his office was in a large Nissen hut. It had been erected as an extension to part of the main building where the Colonel had his office. I had seen it all before! Fortunately, the Adjutant (Captain) was a regular soldier and knew something about Unit Accountants (I was to discover that apart from some regulars, nobody in the wartime RAPC Pay Office had ever heard of an RAPC Unit Accountant). He was as much in the dark about what I had been doing as I was about pay. He had my records in front of him and said he appreciated my position. He obviously required time to think what he would do with me and to my astonishment told me to go home and report back in three days. I was not too happy as visions of the Royal Scots were entering my mind again as he had noticed I was medical category A1.

I reported back in three days and without delay was marched into the office of the Second-in-Command, Major Oram. He was a huge man well over six feet tall and in the region of sixteen to seventeen stone. A regular who had come up the hard way through the ranks from Private. He was a bluff, frank but hearty with it and always called a spade a spade. He could be understanding, always fair and even sympathetic at times as long as you were doing your very best. God help you, no matter your rank, if he thought you were not pulling your weight. Because of his attitude he was very popular and like all regular soldiers I encountered, he knew his stuff. It turned out fortunate for me that I came under his influence and discipline.

I was to realise later why the 31st had the name of being a well organised and well-run battalion. The Regimental Paymaster, Lieutenant Colonel Rowbotham was the opposite of "Big Bill" Oram as he was unofficially called. The Colonel was also a regular, but the university trained, qualified accountant, staff college type with expert organising and administrative ability. The type of soldier who proved to be so essential at the very highest level "organising" the winning of the war. The Colonel was a quiet and dignified person and also very popular but nevertheless a soldier down to his boot straps. A command paymaster had to have expert qualifications especially financial as they had a very highly skilled job to do. He was in effect a brilliant desk man and that is where his orders came from. Major Oram made sure they were understood and carried out by all ranks following his sensible disciplinary procedures.

The Major had my record file and asked me a few questions then gave me orders that were quite specific and very clear - and went something like this:

" You will begin a crash course immediately on all aspects of pay and allowances for every rank in the army except officers. Arrangements have been made that you will be given priority and special attention by all sections in the office. Here is a copy of the Army Pay and Allowances Manual, which is up to date, and you will study page by page. I expect you to work like hell as your time limit will be only six weeks. You have a great incentive because if you pass an examination board test it is just possible, being medical category A1, that you may be selected for transfer to the Active Service Field Cashier Section of the Corps."

Then as I recall somewhere along the line, he told me I was to be billeted at home and my only duty would be to take my turn on guard at night. Not for the first time I was completely mystified, which was becoming a normal occurrence with me since joining the army.

The Pay Office worked seven days a week 8am to 6pm although I seem to remember there was always a reasonable amount of free time at weekends. I selected to do all my studying at the Pay Office, flat out six days a week and avoiding any work at home as being the only way to cope. I was given a desk in a quiet spot and had to organise myself to fit in with many sections.

Studying my Red book now regarding my own pay details takes me back to what I had to come to terms with during those six weeks forty-six years ago. I discovered there was a multitude of different grades and rates of pay for every rank, single and married. Voluntary and compulsory contributions to wives and mothers, marriage allocations, children's allowances, extra pay entitlement for special duties and for serving overseas which was a wilderness of pay scales on its own. Special service allowances, kit allowances, income tax, post war credits and so it went on. It must have been a bit bewildering for me at first, but I obviously came to terms with the system. I went round all the sections and was given excellent attention by them as "Big Bill" was keeping an eye on them and me every day. I soon realised the benefit of keeping to the manual. They were amazing publications, and I am sure they still are to this day.

As I write, one section in particular comes to mind which was called The Heartbreak. Quite a large staff was involved and as things turned out was due to increase later. They dealt with communications and correspondence to and from wives and mothers' whose husbands and sons had been killed. Many wanted financial details and requests for help etc. Keeping in mind that every person during the war had worries and concerns about a close relative or friend. Staff of that section had to be able to cope and have a special kind of dedication to avoid emotional strain.

At the end of six weeks, my mind saturated with pay and allowances, I managed to cope with a question-and-answer session from a board of examiners which included the Major, a Group Major, Wing Captain and Section Lieutenant. Afterwards I received the important decision that I would be recommended for transfer to the Active Service Field Cashier Section. At the outset when I was told about the crash course, I wondered why there was such a rush. This had also been noticed by all concerned including the Section Officers because Major Oram was really forcing the pace with them, and they were wondering what it was all about. I had not long to wait for an answer as the Colonel and Big Bill had been privy to perhaps the most secret of all the secrets of World War Two.

Immediately on arrival at the Pay Office at 8am on the 6th of May 1944, I was asked to report to Colonel Rowbotham. I arrived outside his door at the same time as Captain Stoddart, a Wing Officer, whom I knew as he and his family were friends of Norah's Mother, being near neighbours. A Sergeant Thomson, whom I had never met, was also present. We were ushered into the Colonel's office where he was waiting for us along with Major Oram.

The first thing the Colonel did was to read out to us the Code of Secrecy from Kings Regulations and advise us we were within the code's jurisdiction from that moment. He then proceeded to tell us that from that day, 6th May the three of us were being transferred to the Active Service Field Cashier Section and become a Field Cashier Unit with the Captain in command. Sergeant Thomson his number two and I, who would be promoted to Sergeant number three. (He explained that a Field Cashier Unit was always made up of an Officer and two Sergeants.) He then told us we had been selected for special duties but could say no more. We were kitted out in full active service field uniforms, including firearms. We would leave for our destination during the evening of the 9th May and would receive further orders on that date. We would inform our next of kin and make it known we were going to the RAPC Development Centre in the Midlands. That was normal procedure and a regular occurrence for transfer and postings. We were each given a copy of the manual relating to the duties of a Field Cashier on active service and told to read it. We were excused all duties in the Pay Office. We were to report that day to - of all places - Redford Barracks to be kitted out as the RAPC Quartermasters Stores did not keep active service gear. Captain Stoddart would arrange team talks and ensure we all understood the manual. We were to make ourselves scarce and not have any meetings at the Pay Office. We would have them in private at home or wherever it was suitable. We were given complete freedom and trust to get things done and be ready to receive our further orders on the 9th. That was all and we were to leave the Pay Office Immediately. From being told to make ourselves scarce my mind goes blank. I think the three of us caught a tram car to the town and had our first team talk somewhere. One thing I feel sure about and that is we were asking each other the same questions. Delighted to be appointed Field Cashiers but with battle uniforms and firearms - where the hell were we going? We all reached the same conclusion and what a very sobering thought it was, namely the invasion of Europe.

I think we then went to the Redford Barracks and were kitted out in full battle order and firearms. A revolver for the Captain and .303 for Thomson and myself. Thanks to the Home Guard I knew all about the .303 rifle. Battle hardened Royal Scots comments must have been worth hearing at Redford Barracks when they saw three Pay Corps guys in full battle gear!

During the next couple of days, we only met once for a short session being anxious to spend time at home and to prepare all our kit requirements for the unknown ahead. I could only tell Norah, her Mother, and my Mother and Father what I knew, namely going to the RAPC Development Centre in the Midlands. Talk about the second front as it was called, coming very soon was on everyone's lips throughout Britain which was chocked with troops and war machines ready to explode into action. The morale generated by Winston Churchill was tremendous and there was a great feeling of confidence about but also a nervousness within every family in the land. They all had loved ones involved and could sense the coming soon off a terrific battle from somewhere along our island shores. It was therefore in those atmospheric conditions that I said my goodbyes. There was no kidding the family. They knew I was going to be involved somewhere along the line, as my uniform gear alone put the frighteners on them, and they were very concerned. So was I, at very best apprehensive? It had all happened so suddenly and unexpectedly.

So on the 9th May 1944 we reported early evening to the Colonels office for our final orders and we were instantly taken by surprise. He said that what he had told us previously about going to the Development Centre was a cover story. We were leaving from Waverley Station at 10pm on a troop train to London. We would report at the HQ of the Command Paymaster-in-Chief next day. We were given railway warrants and told we would receive further orders on arrival at Kings Cross Station in the morning. He wished us good luck and said transport was waiting to take us to the station. On arrival we reported the RTO (Regimental Transport Office) and come 10pm were puffing our way into the blacked-out countryside which was awaiting us.

A word about my two colleagues. Eric Stoddart would then be about forty. By sheer coincidence he had lived with his wife and daughter in the same road as Norah and her Mother for many years and both families were friends. I had only known him in passing. He had been an accountant but had volunteered for the Pay Corps before the war started and had been granted a commission. He had good looks, was always immaculate and liked being in uniform. He should have been a regular soldier as the army suited him. He had style and knew it and could hold his own with all ranks. He was a good Captain of our team, always did his share of the work and made sure we were looked after and always kept informed. Eventually as the war went on, he became a full Major and when hostilities ended remained in the Occupation Forces for a year or so as Paymaster of Ostend which at the time was a very important appointment.

As soon as we met, Murray Thomson and I were on the same wavelength. He had also been a medical B1, for his eyesight and then like me, was examined again and found to be A1. He was a Carlisle lad and had worked in the accounts department of the LMS Railway. He had been enlisted into the Pay Corps right at the start of the war working his way through various Regimental Pay Offices to Sergeant of a section and was very experienced which was good news for me. He was strong, stalky and a good footballer having had a trial for Carlisle United. He had a great sense of humour and we became great pals.

I feel I can say that I was a member of a very efficient Field Cashiers Unit and most fortunate to be with two very experienced colleagues. After all

I was a real rookie Field Cashier with no experience of the job, thrown in at the deep end - no, too shallow, more like thrown into the middle of the Atlantic - as little did I know then what was ahead of me!

It has always been said that the best armies "march on their stomachs" as being well fed is of prime importance. It also became a fact especially during the Second World War that money became as important ingredient in the makeup of fighting men's morale. This was in the sense that a "money worry" especially at home, relating to his wife and family could escalate in their mind and influence their performance and concentration. Given an assurance that something would be done about it they need not worry and that could give them peace of mind. The Field Cashier was there to listen and do just that.

A Field Cashier Unit always consisted of three RAPC men. Either a Captain/Paymaster or a Lieutenant/Paymaster in command along with his two Sergeant Cashiers. There was always a Field Cashier Unit with a Division (20,000 men or more). When on active service they were usually well away from trouble at Rear HQ. It may not be realised that during the war even when bloody battles are in progress, somewhere and sometimes behind the lines, money must be on hand and financial experience available.

The Cashier Unit Commander would always have his cash boxes with him. They were specially constructed rather like ammunition boxes in design. They would contain appropriate currencies in large amounts and could be very heavy if not containing notes. They were continually on a Unit Commanders mind night and day as they had to be in a safe place under guard as he was personally responsible.

The contents had to be accounted for in the strictest possible detail. Field Cashier Units came under the jurisdiction of the Command Paymaster (who have been mentioned previously in my story) and not the Regimental Paymaster. It will be remembered Command Paymasters were responsible for in effect all finances other than pay and allowances which were the responsibility of the Regimental Paymaster. The Field Cashier was very much involved on both sides of the fence and therefore built up a wide knowledge relating to the complexities of army monies. When Divisions were static and not involved in action all Commanding Officers of Companies, Units etc. within the Regiments required cash and financial aid of all kinds and therefore had responsibilities accordingly. Men had to be paid, supplies of all kinds purchased and the lists being endless. They had to keep account of money received and how it was spent. They were required to prepare a balance sheet which without exception every CO hated. They would therefore greet a Cashier with open arms to help them especially in foreign countries when currencies were involved.

War time tram journeys were quite an experience and could be frightening if evening bombers were about especially during the night. The trains were always packed with service personnel and the general public. It is well to remember that the choice when travelling was either bus or tram. Petrol was rationed and privileged coupons were necessary for running a private car. It could never be guaranteed trains would run to time as the drivers and the guards often had many problems to contend with especially in the numerous target areas. However, be that as it may, they seldom failed to get their passengers to their destination somehow. Night travel could be traumatic with the whole tram blacked out by heavy window blinds and very low wattage bulbs lighting the carriages. In those days the heating came from large steam pipes under the seats, and it could be a hot, sweaty stifling journey.

The troops train we were on was jam packed tight, which was normal. Fortunately, we had a seat, but the unlucky ones had to sit or be on the corridor floor. Kit was stacked everywhere; every inch of the carriages and corridors were taken up. Going to the toilet could be a major and sometimes painful operation, especially for those on the floor as army boots could be very awkward in small places in the dark!

We had what could be called a good journey until we were on the outskirts of Greater London. A raid was on, and we were at a standstill for quite a long time. We eventually crawled along and arrived at Kings Cross Station I think around 9am. We reported to the RTO who told us to walk to Development Centre which was near the station. It had a NAAFI and we tucked into breakfast. We very soon realised it was also a Collection Centre for Field Cashier Units arriving from all over the country as the regular appearance of an officer accompanied by two Sergeants was quite conspicuous.

Eventually we were collected together, transport arrived, and we proceeded through the city continually making bomb damage detours, crossed one of the famous Thames bridges and arrived at a large house in its own grounds somewhere in outer London known as the Surrey belt (nowadays known as the stockbroker belt) which turned out to be the HQ of the Command Paymaster in Chief. I should remember where it was but cannot as some years later when working in London, suddenly on my travels I recognised the house and grounds. I recall the journey through London that day and I doubt any of us had appreciated the enormity of the bomb damage. It was incredible to us despite the awful devastation surrounding them the people in the streets had a "business as usual" attitude and cheerfulness. We were looking at people who had been bombed to hell night after night. Many had suffered the loss of whole families, children, relatives and friends and also complete destruction of their homes and possessions. Yet there they were with indomitable spirit and courage showing on their faces. They were the ultimate example to the whole country.

We were each very carefully checked in and reminded again about obeying the code of secrecy. We were issued with a carton of the famous 'K' rations which had to see us through the rest of the day. I think there were twenty maybe a few more Units of three present and we were all ushered into a large room, and all seated for a briefing session. The Paymaster and a Bombardier opened the proceedings then a Colonel took over. He told us we had been chosen to play our part within the organisation which would culminate in the invasion of Europe by British and Allied Forces. An operation which would be code named "Overlord" but we did not know when and where the invasion would take place as it would be Top Secret until the last possible minute.

Immediately following the briefing, transport would be waiting to take each Unit to separate camps which were prepared and ready and located throughout the South of England. They would take thousands upon thousands of troops, and before leaving each Unit Commander would be given the code number of the Camp he and his Sergeant would go to. Camp locations would be divided into two separate areas. Troops would arrive at camps in the Assembly Area where they would remain for a few days. They would then proceed to a camp in the Embarkation Area for only a short time. When the Assembly Area camps were full, they would be sealed with no movement in or out except under special circumstances. At a given time we would receive our cash boxes which would contain large amounts of cash in notes of the currency required by the troops going through our camps. Each cash box would be coded and positively no box was to be opened until orders were received to do so. This point was hammered into the Unit Commanders as it was an order to them from the "Overlord" Command HQ and no order could come from anywhere higher than that. Later we were to appreciate the significance of it all.

Each camp would have a Commanding Officer and the Assembly Area camp would have quite a large staff including catering, medical, security, transport, admin etc. every necessity was covered including us. It was explained that we would be a very important part of the camp CO's set up but be self-contained as our orders would come from our own Command HQ. He would rely on us for cash requirements and all things financial for the running of the Camps. Arrangements had been made with local banks and we would carry out standard routine transactions in that respect and a separate set of cash boxes was laid on. However, the most important part of our duties would be when the time came to give maximum attention to the troops who were passing through and be prepared to work all hour's day and night on their benefit.

The briefing session ended and writing about it brings back to me the atmosphere of excitement and tension as we all realised the invasion of Europe was about to take place very soon and we were going to be a part of it. Our destination was Camp J7. Outside were rows of small, camouflaged utility trucks with military police drivers standing by them. We soon were on our way to Camp J7 which was near Uckfield in Sussex. We duly arrived late at night, dead beat after a long and exhausting and tension filled twenty-four hours. Camp J7 had been a huge estate near Uckfield covering many acres and included a couple of farms within its boundary. It had belonged to the local Lord of the Manor, whose name escapes me and had been requisitioned lock, stock and barrel including the beautiful manor house which had been emptied of all its contents. The estate was very wooded. There were large lawns, gardens a lake, stables and outhouses. It had been a lovely place.

The day after our arrival, 10th May 1944 the three of us spent our time looking around and were staggered at what we saw. There were hundreds of large, camouflaged marquee type tents erected all over the estate under trees and out of sight. What we would call nowadays a tented village. There were long canteen marquees full of wooden tables and bench seating and next to them great field service kitchen facilities and stores. The Camp staff were quartered in the outbuildings near the house and Nissen huts were at hand. The staff set-up on its own was quite something with all the Corps and more that were mentioned at the briefing being represented. The manor house had the necessary admin offices for the Camp Commander and senior Corps staff, also the Officers' quarters and mess and the Sergeants mess.

The Camp was an amazing sight now empty but was to be a fantastic and frightening place sealed with thousands of men in full battle order waiting patiently for the order to move on into battle to fight and many of them certain to die. It must be remembered that there were similar Camps to ours with Field Cashier colleagues situated right along the South Downs and forests. The 21st Allied Army Group of nearly a million fighting men and machines also had all their supplies under the command of their General, Sir Bernard Law Montgomery, were about to be hidden ready for action across the Channel when the order was given by General of the Armies, Dwight D Eisenhower the Supreme Allied Commander.

From our arrival we got on well with Major Russell the Camp CO. He had discovered that a room on the ground floor of the house had a large Chubb Strongroom built into it and had obtained the key and reserved the room for us. It was a good size and ideal for our office. He also had the good sense to allot the room next door for Murray and me as our living quarters. It was small but adequate with two barrack room beds and basic furniture. We made it comfortable, it was good, and our Mess was near at hand. Sto (as we came to call him between ourselves) was in the Officers' quarters upstairs, one of the few who had a room on his own.

I think that would be the first occasion I realised being a Field Cashier was a bit special. Whenever you happened to be with the CO no matter his rank, he always went out of his way to make you welcome. His orders were "make sure the Cashier and his boys are looked after", why? Because you could solve his Regimental, Battalion, Company and whatever pay issues and financial problems at a stroke and so he thought but above all help him balance his hated bloody accounts. Major Russell was no exception and similar thoughts had been running through his mind long before we appeared on the scene. We soon became organised and into a routine, Murray and I discovered Sto was a bit fussy and a stickler for going by the book, but Murray gradually made him realise due to the very special circumstances corners had to be cut and he agreed. We respected him even more for that and we developed into a good team. Sto and Murray were very good to me personally. Knowing I only had a crash course they made sure I understood the Pay and Allowances

Manual. It soon became apparent to me just how important it was that I did know my stuff.

We soon got to know the staff especially the Sergeant and the Warrant Officers in the Mess. They tended to become our friends as they soon got round to a pay or family allowance problem. It became that we had an open office door for all the camp staff and sorted out their financial queries. We went to the bank at Uckfield, and made our cash arrangements, and made sure the CO's account was on the right lines as such a large camp involved a lot of financial transactions. Towards the end of the second week, we received a two-day advanced warning that a General Officers inspection would take place. The regular soldiers and the camp staff gave us all another warning what to expect and it was a real eye opener for the Pay Corps lads like us.

We had all heard and read about the great British Armies throughout history had won their battles by strict training, strict discipline and spit and polish. It had become legend at the time that was exactly how General Montgomery won his great battles in the very recent past. It therefore came about that for two long days everything in sight inside and out was scrubbed, polished, dusted, swept, lawns cut, and paths raked. Uniforms, although in battle order were creased in the right places and belt buckles and boots polished. The CO inspected every man and nook and cranny of the camp. He was satisfied that nobody was going to let him down.

Mentioning Monty as he was affectionately known by everyone reminds me that he was equivalent to God in the eyes of his men and every ounce of their confidence was with him as their leader. It was a fact that he demanded the Divisions and Regiments he wanted, and the senior staff he wanted, and he got them. He would not move an inch until he was satisfied, they were fully prepared and ready for battle. Both Churchill and Eisenhower knew that only too well from experience. The detailed inspection of every Regiment, Battalion, Unit and even every Camp when empty was Monty's way of making sure every soldier under his command was on their toes, not only just ready for action but as he always put it, ready to win!

The third day arrived when out of a chauffeur driven car stepped a Brigadier and two senior Staff Officers. We had been told to be at our posts which for us was the office. We thought it most unlikely that the "red tab" would come our way as we would surely be on the bottom of his list.

After a couple of hours or so we thought the inspection was over as the grapevine told us they were in the CO's office. Suddenly a knock came on the door, and it was a message from Captain Russell saying the Brigadier wished to see Captain Stoddart immediately. Sto was not exactly in a state of shock but certainly shaken maybe thinking he was for the Tower of London! He was a long time away and Murray and I began to wonder what the hell was going on. When he did return, he had an amazing story to tell which was to cause us problems plus a situation to come of unforgettable tension.

At the briefing in Surrey we were told that the cash boxes we received would have special code numbers on them. Sto had been told by the Brigadier that the Commanding Officers of the troops who were in the camps for landings "on the other side" on "D Day" would be given a similar number to that on one of our boxes. When the numbers were linked by Sto and checked by Major Russell and the order from Overlord Command HQ to open the Top Secret sealed orders for they would be inside, along with the currency necessary for where they were going. The envelopes with the orders would be handed to the CO's by Sto. Similar procedures would take place at all camps. It was to be an operation of great intensity and a mistake was just out of the question. That had been made very clear!

I do remember immediately the Brigadier had gone, the CO came to our office warning us to be careful as it was already round the whole camp that Captain Stoddart had been in a long meeting and other than the CO he had been the only camp officer attending. We were sure to be "pumped" for information from all quarters and that is exactly what happened. Sto had told Murray and me the whole story and the three of us realised it was a very serious business we were involved in and a single word out of place could be fatal. However we survived, especially in our Messes as there was a sort of code of conduct in the Services about knowing when a person would not and could not give an answer. It blew over as everyone had other things on their minds.

CHAPTER TEN:
MY PART IN OPERATION
OVERLORD AND D DAY

May and the weather was glorious and things quietened down. We could write home and receive mail, but the outgoing was censored as we could not give a clue to where we were. It was all done through the Army Post Office and the address being c/o APO Box J7. The staff were allowed in groups to the local village a mile or so away which had two pubs. It was a pleasant country walk there and back. We became friends with the locals, they knew what was going on but would never ask or bring the subject up in conversation. We had the freedom to go out at any time in two's as one had to be on duty. Murray and I took turns at going with Sto to Uckfield usually on bank business. He would take his turn at looking after the shop to allow us out and sometimes we would join other members of the staff. We were all under very strict orders to keep our mouths shut and a limit was put on drinking. We were careful as Military Police were all over the place. The public by then had a deep sense of involvement and were security conscious as they could not help but be part of what was going on in their minds.

Everything had been checked and double checked throughout the camp and everyone had very little to do. We were well aware it was the calm before the storm. It was then that what could be termed a therapeutic event took place and it was all started by Sto. It seems so incongruous now but definitely true.

Sto was a keen gardener and noticed that what had been beautiful flower beds, each very large and plenty of them, were overgrown and in a dreadful state. Following his instructions Murray and I joined him tidying them up and in no time, we had a real army of helpers as most of the camp staff joined in. I remember we even borrowed tools from our village friends. I personally must have cut back hundreds of rose bushes, and any knowledge I have about doing so comes from that experience. The gardens were dug over and cleaned up surely as never before.

During the last week of May I accompanied Sto into Uckfied in a utility truck and we could hardly believe our eyes. Every wood, copse, and thicket on every road and lane was in use. Tanks, guns, armoured vehicles of all kinds, supply trucks and tankers were on the move to parking places and with many already parked and camouflaged. The heavy stuff of the 21st Allied Army Group were being hidden down near the ports ready for the off. This was happening right along the South Coast countryside. It was truly an amazing sight and will always be a vivid memory to me.

Since Moira and David made their home at Chichester in West Sussex twenty or more years ago, Norah and I have become well acquainted with the South Downs. When we drive along the roads of that beautiful part of England, Norah just waits on a remark I am certain I make every time " An army of a million men and machines were hidden down here before the invasion of Europe in June 1944, and they were never discovered by the Germans."

The smell of the flowers, the sunbathing, the serenity of it all - suddenly came to one hell of a shattering halt! An armoured car came roaring along the main drive and shuddered to a halt outside the main house and out stepped an RAPC officer and our large, numbered cash boxes were unloaded. Within an hour the "Standby" signal was given throughout the camp, Military Police appeared from nowhere in strategic positions including outside our door and we all knew the next signal would be "Assembly" meaning the troops were on their way. The adrenalin started to flow.

It was the 30th of May and early afternoon when the troops started to arrive and continued to do so all that day night and the following day until the camp was full by the evening of the 31st and sealed. I think there must have been four to five thousand troops in full battle order and armed to the teeth and primed ready for action.

I recall for sure the Welsh Regiment was represented and I think the Gloucester and also the Essex. A large contingent of the Signal Corps also comes to mind and there were a lot more. Many of them were the "D Day" and "H hour plus" lads who would be among the first on the beaches across the channel.

Relating my experience of "Overlord" I am only mentioning British troops. It must be remembered that no way could we have smashed the German Army on our own. Dotted all over the countryside in similar situations were troops of the mighty United States 1st Army and also our Canadian cousins being part of the British 1st Corps. I include in the following page the complete structure of the 21st Army Group ready to invade the beaches of Normandy which gives some idea of the monumental operation "Overlord" was and about to take place. The moment the battle troops arrived the staff closed ranks as we all had the same desire which was to give those men our complete attention and concentration. They were loaded with gear, fighting fit and in good spirits and letting go through army slang and humour amongst themselves. I think it was then that it hit me that we were the lucky ones and that these men were ready and prepared to go into hell. They had sweethearts, wives, kids, Mums and Dads but they all knew it was more than just possible that their days on this earth were numbered.

The war had been going for more than four years and we were all hardened to bad news about relatives and friends and people. But in that instance and at that particular time, those involved felt so close to the reality of war, as I know I did, that it had a very subdividing influence on us all. When the troops got settled in, they soon got to know that we were in the camp to help them, and we soon had a steady flow through our office. We could clear some of their questions straight away but for many others we could only write to the various Regimental Pay Offices and promised them the Pay Office would look into it and contact their wives or whoever their next of kin was. We did our utmost to comply with our orders which were to ensure that each man was as content as possible regarding his financial situation and to free him from any such worries. It immediately became routine that the three of us sat writing memos to all the necessary Pay Offices well into each night as the Army Post Office arranged a special collection from us each evening.

I do recall a problem we were not prepared for as it was really not our line, namely the preparation of a will. Every soldier was advised to make one especially before going into action. The advice was to do it privately through a solicitor or following the instructions and forms included in every soldiers Service Pay Book. (As I write I am looking at them in my tattered Service Pay Book still in my possession having made my will privately). Some of the men on the camp had ignored the advice and suddenly realised its importance and asked us to help. They had certainly left it to the last minute! I know we found a legal fellow either from the staff or troops to ensure we were following the correct procedures. It was my job to find the soldiers CO to sign as a witness and be present when all the signing was done. The CO's had more than enough on their plates and the poor chaps would get hell for leaving it all to the last minute. I may say helping someone to make out a will when it was on the cards that it could be put into use within a few days was quite a sensitive experience. We made sure they got to the legal department.

The grapevine was rampant forecasting "D Day" for Sunday 4th June. It is difficult to describe the intense atmosphere caused by so many battle-ready troops together in a sealed camp just waiting for something to happen. The majority of them spent their time cleaning, oiling, checking and re-checking their rifles, automatic weapons, machine guns and all sorts of weaponry. Many had happy go lucky - what the hell attitudes, and would shout "catch" chucking live ammunition to each other and had a habit of leaving grenades and hand stick bombs lying about which put the fear of God into soldiers like me!

They also spent a lot of time eating and drinking tea. The food was excellent and always available. Tea was on brew continuously day and night. The Catering Corps did a magnificent job, they just never stopped. I am sure everyone who was in Camp J7 on Sunday 4th June will remember that night. I have mentioned, we had a large contingent of the Welsh Regiment in the camp. Very late around midnight one man suddenly started to sing then another and another until every Welshman joined in singing as only a massive Welsh choir can sing. They sang many of their well-known favourites and finished off with God Save the King followed by the Welsh National Anthem. I can hear them now. I doubt there was a dry eye in the camp.

The camp had been restless on the 4th of June. There was a feeling all round something should be happening. After the singing it was a sleepless night with a lot of movement and one could sense the atmosphere. By the morning of the 5th the weather had changed to heavy rain and strong winds. Moral lowered a bit as that was the last thing the men wanted to happen. They had experienced flat bottomed landing craft in rough seas when training and did not like it.

The camp was wide awake early on the 5th. The feeling was rampant, something was going to happen, they wanted it to happen, and it did. Early afternoon Major Russell called Sto and all the Commanding Officers to a meeting to tell them he had received the " Stand by for

Overlord" signal but no order for the opening of the boxes and therefore they had to stay shut. The CO's expecting their sealed orders but not getting them, they were edgy, frustrated and downright bad tempered. Very understandable as Lieutenant Colonels and Majors were anxious and ready to get on with a battle, they are not the easiest people to deal with. Eventually much later in the day the remainder of the signal "Paymasters to distribute currency" arrived and we immediately had all the CO's, I think twelve from memory, descend on our office which suddenly became the centre of activity and a kind of excitement.

Each CO gave Sto his code number. A large heavy wooden box with the equivalent number on it was opened by Murray and me and on top of the contents which were spanking new French franc notes was a manila envelope, again with the number, a red seal and Top Secret printed on it. Sto checked the numbers again and handed the envelope to me and I handed it to the CO. The tension was such that very little was said. We asked each CO to send over an officer and some men to collect their boxes and give free issue of francs (I cannot remember the amount) to everyone. It was these boxes that confirmed the invasion would be in France as speculation as to where it would take place had been rife throughout the whole country for months. We were to discover later what had caused the frustration and restlessness on Sunday the 4th. The invasion had been scheduled to take place on the 5th of June but because of the very bad weather and stormy seas, on the advice of his meteorological officer, General Eisenhower, the Supreme Commander, had to make the most difficult decision of his life and postpone Operation Overlord by twenty four hours.

I remember the evening of that June 5th day which was to take us into one of the most momentous days in all history. Our boxes had gone. Our office which had been a place of hectic noise and emotional chatter was empty and the three of us were silent. We suddenly realised the whole camp was very still and quiet. It was an occasion when every man was in his own private world with his own private thoughts and preparing himself in mind and body for what he was about to experience. The impact was devastating to all of us who were there.

About midnight the "Proceed to Embarkation Camp" signal was received and from there on transport appeared from nowhere and the troops were on their way during the early hours of the 6th to Newhaven, their embarkation port about fifteen miles away. The "D Day" lads, as they were known, only passed through the Embarkation Camps which were very close to the ports for final checking and then went straight on to the boats. Faultless organisation all along the line.

When the dawn of that momentous day of Tuesday 6th June arrived the last of the troops had gone and the camp was empty. During the night the staff started to clean up. It was a huge task and every single member including ourselves, gave maximum effort as more troops were expected during the day. Excitement and tension were at bursting point level as news was eagerly awaited of how things were going both during the channel crossing and on the beaches. We could not help but feel very much involved as we knew that many of the lads, we had been speaking to just hours previously could be in the thick of action.

The furious clean up taking place helped to keep our minds on the job. That could mean anything from cleaning out tents to scrubbing tables for the catering boys or attending to busy field telephones, to carrying stores. The circumstances were such that rank was forgotten as we all realised life and death were rather close at hand and everything had to be no less than one hundred per cent ready for the next intake. The all-important news eventually came through that seaborne troops had landed on the Normandy beaches at approximately 6 am and had established a beach head. It was a few days later we were told our J7 friends were involved on "D Day" and "D Day+1". Their landing areas had been Sword and Gold beaches. They had taken an awful hammering from the Germans, and many did not make it but those that did established a good beach head. We all had such deep feeling of sadness coupled with a great sense of pride for the heroes we had been associated with. Records confirm that 150,000 men crossed to Normandy on 'D Day".

The next five days were the toughest I experienced in the army, as they were the most crucial days of the whole war. We worked continuously until we could go on no longer, had a little sleep, then started again. There was continual movement in and out of camp. The back-up troops to the initial attack and the reinforcements were coming and going. There could be a few hundred or a few thousand of many Regiments and Corps. It all depended on the requirements in Normandy. The numbers in camp varied every day but we always seemed to be full. It was a hectic time with the camp staff always under pressure and requiring the utmost concentration to cope.

Regular news came through from the beaches. At the beginning it was bad as the going was very tough but gradually things got better as a breakthrough developed from heavy fighting. The attitude of the troops in camp was quite different to the "D Day" and "D Day +1" men we had at the beginning. They were not sure what to expect and did not know where they were going until the last minute. All the troops following on knew exactly what to expect and where they were going and waiting caused frustration and it showed. They were anxious to get at the enemy. They were superb as they too had such tremendous confidence in their Commander. From "D Day" the same words were repeated "We'll be ok. Monty will see us through."

Although the main concern of Sto, Murray and myself was attending to the troops we also took over all Major Russell's camp finances. He was having a hell of a job coping with the "Overlord" organisation and the most vital time schedules. He was about sleeping on his feet on occasions. Although the camp was still sealed certain members of the staff including ourselves, were allowed to do many important tasks essential for the running of the camp. Our visits to Uckfield were still very interesting as the roads were packed with war machines and military transport, more so than at the beginning.

During those five eventful days a bridge had gradually been established on French soil. It started on "D Day +2 and 3" when British and Canadian troops pressed on towards Caen and Bayeux. By " D Day + 6" a real solid front had been established in Normandy and the battle for Caen was about to begin. I find it difficult to explain my own feelings at that particular time, being so close to the men involved and being aware how they felt. It was all to do with the kind of tension being generated by thousands of individuals in the face of fearsome expectations. I think I was also quite bewildered by the enormity of the gigantic operation going on around me.

Perhaps my best way of explanation is for me to quote the official "Overlord" published records, which say it all. During those five days - June 6th - June 10th inclusive: 326,000 troops, 54,000 vehicles and 100,000 tons of supplies including a military floating harbour crossed to the allocated beaches in Normandy. 5,000 Naval and merchant ships took them across and continued a shuttle service. On "D Day" alone Allied Forces flew 15,000 sorties and dropped 10,000 tons of bombs. During the five days allied bombers pulled gliders which contained 13,000 men who dropped by parachute behind enemy lines.

Between "D Day" and July 19th the day Caen was eventually taken after a terrible battle, and which was the real breakthrough for Allied Forces - The British 2nd Army alone lost 34,700 officers and men. Add to that the huge casualty list of the US 1st Army. The 21st Army Group certainly did not get off lightly and paid a huge price.

After all these years I could not help but feel a tinge of sadness when reading the "Overlord" information record, that on "D Day" 630 men of Force 5 were killed, wounded or missing during the landing on Sword beach. The men who left Camp J7 during that night for embarkation on " D Day" morning were in Force 5.

The month of June went on into July and we had become used to the intermittent troop routine through the camp. The advance of the 21st Army was slow as the Germans were putting up terrific resistance on the way to Caen and there was still no real breakthrough. Many beach heads were still being established by fierce fighting and the long front line in France was like a huge jigsaw. The reinforcement troops were the "pieces" which had to be fitted into the pattern of the overall battle. The "pieces" were the troops in camps like ours always ready to be moved at a moment's notice. (It must be remembered that all the assembly camps dotted along the Southeast Coast were involved in exactly the same way as J7.)

The three of us were working hard on our duties when on the 8th of July we really did receive a surprise which made us come to a sudden halt. A message arrived from our own Command Headquarters and handed to Sto. Our order which said in effect " The Field Cashier Unit Commanded by Captain E Stottart, will proceed to the Embarkation Area Camp J3 on the 10th of July. A replacement unit for Camp J7 will arrive later today." Sto's instant reaction is very clear in my memory "Bloody Hell surely not at this early stage". He did not need to include the words "going over" as we knew what they meant. It was on the cards that once the real advance into Europe got started, we could "go over" with a Division. We tried to convince ourselves that the battle front was still far too close and no place for Field Cashiers. We were not very happy as we knew there were no Cashiers at the Embarkation Camps and Sto could not find out what was going on. To make matters worse our replacement unit arrived before we could calm down.

During the remainder of the 8th and part of the 9th of July we put our replacements in the picture. We packed our kit and said our goodbyes to our good friends the camp staff. Such a lot had happened in the two months since we arrived. We had been members of a wonderful team playing our part in a military operation which would go down in history as one of the greatest ever undertaken, perhaps "the" greatest. We were very proud and to have served with such a brilliant Camp Commander.

So, on Monday 10th July 1944 we left Camp J7 behind and were transported about ten miles into the Embarkation Area en route to Camp J3. Our route took us through the town of Lewes and south until we reached camp J3 which was situated a couple of miles or so south of Newhaven. The roads were still very busy with service transport of all kinds, and we were able to discover that Newhaven was a very important "Overlord" port.

J3 was another estate but much smaller than J7. The embarkation camps did not require anything like the space of the assembly camps as they were only set up and prepared for speedy through put of troops. They did not remain for any length of time, an average of a few hours. The camp had the large marquee style tents, but they were only for rest and shelter. Catering facilities were included but just for the inevitable tea and short snack. It was where the Commanding Officers issued their final orders and told the men which ship they would be on for the sea crossing. On "D Day" and the early days of the invasion those camps must have been tense places to be in. Immediately on arrival at the camp the fears the three of us had were put to the test. A staff officer from our HQ was waiting to explain.

It was D+35 and following great land, sea and air fighting success the Allied Armies had established many permanent bases all along the French coast. More than half a million had crossed the channel since "D Day" and the big battle was on for the key position, the town of Caen, which was expected to fall into the Allied Forces hands at any time. The officer told us it had been decided because of the established basis that a Field Cashiers Unit had become necessary at each of the main embarkation ports because two-way travel, incoming as well as outgoing, was about to develop and we had been appointed at Newhaven. We would have the addition of being involved with important civilian personnel and currency exchange and we had a load of cash boxes which contained British and European currencies. Murray and I got a surprise when shown to our quarters - a large bell tent. All members of the staff except the officers were under canvas.

J3 had been a beautiful estate with a large and elegant manor house surrounded by gardens and lawns. It must have been a lovely family home. The staff tents were near the house on estate grassland and sheltered by trees. The officers had their accommodation and mess in the house. All other messes including ours were in huts adjoining the house. There were the usual many outhouses and stables etc but they all contained very important communication equipment, manned and guarded by the Royal Signals personnel who were on the staff. It was all a bit hush-hush and was the cause of daily and nightly visits to the camp by General Staff Officers. It was obviously a battle control centre or the like and we knew not to ask questions.

All I can remember about the camp CO is that he was a very tall Major with a French sounding name. He made sure we were looked after having allocated a large room on the ground floor for our office. We had not the luxury of a strong room so had a twenty-four-hour armed guard on duty as we had a lot of cash and important documents within our responsibility. The camp staff at J3 was much less than at J7 and we were therefore a small compact community. Living under canvas in a bell tent was a new experience for Murray and myself. We had really no discomfort having a table and chairs and electricity laid on from the Signal Corps generators.

Our work routine was quite different from what we had done at camp J7. We had very little to do with the troops coming through from the assembly area. They were only in a few hours as their schedules were geared to ships and tides, however the atmosphere of "expectation tension" I think it was called, was always there with the thousands of men in transit. A great battle was going on and men were being killed and wounded in great numbers not all that far away and the momentum and discipline of the whole fantastic operation was still in top gear.

We were at liberty to move between camps and the docks at Newhaven. We became involved with the coming and goings of both military and often civilian high-ranking personnel of all countries connected with the invasion as we always had cash and the necessary currencies available. Newhaven was a short sea route and very accessible and all kinds of "experts" from all the countries wanted to see for themselves what was going on across the channel and did not appreciate a bloody war was raging almost within ear shot and they were being a bloody nuisance!

On occasions we attended incoming ships which had "walking wounded" on board going to hospital reception centre's near to the port. We would ensure they had no immediate cash problems and if so would help them out. We were also able to inform their Pay Office that they had returned safely and were in hospital. I shall explain later the important part played by the Pay Officers. It was a very interesting time for the three of us as we gained tremendous experience which was to be of practical advantage to me personally later. We were again working twenty-four hours per day and caught up with sleep when we could as port involvement always seemed to be busiest during the night. We had also taken over all the camp finances leaving the CO free from that worry as he had enough on his plate. We had to make regular visits to Lewes where we had banking arrangements. At the time it was a very busy and important town as so much was going on around it.

CHAPTER ELEVEN: AVOIDING A V-1 FLYING BOMB!

From the day we arrived at J3 our hearing became very acute and sensitive day and night, the reason being Hitler's promised secret weapon to win the war - the V1 Rocket - the flying bomb. A real nasty piece of work. I quote from an official publication: - "It was a pilotless aeroplane, wingspan sixteen feet, armed at nose with explosive head like torpedo. The explosive charge was over a ton and the blast at ground level was very powerful and destructive. They were ejected from ramps in Germany and flew at 360mph. They were the very earliest of jet propulsion making a roaring noise with red flames belching from the rear and guided towards targets in Britain. The complicated engine mechanism was set for the engine to shut off over the target and then noiselessly glide down to earth and explode."

The Germans started sending over the V1 rocket flying bombs in mid-June, not in any great numbers and only occasionally, as it transpired, they had trouble with their reliability early on. They only concentrated them on London in the beginning. When at camp J7 we had heard the odd one in the distance but never actually saw the thing. However, by the time we arrived at J3 the Germans really had them working and knew by then our embarkation ports and troop encampments in the south and were dispatching a steady stream of them every day.

They were targeted to hit Portsmouth and Southampton docks and the surrounding area and did a lot of serious damage. They flew at about three thousand feet and making for those targets their flight path was almost right above us. We got used to them, watched them go over and as long as the engine did not cut out, we took no action except to hope the RAF were around that area of the sky and would spot them. The RAF very quickly got the measure of the "Doodlebug" as the infernal machines became popularly known but what a dangerous operation it was. We used to watch with awe inspiring appreciation at the bravery of the fighter pilots. The method they adopted was to fly alongside at the same speed and wait patiently until they spotted open fields on the ground below where hopefully minimum damage would be done to property and life. They would then move in close until one of their wings was just under a wing of the V1, judge exactly the time they would be over the selected open space then suddenly tip over the V1 wing making it plunge vertically to the ground. At the same instant they would take evasive action out of the way. If the pilot miss-timed the manoeuvre the V1 would go into a long shallow dive and could cause tremendous damage with loss of life if it hit a town or village.

The pilots were usually successful and the unknown thousands of people watching from the ground would, as one, raise their arms to the sky and cheer and shout their appreciation when they saw the V1 rocket tip over and plunge to the ground. I remember standing in the dock area at Newhaven and watch the amazing performance of a pilot tipping one down just in time for it to land on the beech a mile or so away. We were shaken by the large number of explosions which took place and later told that it had activated dozens of mines, which had been laid along the shore in case of invasion by the Germans. I have always maintained it is just as well Hitler did not have those bombs at his disposal a lot earlier in the war and when he did only for a short spell after we invaded. Their psychological and nuisance value added to their devastating destructive power could have been a tremendous asset to our evil enemy.

At night during darkness, we all became like cats, sleeping with one ear open. If we heard the missile with its destructive rasping engine roar, we knew it would fly on and not bother us. If however, the jet engine started to splutter, experience told us it would cut out in just thirty seconds. When it did splutter every person within earshot, which could be thousands upon thousands covering many miles, wherever they were became alert and ran outside looking at the sky. The reason being it was essential to see the jet flames coming from the rear before the cut-out so that you would know from which direction the bomb was coming, or going, then when it did cut-out and became noiseless you could hopefully judge the silent glide path it would take towards earth.

Then again hopefully take the necessary action to avoid it. It will be realised it was quite a terrifying experience and although it happened thankfully during a small period of time in my humble opinion, I think wartime historians and writers often forget to mention the V1 or treat it as a minor happening. That also includes by far the more terrible bomb the V2 which was to follow much later.

If I am being rather precise about the V1 pilotless rocket bomb, it is because I have good reason never to forget it. During my army career there were only two occasions, that I was aware of, when perhaps I thought the end of the road for me was sign posted "No Return!" The first was at camp J3 and the second when overseas and that will be mentioned later.

It was a beautiful day with a blue cloudless sky. It was a most unusual day because the camp was empty due to a twenty-four-hour lull in troop movement control to us from the assembly area. The CO issued an order declaring it a complete rest day for everyone, a one-off occurrence but an intelligent decision as we had been working nonstop night and day.

Following a lie-in and lunch in the mess, Murray and I decided to stretch our legs and walked across the estate to the perimeter road which had been built by the Royal Engineers in the usual style which was solid concrete. We found many of the camp staff under some trees laying in the sunshine and joined them. We had been there maybe an hour drowsing and not saying much. We heard the familiar sound coming our way and paid little attention as it was obviously going along the coastline on the usual route. Suddenly the engine spluttered and stopped immediately without the usual delay. We were all rather dopey and quite casually got to our feet. What happened next was that we ran 150 yards faster than any of us had run in our lives. The torpedo like winged bomb with a ton of explosives in its nose was in a long silent glide coming straight at the camp in our direction!

The 150 yards were between us and the nearest tents. Fortunately, split trenches had been dug close to all tents and marquees at all camps anticipating visits from German bombers, the usual kind, as nothing was known about the V1's until they arrived on the scene. All I can remember is running like hell and diving arms outstretched in front of my face into the trench and stocky Murray landing on top of me as simultaneously there was a deafening explosion and blacking out. I came to sometime later, lying on a stretcher under a tree.

The perimeter road went through a large square section which had been built at the same time to park heavy transport vehicles. The V1 had landed plumb in the middle of this huge parking area which was about 100 yards from our split trench. It was later explained to us that being as close to such an explosion and fortunately just in time being below ground level, we would be caught in its down draught which would suck out air from the trench and our bodies causing us to black out.

What happened during the incident was just amazing. The RAF realised J3 had received a direct hit and immediately put out a full red alert for the Newhaven and Lewes area. Hospitals for miles around received the "Standby to receive casualties" alarm. Service and civilian ambulances, jeeps and cars with doctors and nurses rushed into the camp - to find it empty! It must have been the only day during the whole of the

"Overlord" operation when any camp was empty. Normally at the very least a few thousand men would have been inside, and the result does not bear thinking about.

I am sure no members of the staff were killed although some were seriously injured by flying metal, shrapnel and chunks of flying concrete. Tents large and small were torn to shreds. Catering tables and equipment outside had just disappeared, up to three London buses could have been stored in the bomb crater and trees close by were uprooted and split in pieces.

I certainly was one of the lucky ones. All I had was a bruised shoulder and a sore back caused by Murray landing on me. I had nothing broken. I was put in the camp sick bay with a few others and kept in bed for a day and half. We were carefully watched over at the time I think it was a shock reaction symptom as they were concerned about us being so near to the blast. I was back on duty in a few days obviously none the worse. Murray, however, was not as fortunate and ended up in Hospital.

He mistimed his dive into the trench and hit his face on the side of it. He was very badly bruised and swollen. The air extraction had also caused him some trouble. It was a week before he was back on duty. I recall the house and outbuildings had only minor damage not being in the path of the explosion blast. The communications centre was not touched but we wondered at the time if Gerry had in fact made J3 a target because obviously it was a very important place.

One thing was certainly proved that when a Red Alert went out in the Lewis - Newhaven area, they were well prepared to respond to an emergency. Despite all our defences including large balloons, anti-aircraft guns and the bravery of our fighter pilots many V1 flying bombs got through. They did tremendous damage to property in London and all over the South of England. Thousands of civilians were killed and seriously injured. Eventually our bombers got at and flattened their launch sites and silenced them. However official records show that from 13 June to 4th September 1944 more than 8,000 V1's were launched against England.

Much more was to come, and Hitler still had up his sleeve the V2 rocket bomb which was fired from launch pads in the Netherlands. They began coming over on the 8th of September 1944 and were the most horrendous things ever invented at that time. They weighed 3 1/2 tons, carried 1 1/2 tons of explosive at 3000 mph. They descended at 2000 mph, nearly three times the speed of sound and it took only five minutes to fall on London or their other targets. They were in effect noiseless as the rocket bomb arrived at its target well before the noise of its passage could be heard. During seven months of attack 1,050 fell on England about half of them on the London area. They killed 2,754 civilians and seriously injured 6,253. Only when allied armies advanced far enough to cut off the railways which took the bombs to the launching grounds near the Hague and Amsterdam, was the grim ordeal ended.

The nearest I ever came to a V2 was hearing one explode a long distance away when I was visiting Mum and Dad at Liverpool. They scared the hell out of everyone as it was so frightening to realise, they could arrive without any warning and such suddenness and with such devastating effect.

CHAPTER TWELVE:
BACK TO EDINBURGH. A CHANGE OF RANK. FOOTBALL

Come mid-August 1944, the three of us realised our days at J3 were numbered. We were told that the Field Cashier Units had been allocated for Europe and we were not one of them. We were bitterly disappointed.

From the yard-by-yard breakthrough on the Normandy beaches the 21st Army Group battering its way forward and on the 20th of August reached Nantes in France. They had by then complete command of the sea and air, therefore the crossing from the embarkation ports were plain sailing. Many camps were closing and the few remaining open could easily cope with the two-way traffic which had developed.

As I think back and write about "Overlord" I realise it has left a very sensitive lasting impression on me after all those years, especially Camp J7. I can still feel the atmosphere, tension and excitement which lasted all the time I was there and can "hear" the rough army banter and rogue language. I can "feel" the tears running down my cheeks the night the Welsh boys sang and "see" the anger, frustration and bewilderment on the faces of the Commanding Officers when the delay took place, and we could not give them their Top-Secret envelopes. Their frightening responsibility was showing. I remember their great dignity when the time came to do so, each one saluted, thanked us and shook hands. It was their way of apologising, and we were deeply touched. Although full to capacity the eerie silence of the camp the evening before "D Day" is still with me. The hushed noise of the departure of the 5,000 or so men. Then came the dawn silence again as they had all gone and the camp was empty.

I have tried to explain what it was like to be involved, listening, helping, sharing jokes and just talking to men sealed in a camp for six days when each of them realised that when they left the camp their chances of survival were at the least only fifty-fifty. They knew they were going into hell.

Maybe this is the time to quote from the official records. From "D Day'" 6th June 1944 to 7th May 1945 the day Germany surrendered ending the war in Europe. The Allied armies had 187,000 men killed in action,11,000 missing and 546,000 wounded. What can I say as that says it all?

Apart from the V1 Flying Bomb incident my memories of Camp J3 are of being on duty day and night and catching up with sleep whenever possible. I did not realise it at the time, but the many varied investments mentioned previously were a very important part of active service field cashier work and of great interest. As days passed a personal concern was in our minds. Where would we be posted? Would it be individually or as a unit? The posting order eventually arrived, and we could not believe what it said. We had to report as a unit back to the 31st Battalion in Edinburgh on the 20th of August.

At J3 just like J7 we had been part of a super team of great comradeship all working together again for a Camp Commander who was an inspiration to us all. So, what about our little unit as the end of this amazing time together was near. Eric Stoddart our Captain (our Sto) from day one was a fine leader and Murray, and I soon developed the utmost respect for him. We were his priority in all circumstances and events, many of which were difficult, to say the least. As his two sidekicks we got on really well together and I know we gave him 100%. He said from the start our load would be shared equally by three and he kept to it.

"Overlord", what an experience it was to be there. Looked at within the context of the whole mighty operation my insignificant contribution is really not worth a mention. However, I have to realise that the genius who took on the colossal task of planning the whole thing, needed me just as he needed the other hundreds of thousands to be in their allocated place at the right time to work, to fight and to die if necessary, to win in what Winston Churchill called "The greatest land, sea and air operation in the whole history of warfare."

My Red Book informs me that on the 20th of August 1944 after a long train journey from Brighton via London the three of us reported at the Regimental Pay Office, Edinburgh and were immediately given a week's leave. On our return from leave our old friend Major "Big Bill" Oram was waiting for us in his office. We realised immediately that urgency was in the air and not much mincing his words as usual said " Maybe Overlord was the supreme example of organisation and planning but they forgot to organise and plan what was going to happen afterwards on the Pay Offices". We soon realised the Pay Office had not been aware of the procedures in the Camps until sometime after the event which was due to the long strict blackout of information. They had done their best with the extremely urgent cases but reorganisation to cope was urgent also keeping in mind that by then the volume of work was increasing daily from the battlefields of Europe. I know we left his office with "You have a free hand, now get stuck in!" It was most certainly in much stronger language from the old tough regular soldier!

Unfortunately, a disappointment was awaiting me, they had to take away my Sergeant's stripe. Their Sergeant establishment was full and there were added complications with me being a Field Cashier. Major Oram had obviously tried hard for me but without success. He did give me the assurance that I would remain in the Field Cashier Section of the Corps.

I was certainly not happy knowing that the lowest rank in the section was Sergeant. However, I kept to my "plan" and accepted the situation and soldiered on after all I was staying at home.

I had been paid acting Sergeant, so the loss of the extra money was tough. It is interesting to look at my pay structure when I was demoted and became a Corporal again. My pay was 7/9 (39p) per day. I allotted to Norah 3/- (15p) which left me with 4/9 (24p) or £1.13.3 (£1.68) per week. Norah received £1.7.6 per week married allowance from the army, add my allotment £1.1.0 so she received a total of £2.18.6 (£2.93) per week. She was working hard at the Scottish Insurance Corporation saving every penny of her salary that she could for us to have our own home after the war. As we were living with Norah's Mum, I was able to give Mrs McGavin the ration and lodging allowance I received which was 6/6 per day (£2.27) per week plus of great importance an extra ration book which was worth its weight in gold. Compared to many we were quite well off.

What was the cost of living like in 1944 in today's money? A really good four course meal in a first-class restaurant 25p. 20 cigarettes or 1oz tobacco 5p. Return rail fare between Edinburgh and Glasgow 17p second class and 25p first class. A one-hour tram car ride from one side of Edinburgh to the other 5p.

Murray and I wasted no time in making a start with the new section and from our experience gained with the help of Sto soon recruited and trained service and civilian staff usually from other sections in our office. We had realised at once that apart from the lack of knowledge about "Overlord" the real weakness was the lack of understanding and terms of reference between a Regimental Pay Office (RPO) which dealt only with Pay and Allowances and a Command Pay Office (CPO) being responsible for other army finances including Field Cashiers having money and distributing it for all sorts of purposes including pay, when necessary, in the field.

It took some time, but we eventually cleared the back log emanating from "Overlord" and were dealing with the European operations of all the Scottish Regiments fighting their way across Europe. Not forgetting the Burma Campaign in the Far East where many of the Scottish lads were involved. The new section developed until we had eventually about twenty-five staff with a Lieutenant in charge. Down the line ranks established and all the necessary links and feed backs arranged between the war operation the CPO and the RPO. Sto having given us a free hand and only kept a watching brief was very happy to have the new section in full working order. Needless to say, so was Major Oram.

I am sure the situation helped me and Murray. So far as I was concerned, I shall never know how Colonel Rowbotham arranged that I remained in his establishment as a member of the Corps Field Cashier Section - medical category A1 as a Corporal and for nine months. Again, it surely was being in the right place at the right time!

By the end of 1944 the new section was well established, and Murray had been transferred to another section of Sto's wing as their Sergeant, which would lead him to promotion as Staff Sergeant, so well deserved. Sto told me that Major Oram had given him assurances that he could keep me as long as I was allowed to stay with the Pay Office. I had established essential communications with the Command Pay Offices by obtaining feedback from the Field Cashiers with the Divisions in the battle zones which was so necessary for the new section. The CPO system was a bit of a mystery to the RP Offices as the necessary liaison was only in use during war time. As my story explains from the first day, I joined the army until I arrived at the Pay Office before "Overlord" I was in the CPO system and never really left it during my service. I seemed to be the only person around who understood both systems hence the reason Sto had his clappers on me.

During my nine months at the RPO I was known as either "Field Cashier" or the "CPO Corporal". It was a great working office, and we were all good pals, but I was not "one of them". Field Cashiers were "different" being in a special section of the Corps. Like my Unit Accountant days with the Royal Engineers, I was also "different" and once again I was being treated as a single unit with more or less a free hand. Be that as it may I had been long enough in the army to know my way round and wise enough to ensure I took part in certain duties. I always took my turn at guard duty from 8pm to 8am. I made sure I attended weapon instruction and practice at the firing range up in the Pentland hills. I continued to ensure my inoculations and vaccinations were always up to date. There was regular square bashing almost every day but I was never asked to take part and certainly never volunteered. Field Cashiers had done all that stuff, or so they thought!

I have explained previously the make-up of a Pay Office. So many sections to a wing, so many wings to a group etc. Well, they were football crazy at Edinburgh and had a well-known service team. They held an inter-wing tournament which was taken very seriously. One day our wing was short of a player and could find no one available and very much as a last resort asked me if I could possibly help them out. I said yes and little did I know where that was going to lead me.

The mention of football reminds me of quiet an amazing occurrence during the latter part of the war in Europe which I feel is well worth recalling. It would be soon after "D Day" when the RAF had complete command of the sky and it was safe for crowds to gather. Churchill and the War Cabinet with the blessing of all the Service Chiefs encouraged Football League Clubs and all minor league clubs to start playing again on Saturdays. The interesting thing for the spectator was that teams would seldom be the same each week as it would depend on players stationed locally being available. This meant that very often lesser known and small-town teams could have First Division and possibly international players in their teams. Commanding Officers of all three services cooperated and if it was possible, made sure footballers were off duty on Saturdays.

Whoever thought of it, maybe it was Churchill himself, it was a wonderful idea as the grounds were full and causing great interest. The importance of it all was that it took people's minds off the trauma and worry of the war for a few hours. I am sure it was said at the time that next to the news that another battle had been won, it was the greatest morale booster for servicemen and public alike. It acted as a stimulus and recharged the batteries.

Eventually a high-ranking Sports Officer was appointed and ordered to collect all the most famous footballers no matter what rank or service they were in and make up a squad to send on tour to the war zones of Europe. Arrangements were made for a similar team to be put together in Southeast Asia to play for the troops in that war zone. Both teams were a sensation, and I am sure are still talked about today when war time pals meet, and reunions take place.

I was fortunate to see both teams. One in Glasgow at Hampden Park when a Scotland via England match was arranged. Every player on the field was a famous household name. More than a 150,000 in the ground. No crowd restrictions then and I thought I was going to be suffocated and deafened but survived. Unfortunately, Scotland lost. The second time was the marvellous Southeast Asia Command team playing at the famous Eden Gardens ground in Calcutta. More about that later.

Reverting to Pay Office football. I was trained (coached was not the sports vocabulary in those days) to play rugby at Stewart's College in Edinburgh when I was nine. I played at junior and senior school level every winter when I was there, but never made the top teams, being I suppose at best "good average". I could run fast, kick a ball and from the start was taught how to cope with the physical contact which the game of rugby is all about. When I left school, I only played a few games with one of the Former Pupil teams and gave up rugby as golf had always been my first sporting love and it took over.

I had been brought up in a football environment from a very young age. As a little lad I was taken regularly on Saturday afternoons by my Uncle Jack to watch Falkirk play at Brockville Park. The days when youngsters were carefully passed down through the crowds of spectators to the front and were as safe as houses. I was also a keen supporter of Stenhousemuir when at Larbert and when we moved to Edinburgh the Hearts of Midlothian was my team. I played for the Scouts and many a scratch side with my pals the Taylor boys when the occasion arose as I knew the game both on and off the field.

I think I played for the Wing team twice. The Battalion team was good and well known in and around Edinburgh. Outside it was surrounded by a bit of a mystery and was "talked about". How was it that the Pay Corps, who were supposed to have men of the lower medical grades, had one of the best football teams in Scottish Command? The reason was because the Corps had Staff Sergeant White (Chalky). He had been trained by a Scottish second division club and seemed to know every player in the Scottish leagues. He was therefore capable of arranging some crafty "transfers" to the Pay Corps in Edinburgh. Chalky organised, trained and chose the Battalion team. Knew what he was doing and ruled with a rod of iron which brought success.

After playing for the Wing team one day, he approached me saying he had watched the game and would I like a run out with the Battalion team. I really thought he was joking, replying no way as I would be right out of my class. I knew the team contained at least five or six professionals and the remainder being very experienced armatures. Being somewhat surprised by my lack of enthusiasm Chalky the old devil of course held the trump card and pulled rank on me, so I had to obey! He must have noticed football ability in me that I did not realise was there because I shall never know how I kept my place in that team. He put me in at right back, and I retained that position throughout. His match instructions to me were always the same. Run fast, tackle hard and thump the ball towards the opponent's goal. When defending, keep in mind our motto, they shall not pass. We had the use of a super pitch which belonged to the Scottish Rugby Union. It was behind the standoff the famous Murrayfield rugby ground. We also had use of the facilities and dressing room used by the Scottish International rugby teams and their opponents.

I played at many of the local football grounds and as far afield as Fife. We played against the Battalions of local regiments and Corps, the RAF and the Navy. Our most exciting match as I recall was always against a civilian side called the Civil Service Strollers whose home ground was at Burntisland. They were recognised as the top team. As the name implies, they were Civil Servants who were exempt from war service. I think they related to the Navy as an awful lot went on and around the River Forth during the war.

I am sure the notorious Chalky's duties were arranged so that he could spend most of his time on football with the Colonel turning a blind eye. He could stick out his chest to his pals in the Officers mess at Command HQ. The Royal Scots and the other regiments just did not like being beaten by the Pay Corps at football. The football we played was of quite a high standard and could be rough and tough but in the main we held our own and were always recognised as a top army side. We had a very enthusiastic following and like all the other team players became well known individually throughout the Battalion.

The situation reached a high for me when to my amazement I was chosen to play for Scottish Command against another Command the name of which I cannot remember. I do not recall anything about the match or the result except it was played in front of a large crowd at the old Meadowbank ground which I think at the time was the home of Leith Athletic FC long since defunct. The interesting point is it was the ground which many years later was completely redeveloped and on it built the renowned Commonwealth Games Stadium which was to become famous the world over.

My football "career" to this day is still a bit of a fairy tale to me but it did happen. I am sure Norah will confirm I was always on duty on Saturdays playing football and remembers visiting me in an Army Field Medical Unit in a large house at Roseburn, where I was detained for a few days recovering from a football injury. Chalky even had the Royal Army Medical Corps organised on the team's behalf!

Reading back what I have written in the last few pages may sound incomprehensible, after all there was a war on and at a critical stage. Terrific battles were taking place across Europe and in the Far East. Thousands of families were losing forever husbands, sons, grandsons and uncles and every day news came through of them being either killed or missing at the battle fronts on land, at sea and in the air. Every person throughout the land, including us and our nearest and dearest were in the same situation, living from day to day, worried about the future but all sharing each other's problems.

The people of Britain had the courage and indomitable spirit to carry on with life as usual which played such an important part in what I would call the psychology of winning the war, something the Germans and others just could not understand. I have just happened to mention as part of it my true involvement in football at the time. Everybody was involved in something and trying hard to carry on with life as usual and through all the sadness, the tears and the joy they succeeded, and the war was won.

Being in the football team I had to train two mornings per week 7.30 - 8.30 when the other lads were square bashing. We did so on a pitch near at hand where Chalky put us through a hard session ready for the weekend match. Believe it or not all other times I was really in the army and although in effect at their command twenty-four hours each day I must admit to being left alone to get on with my job. From the beginning of 1945 I was dealing with special field cases which came in from the Command Pay Offices. By February/March the allied armies had the

Germans on the run in Europe following many battles being won and I was kept very busy and worked long hours. I was really accepted and treated as a CPO single unit attachment and as I have mentioned before I was not an RPO man which suited me fine. If I had a problem, I still had good old Sto to fall back on. He was still my boss and had direct access to him although he was very happy to let me deal with the awkward cases without bothering him too much.

I was very lucky staying at home with Norah and her brother George, which was tremendous. I was not special in that respect as all ranks who were from Edinburgh lived at home. I was most careful with off duty orders but the powers that be were always very considerate about giving time off. I was uneasy as time went on at the Pay Office being Medical Category A1 and a Field Cashier as a Corporal which was just not on any of the regulations. The fear of being found out by The Royal Scots and them pointing a finger at me for their famous infantry regiment was never far from my mind, especially when I was quite well known to them on the football field. However only the Regimental Paymaster himself, Colonel Rowbotham and maybe Major Oram knew the answer to that problem, as I was certainly not going to break my rule of saying anything.

My fears about the Royal Scots really came very close to me when out of the blue towards the end of April I received an order to report to the Chief Medical Officer, Scottish Command for an examination. I was given a real going over, including the exhaustion test and heart check. The verdict was great physical condition category A1. On the 29th of April 1945 I found myself standing in front of Colonel Rowbotham in his office. He told me I was immediately going on embarkation leave as I had to report to the RAPC Overseas Deployment Depot in London on the 13th of May. He confirmed I was remaining in the Field Cashier Active Service Section and due to my good work on "Overlord" and since then with the Battalion he was recommending me for a commission.

Norah and I went down to Wallasey staying with Mother and Father but also managed a few days on our own at Heswall in the Wirral. The bombing had long stopped, and Mum and Dad had returned some time back from Ormskirk. They had survived but a few of their friends were not so lucky. The experience had taken its toll on Mother and left her with a nervous disposition which was to remain with her.

My embarkation leave will always be remembered for a date which will go down in history - 7th May 1945 - VE Day. The Day Germany surrendered. The 21st Army Group with all the heroes who set off on "D Day" 6th June 1944 had completed their task brilliantly led by General Montgomery and won the war in Europe and Hitler was dead. There were tremendous celebrations throughout the land in every town and village on Victory in Europe Day. However, the great success was tempered with some worry and anxiety because everyone realised only half the war had been won. Thousands of miles away in Southeast Asia in conditions so different from those in Europe the other half of the war was still in progress. Our sailors, soldiers and airmen along with our Colonial and American Allies were fighting the vile, cruel and despicable enemy - the Japanese. It was jungle warfare taking place in searing heat, monsoon rains and awful humidity. It was obvious that many brave men who had survived the North African desert campaign and the European campaigns with their regiments to SEAC (Southeast Asia Command) would be necessary to strengthen the 14th army Group Command by another superb leader of men, Admiral Lord Louis Mountbatten the Supreme Allied Commander, South East Asia. It was anticipated the war against Japan could last a few years as they seemed to have an endless supply of fighting men who were fanatical about dying for their country having committed themselves not to surrender.

Saying goodbye to loved ones following embarkation leave was a common enough occurrence but it was so special and important to the people involved therefore unlikely ever to be forgotten in the memory. I left behind my Mother and Father at Wallasey, then later Norah and her

Mother in Edinburgh. I recall a great feeling of anti-climax as one minute we had been rejoicing a great victory and the next being very unsure and worried about the future. When the time came to go, I felt very sad and apprehensive. On my departure day I had reported to the Pay Office and the Adjutant had given me my documents. The important one read that I was being posted overseas as a single unit and my destination would be confirmed when I reported to the RAPC Deployment Depot in London. So late on the 12th of May 1945 I was on the night train to London. Off on my own into the unknown wondering when, or if, I would ever see Norah and my family again.

CHAPTER THIRTEEN:
COCA COLA AND THE
QUEEN OF BERMUDA

Night travelling conditions had improved due to blackout restrictions being lifted but trains were still packed to capacity. I arrived once again at Kings Cross Station early morning and reported at the Corps Overseas Depot, then breakfasted in their NAFFI. It was for me, the beginning of a most extraordinary day.

Very soon I was in a room with two RAPC Staff Officers being asked questions and pumped for answers because in their experience, I was a most unusual case. Eventually they let me know why they had reached such a conclusion. I was to report personally direct to the War Office. They just could not understand why a Corporal Field Cashier, with there being no such rank, and a single unit, had to report at the War Office department for Overseas Postings. They had to convince themselves " Yes that's what the War Office order says and gives no further information". I also had to convince them I knew absolutely nothing and was just as bewildered as they were. I then had to wait quite some time as it was realised I would require a special pass and documents all stamped and signed to get into the place. Eventually I set off with all my gear to Whitehall and sure enough they were expecting me.

A Staff Sergeant took me into an office saying I would be called for an interview by the Officer in Charge of Secondments. That really complicated my mind, and it was then I must have wondered what the hell was going on! In no time I was sitting in a Majors office trying to take in and digest what he was telling me, which reaching into my memory bank with a lot of confidence went something like this:

"You are being seconded to the RWAFFR - The Royal West African Field Free Regiment. In a few days you will leave by troop ship for Accra capital of the Gold Coast Colony. You will be there for six months to become acquainted with the regiment and crash course of the language. You will go before an Officer's Commissioning Board and with expectation of being accepted will be posted as 2nd Lieutenant Active Service Field Cashier to either 81st or 82nd Division of the regiment at present battling away with the 14th Army Group in Burma. The Gold Coast is one of the hottest places in the world therefore on-board ship you will receive all the necessary inoculations and vaccinations. As from today 13th May 1945 your secondment will take effect and be posted accordingly on War Office orders. You will report tomorrow at Quartermasters Stores to obtain full tropical kit including shoulder tabs with RWAFER on them which you will always need as part of your Royal Army Corps uniform. You will report each day at 9am to this office until you have a sailing date."

He obviously had my record file in front of him and explained that secondments were very important and required special transfer arrangements from a British regiment or Corps to a Colonial regiment or Corps, hence the reason they were carried out by the War Office. He also confirmed I would be a single unit all the way to Accra. He was fine up to this point then his mood changed when he started to tell me the hell of a job, he and his staff had finding me accommodation. He explained how an American Army Colonel friend had come to his rescue by finding me a room in the U.S. Armed Forces Hostel where I could use all their facilities. I am sure at the time I thought, here we go again. Just like the Black Watch at Perth, the Ordinance Depot at Stirling and occasionally at other times and places along the way - free-lance Stark - just a bloody nuisance!

After being given another handful of passes, permits and official stamped and signed documents, including U.S. Army this time, I got through the War Office security set up and was on my way again! The U.S. Armed Forces was for American servicemen visiting London on leave where they could rest up relax and have a look round. It was in the Bayswater Road near Marble Arch and was just like a hotel. It had been quite a large hotel before it had been requisitioned and fortunately had avoided serious bomb damage. What a place to be billeted, I just could not believe where I had landed.

I was given a room to myself, small but adequate. The American food suited me and was always available and plentiful. I received a G.I.'s ration, a packet of cigarettes or tobacco per day and as much Coca Cola as I could drink - all free. They had a nice comfortable common room. I was suddenly living in the life of luxury. I was an oddity being the only British soldier on the premises. As soon as I opened my mouth I was called "Scotty" and recall they all seemed to have Scottish ancestors! They were very friendly and easy to get along with and we had many interesting chats together into the small hours drinking the inevitable Coke. Liquor of any kind was not allowed on the premises.

The morning after arrival I duly reported at the War Office on the dot and was sent to a Quartermasters Stores somewhere and obtained all my tropical kit. I went out quite often with my American friends. A favourite place was the famous Stage Door Canteen in Piccadilly. Top big bands and stars both American and British were on stage every evening. You never knew in advance who it would be. The entrance fee was a small price for a big snack. The atmosphere was tremendous and the shows super. They would always go on until after midnight.

I know I went to Lords cricket ground that week and watched a wartime services Test Match between England and Australia with famous players on both sides. I have never been to another Test Match not being a cricket fan. I have no idea how or why I happened to be there as my memory is a complete blank, which has not happened very often since I began my story.

The main thing that comes to mind about that week is Coca Cola. There was a popular saying during the war that American soldiers would not go into battle unless they had a bottle of Coke at hand, and I came to believe it. In the hostel it was the first time I had ever seen a Coca Cola dispensing machine - nor for that matter any other dispensing machine in those days. I was fascinated the way the famous bottle appeared with the contents chilled to the exact drinking temperature. I very quickly discovered you had to drink from the bottle as it was a crime in the company of an American serviceman to put the Coke in a glass, and they meant it! A dispenser always seemed to be within reach, and it appeared to me they were never without a bottle. I concluded it was like a drug to them and most certainly habitual.

I have a good reason for going on about the famous drink. I think it would be during 1950 to 1952 that one day at my office in London a very American voice was at the other end of the telephone line. He said he was a Mr Baraldi of the Coca Cola Corporation of America. He understood I represented Waddies of Edinburgh who had been recommended to him as a first-class printers and die-stampers not only in the UK but as exporters overseas. To cut a long story short Jimmy Baraldi had been sent to the UK to organise bottling plants and distribution outlets, advertising and marketing as Coca Cola were going to set up in Britain in a big way.

I booked an opening order for die-stamped letterheads, envelopes and other stationery which was a real big name winner for Waddies and if I may say so a feather in my cap. As we all know Coca Cola took off not just in Britain but in Europe and my initial order escalated into big business for the company. Jimmy and I became good business friends and as luck would have it, he was a golfer. He eventually became Senior Vice President and Manager of the Northern European Area of the Coca Cola Export Corporation. I shall never forget the first time I entered his office. A Coca Cola dispenser was part of the furniture and he immediately asked if I would like a Coke and I said, "Yes please but could I help myself?" Fortunately, I remembered how to do so and then drank from the bottle. He showed his surprise and said so saying his British visitors usually declined but if they said yes waited until he had extracted the bottle then poured it into a glass provided. I knew he considered my doing the right thing a great compliment and always felt my action cemented a friendship right at our first meeting especially when I explained where I came to know about the correct way to drink Coca Cola.

I must not forget to say something about good old London. It had been at death's door a few times but had survived and was recovering from the hangover of celebrating VE day the previous week. The quickest way to get around was to walk as for cars, buses and taxis diversion signs were everywhere. The underground trains were running as best they could, but it was quite a surprise at times to look deep down over a barricade and see them running through what had been a huge bomb or V2 crater. The City and Inner London were just devastated ruins caused by the bombings. The monumental task of cleaning up, repairing and rebuilding had begun but would take years to complete.

On my eighth day, 21st May 1945 at the hostel early in the morning a dispatch rider arrived with a message for me from the War Office, saying I had to report without delay and before 9am which I duly did. The Major certainly had news for me, which again went something like this: -

"Your original orders have been cancelled. You will now proceed to the Forward Base Pay Office of RWAFFR which is at Meerut in India. You will embark on a troopship which leaves the River Clyde tomorrow. You will be on the midnight train to Glasgow tonight. All your new documentation and warrants are being prepared and you will collect them this afternoon".

I was shown a map of India and discovered Meerut was about fifty miles northwest of Delhi and that was a long, long, way from home. I had been keeping in touch with Norah and my Mother and Father by letter which were censored as when waiting embarkation to a theatre of war (SEAC) Kings Regulations were very strict. However, I am sure I arranged for information to get through to Norah, word of mouth via movement of pals I had between one of the London Pay Offices and the RPO in Edinburgh.

So, after obtaining everything I required from the War Office in the afternoon then during the evening I had a meal and said goodbye to my American buddies at the hostel. Then stacked with enough packets of American cigarettes and tobacco to last me to India and bottles of Coca Cola for the train journey I set off for Euston Station.

When I reported to the Railway Transport Officer at Euston Station, I suddenly realised I was really on my own. The fact had not bothered me until then. What happened there was to be repeated on so many occasions before I reached Meerut. As I recall, fortunately, whenever I happened to be reporting, my name was always on usually an officer list or schedule and he would say: - "You are 7680868 Corporal Stark J. RAPC (RWAFFR)? "Yes sir." followed by, in a surprised tone of voice - "You are a single unit?" "Yes sir." I would then hand my documents which raised eyebrows and caused a surprised look when it was noticed they were from the War Office and not as expected Corps or Regiment. Then almost without exception the question, "What does RWAFFR stand for? And sometimes followed by " Have you something to do with the Royal Air Force Regiment?" I had to explain again and again as I did hundreds of times from then on, every time my shoulder tabs were spotted.

My immediate clearance would follow usually without any fuss or delay, and I soon sensed why it was so - because I could be a responsibility problem being a single unit - it was the bloody nuisance factor again! There is no doubt there and then at Euston Station I realised I would have to fend for myself come what may all the way to India.

It started at Central Station Glasgow the following morning, 23rd May. I had to report to the RTO there who went through the expected routine already mentioned. He finished by telling me the dock number I had to go to where the troopship was berthed. Good, but how was I to get there? After quite some time, which included a lot of comings and goings, the problem was solved. I was found space on a troop transport vehicle going to the dock. I could read their thoughts in the RTO's office. A certain RAPC Corporal was just a bloody nuisance being on his own!

Docks and large ships have always been of great interest and caused excitement to me as I had been brought up in that atmosphere. From a very early pre-school age until after I was married because Norah became interested, part of my life was to be on Father's ships. Large cargo vessels or cargo-passengers of the Ellerman Hall or Ellerman Lines. When Dad returned from long voyages having been to New Zealand and Australia or South Africa or India, Mother would travel over to meet him at the European arrival port usually Antwerp or Rotterdam. She would then sail with him round the UK ports where cargo would be unloaded, usually Hull, sometimes Newcastle, then Dundee, Glasgow and finally his home port, Liverpool, where he would obtain his well-deserved leave. Only wives of the Captain and the Chief Engineer were allowed to sail with their husbands in those days and only around the coastal ports. It therefore follows, with Dad being anxious to see me, that at one time or another I was staying on board a ship when in dock, often at all the UK ports mentioned. Later on, when Dad became Senior Chief Engineer he had to spend some time at the builders dockyards being responsible for the engineers when a new ship was being commissioned and be on board on her trial run. If all or part of the programme coincided with my school holidays, Mum and I could be living on board at the builders' dockyards for some time. I can remember being over in Belfast for six weeks when I was nine or ten at the Harland and Wolfe and Workman Clark dockyards when a new ship was being fitted out. I was not long out of the cradle when I got to know all about ships and why geography was always my best subject at school. I knew all about them and could tell the shipping line company of every vessel by the colours on the funnel and the flag on the foremast. The dock areas were therefore my favourite parts in all the ports, rough and tough as they were. I knew the River Clyde docks in Glasgow quite well, but it was the huge Mersey docks at Liverpool I could find my way round as easy as streets at home.

I was dropped from the army truck and walked along the dockside looking up at the huge liners . She was camouflaged but I recognised a "Bermuda" class vessel (I think of the White Star Line), and she would be either a "Monarch" or the "Queen" as I had studied them both when berthed at Liverpool. She was the "Queen of Bermuda" a magnificent ship. There is no doubt I would be excited climbing up the long gangway and also realising they were the first steps on my way to the vast subcontinent of India. I had been told stories about India and Ceylon by Dad who had been there many, many times on ships carrying home huge cargoes of jute and tea. In my wildest dreams I never imagined I would see it myself.

CHAPTER FOURTEEN:
A PASSAGE TO INDIA

My entry in my Red Book tells me I sailed from Glasgow on the end May 1945. The Queen of Bermuda like all big liners at the start of the war had been refitted from a beautiful passenger liner to a troopship able to carry thousands of men and she was packed to capacity. Loaded troopships were leaving our ports every week at that time for Southeast Asia as the other Army Group required all the reinforcements they could muster to battle with the Japanese.

I was allocated a bunk in an inside cabin on one of the lower decks along with five other lads. There were three bunks one above the other on each bulkhead. I was on a top one. There was no more than three feet of floor space between the two sets of bunks. A wash hand basin with cupboard above was at one end and the cabin door at the other. There were small cupboards at the door end of each set of bunks for clothes and gear making the cabin approximately ten feet long by nine feet wide for six of us! Like all cabins we were very cramped for space and movement. My immediate reaction was that it would be hell in the hot weather - and I was right. I was amongst the last on board and we sailed down the Clyde and away from Bonnie Scotland on the late afternoon tide.

I was caught up in the general feeling of apprehension on board. Everyone's thoughts were of home and the families and friends left behind also anxiety of what the future had in store. The ship was quiet, and she stayed that way for a day or two.

I remember the voyage so well as to me it was a great adventure. I was like a school kid having a dream come true. I had visited some good-sized passenger ships with Dad but to be on a 30,000 ton liner on the way to India, although in unfortunate circumstances, was just terrific. After a few days at sea the ships company settled down into a routine. It was obvious, being a single unit, nobody in authority was going to pay the slightest attention to me which was fine. I was very lucky early on to meet a fellow Corporal who was also a single unit as we must have been the only two on board. We met in a queue for a mug of tea and from then on became pals for the voyage. I do wish I could remember his name. He stood out in a crowd as he was well over six feet tall, half coloured, good looking and of superb physique. He was a quiet, well mannered, reticent lad which really surprised me when after some time and many chats together he confided in me on condition I told no one. He was a member of the most elite section of perhaps the most elite regiment in the British Army - the Special Air Service (SAS) of the Parachute Regiment. The chaps who were dropped behind enemy lines, caused havoc, then found their own way back to base. He had been involved throughout Montgomery's desert campaigns and had also been on special assignments across Europe. He was going home to India having an Indian father and English mother. It was only when we were disembarking at the end of the voyage that I saw him in full uniform for the first time. He had on the famous red beret, wings and parachute chevrons on his tunic along with the Military Medal. When shaking hands, I wanted to say something but refrained. He had never mentioned about being decorated he was that kind of man. It was a privilege to have known him.

One thing about the voyage that comes to mind, and I suppose was quite unusual for such a long journey - the sea was dead calm all the way. Unfortunately, that caused few sea breezes and continual hot daytime sun. After about a week I must have become bored or had some ulterior motive because I decided to approach the CO Troops. Every troopship had a Commanding Officer who was responsible to the Captain of the ship for all the troops on board. He was usually Army or Navy of senior rank and in our case with so many on board he was a Lieutenant Colonel. The CO always had a small staff and except for the ship's officers had supreme authority over everyone on board. It was a very important and responsible job as all sorts of emergency drills and disciplines had to be carried with great seriousness on a loaded troopship in case the worst happened from air, sea or wherever.

So, I knocked on the door of the CO's office cabin and was confronted by a Sergeant Major. I told him I was a Pay Corps Field Cashier on my own and could I be of any assistance on the voyage? In no time at all I was in the Colonel's cabin with him and a Lieutenant his number two and the Sergeant Major drinking tea, having said I would do his accounts for the voyage and attend to any pay queries - manna from heaven to a CO! Everything worked out well I was in his office sometimes each day. It was really part time work for me as I could cope easily enough and could come and go as I pleased. It got me away from the hell hole of a cabin down below as from when we entered the Mediterranean one of my perks was a reserved sleeping place for me and my SAS pal outside on the upper deck every night all the way. That really was a special privilege as every single inch was taken up on all the open decks as soon as the signal was given each late evening and there was always a frantic rush for places. It was better sleeping between two blankets on a hard deck rather than being almost suffocated down below.

The warm nights were fantastic with clear sky above and just the movement of the engines and the swish of the huge liner cutting through the calm waters. It was only on a very few occasions that deck sleeping was not allowed. I got my pal involved doing odd jobs for the CO office as he appreciated the reserved deck spot at nights. Other perks were cups (not thin mugs) of tea and the odd noggin in the office with the staff. It was also good to know in advance when things were going to happen such as lifeboat drill and where and when we would sight places of interest as we sailed quite near the North African coastline at times. I had certainly made a good decision.

Very soon after we sailed from the River Clyde out into the open sea, we had lifeboat drill rehearsal. We had been issued with life jackets and allocated a position at a lifeboat station. In any emergency at sea and especially on a troopship the ships officers, taking orders from their Captain, are in complete command and must be obeyed by all on board including the very highest ranks. The rehearsals took a long time. It was well over an hour before every person on board found their exact position at their lifeboat station and above all how to get there by the shortest route. The ships officer in charge of each station then briefed everyone what to do in all circumstances which could arise. A lot of careful organisation was always necessary, many lives could be at stake.

A few days later in daytime the emergency bells went off continuously which meant emergency drill and we all made haste to our stations. We really put up a very poor show and took ages to get there. The Captain and his officers reached the conclusion we had not been paying attention to their orders and not taking things seriously. I think we were approaching Gibraltar in the middle of the night when the bells went off and this time at full throttle enough to wake the dead and staccato sounding which we knew meant red alert! We shot out of bed and found everything and everywhere "dull red'. The result was that all boat stations had the "all present and correct" muster called in only a few minutes. The very sudden red alert awakening with the dull red atmosphere had given everyone a hell of a fright as instant reaction was that there was fire on board. When we came to our senses and had our breath back standing half naked on deck, we realised the red emergency lighting was on throughout the ship. It was the first time we had been aware of its existence. The Captain had taught us a lesson and said so, when, with us still at our lifeboat stations, he gave us a lecture over the tannoy system. It was to the effect that did we realise Japanese submarines had been reported as far north as the

Arabian Sea which we would eventually sail through to reach Bombay. We must not forget the Indian Ocean was a war zone and to remember and we had won only half the war! That the Japanese were in many ways tougher than the Germans and ruthless if you fell into their hands. He gave us a real roasting and we did not forget it.

I have mentioned we were allowed to sleep on deck which happened after we left Gibraltar. I have just remembered the very strict "between two blankets" order, which applied to all ranks. We had to lie on a full spread blanket which covered our life jacket placed at the top as a pillow. Then cover ourselves with another full length blanket. This was to avoid "tummy chill".

The importance of this order came later in the voyage in the really hot weather when it was so lovely and warm during the night that it was quite comfortable to sleep without a cover. However, the dreaded chill factor was always ready to strike a bare tummy causing great pain the next day and nuisance to the medical staff and ships hospital. Disobeying of the order came within the "self-inflicted" act section of Army Regulations. The Officers of the Watch were always on the lookout for offenders. It was quite a serious pay stopping offence which is why I remember it so well as I was usually involved in the CO 's office. It surprises me how those small incidents come to mind. Mentioning the tannoy system reminds me of the Bing Crosby record which was the huge hit of the time "Don't Fence Me In". It was played two or three times each day and eventually drove us up the wall - or should I say up the bulkhead! It is still played on the radio to this day and always reminds me of the Queen of Bermuda.

I shall concentrate now on the route we sailed the places seen from the ship as we were never allowed off until we reached India. When we left the UK behind, we sailed south through the Bay of Biscay down the west coast of Portugal and into the Straits of Gibraltar and anchored at the famous rock for some hours. I was fascinated watching the continual comings and goings of ships and tonnage including naval ships making their way gently through the surprisingly narrow Straits. When we got under way and entered the Mediterranean Sea, I shall never forget the blueness of the calm water and the hot sun shining from a cloudless blue sky. The weather remained as such without a break for the two thousand or so miles from Gibraltar to Port Said. The only land I defiantly recall seeing from the 'Med' was when we entered the Nile Delta and that was during an evening. We sailed quite close inshore to Alexandria just when darkness was falling. The huge town was lit up, a most wonderful site. The next day we docked at Port Said and were there for about thirty-six hours disembarking some troops and taking others on board. It was when we stopped at Port Said with no movement from the ship to cause air currents around us on deck that we realised for the first time the real impact of tropical sun heat. Most of us on board had "white knees" army jargon for those who had never been where the sun is really hot.

We thought sunning ourselves sailing through the "Med" would acclimatise us, but we were just kidding ourselves. We had never experienced before anything like the blistering heat of Egypt. After all we were not very far from where one of the greatest battles in history took place, El Alamain. We had read the newspapers, listened to the radio and watched the Movietone News at the local cinema and thought we knew about the 8th Army desert campaign. There and then we realised just what the great fighting men had gone through to win the many battles and wondered just how they had survived and not forgetting the many who did not do so. It was only when in the scorching heat that we appreciated how great and special they had been.

All we could say was "Bloody hell it's hot!" Try and look for a place on board where we could lie down and hide away from the sun exhausted doing nothing! We would learn how to survive by taking the advice of the medical team. Making sure we had all the necessary inoculations and vaccinations. (I had them done early on the voyage and as usual none of them "took" some being for unusual tropical diseases. When my upper arms were scratched and like a pin cushion, the medical officer certified me immune). We were advised to drink a serving of pure lime juice every day and a pint of water with a spoonful salt twice each day. Compared with modern medicine today the above prescriptions may sound daft, but they worked. Having said that the water and salt took some getting used to. We were advised about the importance of fluid intake and the obvious precautions about sunstroke, prickly heat and blisters etc. Some lads knew better of course they were tough and did not require lime and salt drinks. They got scared out of their wits when they suddenly turned yellow and felt they were going to pass out. The Doctors would get them back to normal in a couple of days but then no mercy was shown. They would be on late time cleaning duties and all the dirtiest jobs for the rest of the voyage.

We were glad to be on the move again when our turn came to enter the Suez Canal. I was not going to miss a wonderful experience and never mind the heat I was up on the top deck at every opportunity during the one hundred and three miles from Port Said to Port Tawfiq. A liner like the "Queen" had to proceed very slowly in order to create as little wash as possible, the banks being low and sandy and therefore easily damaged. We were to take twelve hours.

I witnessed the famous sight known to all who have been through. Ships keep about half a mile apart and all one could see on either side were miles upon miles of sandy desert. Ships, especially the large ones like ours, towered above the desert land level giving the impression they were slowly moving through a sea of sand as the outline of the canal was not visible even if just a small vessel was going through, a truly fantastic sight. (I should mention that ships wait their turn at each entrance of the canal to pass through as only one vessel at a time being allowed to proceed in either direction).

The first and longest narrow section of the canal beginning at Port Said terminated at the small port of Ismailia a lovely looking place from the ship and so outstanding as an oasis of grassland surrounding the town and along its shores. We then sailed gently through a small lake called Timsah into the second narrow section again giving the appearance of sailing through the desert then suddenly we entered the beautiful Great Bitter Lake which was fifteen miles long by eight miles wide. We continued into the Little Bitter Lake then entered the third and last narrow section which stopped at Port Suez, quite a large town and its neighbour Port Tawfiq being at the end of the canal and the one hundred and three miles.

The ship had just moved very slowly and quietly all the way stopping and starting now and again for one reason or another. Luckily most of the canal run was during daylight which made everything most interesting. We sailed on entering the Red Sea. What an awful diabolical place that was. Very definitely the most uncomfortable part of the voyage which covered approximately twelve hundred miles and completed four days of sheer purgatory. It is situated in a huge, wide, deep trench like valley. The water was actually red in places due to the presence of millions upon millions of red algae plants caused by both shores being lined with coral reefs and coral islands. As a map will confirm the Red Sea is situated between the deserts of Egypt, Sudan and Ethiopia on the west side and the deserts of Saudi Arabia and Yemen on the east.

It is so humid that the air is always saturated with moisture and with the tropical sun beating down from cloudless skies makes the atmosphere very hot and damp. We certainly realised the importance of drinking our pure lime juice and then pints of salted water in that place. The Red Sea also left an everlasting impression on me. Surely it was close to being in Hell!

Towards the end of the Red Sea, we had an emergency on board. A Royal Marine became ill, and his condition deteriorated and it was diagnosed that his body had stopped sweating. It was decided he required emergency treatment not available by the ship's hospital. Arrangements were made for the ship to be given a clear passage through the narrow straits into the Gulf of Aden. A fast naval torpedo boat would come out and meet us.

The MTB arrived some miles from Aden with a doctor and equipment on board and the transfer took place. We were all very sad when sometime later we heard the poor chap had died. The Gulf of Aden was another scorching place, but the heat was dry and as we entered the Arabian Sea there was a slight but welcome breeze. We were however in a war zone and the ship was blacked out from dusk until dawn.

From the Gulf of Aden to Bombay was a very busy shipping lane and strategically placed as all ships with men and supplies from the UK to Southeast Asia used it. We had to keep in the 2000-mile-long lane to Bombay and often we would see British and Indian Navy destroyers on patrol on each side and when we got closer to our destination many mine sweepers were on the hunt. It made us realise we were coming closer to the war scene and not a holiday cruise.

Approaching the massive city in the distance the first thing that caught my eye was the huge natural harbour packed with shipping of all kinds. Troopships, merchant ships, naval vessels and hundreds of smaller ships and craft. Then closer in, the small boats, the floating barges with their Indian boat traders trying to sell us their wares, yelling their heads off in Urdu English, it was all a most wonderful sight. The tugs came along side and took over. They somehow inched the "Queen" through the conglomeration on the water. It was then I sighted the magnificent and touring stone-built arch called The Gate of India, known to every soldier, sailor and airman who arrived by sea. Across the centre top in letters which must have been at least twenty feet high were the words - Welcome to India This is Bombay. Eventually we were in the dock area, then alongside the quay, the hawsers were secured, and the "Full Stop" bells rang out from the bridge. It was the 13th of June 1945. We had been twenty-one days at sea covering almost eight thousand miles. With thanks to the Captain and all his crew for a safe passage.

Being brought up from the earliest age to know all about ships - not being the least interested in small ones - and having been on many and stayed on many but never having sailed on one, made the voyage for me a terrific adventure. (I had sailed from Liverpool to Belfast but only on a small vessel). So many of the stories my Father had told me about the sea and faraway places including India were coming true. The brain wave I had at the beginning of the voyage to approach the CO Troops certainly paid off as in effect I became a temporary member of his staff which had certain advantages.

I made friends with some of the ship's officers. I mentioned about my Dad and we chatted about ships. They realised my interest was genuine and that I was conversant with ships "language" i.e., all the terms used. The result being I was invited up onto the bridge and down into the engine room. All done on the quiet as both places were out of bounds to all ranks.

I got on very well with the CO Troops and all his staff. I was in his office quarters at some time each day helping out with his routine bookkeeping and finances. The Colonel also found my knowledge of pay and allowances a great help as he had no Pay Corp man on his staff. With so many troops on board I could handle the non-routine awkward queries and problems he received. I had a lot of confidence by then having gained such a wide range of knowledge at Overlord and my months at the Edinburgh Pay Office. I had all the perks which were going, like tea and biscuits, reserved seat in the mess for all the meals not forgetting sleeping place on top deck. However, the best perk of all was being able to leave a fan above my head when I wanted to cool off. A fan was worth its weight in gold!

My SAS pal eventually became a staff temp being a sort of runner or messenger and got to know every part of the ship. He enjoyed it as he had to do something intelligent and very alert, which was not surprising knowing what I knew about him. The staff gang including myself and SAS, I think six or seven in all, had our meals together and all slept within a few feet of each other. We had many a laugh, chat, serious discussions and friendly arguments on all subjects under the sun - not the sun but the stars before going to sleep. It does seem incredible looking back that with only a few exceptions I slept on an open deck covered by only a blanket all the way from Gibraltar to Bombay. The nights were always warm, what we called "balmy", and it never rained. I only used the cabin when I had to like all the lads as it was hell down below. The occasions I had to sleep there were very uncomfortable as the fresh air system was never very good.

We had all been busy in the office a few days before we reached Bombay organising disembarkation arrangements. Many Transit Camps had been built near Bombay to accommodate the thousands of troops continually arriving at the Gateway of India. The camps had become well established as the war went on and played an essential part in the success against the Japanese in Burma and Southeast Asia. Every company or battalion of men on board had to be transported by train from the docks to the correct camp. They would then in time be dispersed to join a Division of their Regiment or Corps in India and then more often or not continue to the Southeast Asia theatre of war wherever it happened to be at the time. It was all part of a huge operation.

The Colonel's job was to have everyone on board down the gangway in the correct order onto the quay side to link up with their gear from the ships holds. It was then that the shore Transport Officers took over. The "Queen" had entered the huge natural harbour early morning and had been berthed in the dock before mid-day and the disembarkation had started without any delay. I had some experience of being on my own in the Army, but I am not likely to forget that day. It was surprising how quickly the ship emptied. Due to the Colonel's experience and know how everything went like clockwork. The second last man would go down the gangway around five pm. The last man was one Corporal J Stark (RWAFFR) who was stranded on board because "his" was the only "unit" for which no movement order had been received.

Enquiries were made through all the usual channels, but nobody knew anything about him. (My SAS pal was on his own, but he was an individual going home) On making enquiries the reaction about me was something like "A single Unit are you sure you never heard of one!" I could sense complication and trouble ahead. A dead end was reached but after some head scratching the Colonel himself came to my rescue. He knew the CO at the Kalyan transit camp and got in touch with him, explained I was stranded and fortunately he agreed to take me. The Colonel wrote a note to him which he gave me for personal delivery.

My memory is a bit hazy from then on. It was dark and late evening when I walked down the gangway. All the troops' trams had gone from the docks but I vaguely recall being taken to a station with all my kit by some of my staff pals. I eventually arrived at Kalyan around midnight and was to discover it was about forty miles from Bombay. It was a traumatic journey, but I was to find out all rail journeys in India were, without exception. So my life as a single Unit in the Army continued. I must have wondered what on earth would happen next and what would be in store for me next.

CHAPTER FIFTEEN: KALYAN, INDIA

My memory is hazy about it but that dark Bombay night must have been quite an experience for me. My traumatic journey would be in a hot humid rather sweaty atmosphere close to strange travelling companions who spoke in a fast-chattering language called Urdu. There would be many peculiar smells, some not so nice at all and others of a sweet spicy aroma coming from cigarette and tobacco smoke. The train would often stop and start with violent shudders and not always at a station. Every window would be down at elbow level which caused a continual circulation of chocking black smoke from the monster of a steam engine up front. I can say all this with confidence without a memory of the journey as I have said I was to become quite an expert on Indian railway travel. However, I obviously got safely to the camp, was accepted and given a bed for the night.

The Commanding Officer of Kalyan transit Camp was a Major Fairbrother. He was white, British and had been most of his life in the Indian army. He had retired before the war started but had offered his services again. His age must have been around the sixty mark. He was steeped in army tradition, rather pukka and all that you know but easy to get on with unless you stepped out of line. He knew all the rules and how to break them when necessary. A great old boy of the colonial school. He was very popular, and I learned a lot from him about India and the army in particular.

My first duty on my first morning was to request an interview with him which I obtained and handed him the letter from the CO on the ship. It transpired that quite apart from asking the Major to put me up until my orders came through the CO had been very generous with his remarks about my cashiering ability. Before I had time to take in "you are the very chap I am looking for old boy" he was rasping orders for my gear from where I had slept overnight to be taken to the staff quarters. He kept going saying a desk was to be made available for me in one of the offices and that I was also to have the use of the staff mess facilities for all meals. I am sure that nothing really surprised me personally in the army. I had decided from the start to take things as they came along and never complain!

Kalyan was a big camp capable of handling high volume troop movement in and out day and night which made administration quite a problem, especially catering, therefore the Major certainly had his hands full. He had a large staff mostly Indian officers, NCO's, other ranks and many civilians. He told me his accounting procedures happened to be a bit behind - that was putting it mildly - and asked me to try and help tidy things up into the correct routine best I could, until my movement orders arrived, and he gave me a free hand to do so. Fortunately, the Indian army system was the same as ours - it was for everything - but my main problem was the currency, Rupees. Until I got used to it, I kept working in sterling as a check. No calculators in those days. I do well remember being a bit apprehensive when the Major took me along to a large hut and introduced me to an Indian Lieutenant Sergeant and seven or eight Indian clerks who were responsible for accounting analysis but fortunately the systems, they used to be the same procedures that I knew well. I was on the job without delay and soon discovered both the Lieutenant and the Sergeant were pleased to see me as, from memory, they were being drowned in documentation and found it difficult to cope due to the coming and going of staff. That situation was a continual hazard as civilian staff in India very soon became "unsettled" so when the going got tough they started looking for an easier time elsewhere.

Making sure I kept my place with the Lieutenant, and Sergeant I got stuck in to help. I got on well with them all in the office and was accepted which was very important to me. I like to think my extra pair of hands and experience just made some difference. The continual troop movement and the problems it caused reminded me a bit about the Overlord camp and how corners could be and had to be, cut within the system to keep pace. I was able to put that know how to good use at Kalyam. After a week to ten days the routine was getting back on the rails again. I was very happy at Kalyan. I had good accommodation being in a large hut with another five or six NCO's. I was obviously interested in the make-up of the huts being my first acquaintance with the typical design. They were well constructed and solid being made to intake every breath of air and be cool but also well sealed and waterproof for when the rains came. We were lucky to have one with a veranda and it was all very comfortable.

As it was to be expected from the day of arrival in India one new experience followed another. Sleeping in a cage took some getting used to, the cage being a mosquito net and it was hot inside. The beds were wooden and sturdy a palliasse was placed on interwoven rope fixed to the frame making sleeping very comfortable. Six-foot canes were fixed to each corner top joined to each other by rope with the net draped over and tucked in under the palliasse from the inside. I certainly do remember the torch limits coupled with cursing and swearing which went on when you got into bed from the tiny little insects. You just had to hunt for it, find it and kill it, otherwise you would wake up bitten to hell. They were expert in biting in the most awkward and tender places - and could they bite!

The last days aboard ship we were all given anti-malaria tablets called Mepacrine which we were ordered to take all the time we were in India and Southeast Asia. They proved to be a very good deterrent. They were bright yellow in colour which usually showed up on the temple. If we were near a river or swamp, we would put anti-malaria ointment on uncovered skin. At dusk, if possible, we would always change from short sleeved shirts and shorts to long sleeves and trousers. Some lads did catch malaria, usually their own fault, which resulted in a rather nasty fever. The real problem was that it could occur on occasions during the remainder of your life. There was a sort of myth in the army that the mosquito in the bed cage was a carrier and Mepacrine or not it had to be slaughtered hence all the commotion and keeping people awake most nights!

I think it was during my second week at Kalyan when another experience came my way. The baking hot sun from a bright blue sky started to gradually disappear as the wind got up causing a very unpleasant dust storm followed by the appearance of fearsome black clouds. The weather change was sudden and dramatic. There was a surprising reaction from all the Indians who became excited and happy because the monsoon was on its way. It is welcomed with great rejoicing and thanksgiving in the hope it will be heavy and lasting which would mean good crops. A short and light monsoon means poor crops which can often be followed by the greatest dread of all Indian people - famine.

I suppose I had experienced rain like it at home at it's very heaviest but not keeping on and on for days without any let up. It was a relief to be rid of the continual baking sun, but the rain became tedious. We got used to being continually soaked. The routine was to sit outside the hut clad in only a pair of swimming trunks and let the hot rain beat down on you. I have always sun tanned easily and by then from the voyage onwards I was always brown. It made me think I could maybe be mistaken for one of my Indian friends. The monsoon continued all the time I was at Kalyan. Fortunately, it did abate a bit and settled down into a stop start routine. In between it could be very hot and very humid, and we looked forward to the rain starting again.

A great effort by everyone concerned, when we had a lull in troop movements and an almost empty camp, helped us obtain an even keel with the admin and accounting which brought a large grin to the face of

Major Fairbrother. Eventually I was able to help with pay and allowances. I wanted to be sure I understood the overseas system involving the different currency changes which I was sure would help me when I did get to Meerut. There was no sign of movement orders, and I was not really bothered. I was finding everything interesting and quite exciting. All my colleagues black and white were friendly and helpful and I was learning a lot about the country. The "old boy" as we called Major Fairbrother was always hovering around being very considerate to me and appreciative of what I was doing. I soon got to the stage I could get time off and leave the camp.

Kalyam was a fair size and quite a pleasant town which housed in the main middle upper class government civil service types who commuted by train to Bombay each day. There was a British Colonial Club in the area not far from the camp that before the war had such activities as polo, tennis, cricket etc. It had just managed to keep going by allowing not only officers but surprisingly also noncommissioned officers from the rank of Corporal and above to join as temporary members. They had however to be accompanied by another member. I was certainly taken by surprise one day when good old Fairbrother told me I was in!

It was within walking distance, and I got there as often as I could, especially when it was not raining for a swim to cool off, have a change of atmosphere and a drink. Some of the staff NCOs were regular visitors and I went along with them. It had been a beautiful place and was still in quite good shape. I shall never forget it had a very large quite spectacular circular swimming pool with an island in the centre. I was a very poor swimmer and could just about keep myself afloat but by the time I left Kalyam I could actually swim to the island, which I may say was not really all that far away and back again. What made me pleased with my accomplishment was that the pool was for "real" swimmers as it was very deep throughout and had no "shallow end". For me it was a case of swim or sink. I was scared stiff at first just jumping in but could not let King or Country, the RAPC, the RWAFFER and the Stark name down! The club still had a few old Sahibs who would sit on the veranda with their drink. I can see them now.

I visited Bombay twice, each time for a day again with some of the camp staff. Travelling to the great city by train really was an experience and for a first timer like myself quite frightening. It was a main line train from Kalyan, the journey taking more than an hour. Indian engines really were huge and, on that line, pulling up to twelve very long coaches. Saying they were packed to capacity is a huge understatement, as they were over packed far beyond any possible railway safety regulations. Every inch of seating and standing pace was taken up inside but the astonishing thing was that every inch of hanging-on space was also taken up outside, quite unbelievable. When the sun was out and beating down with all the large windows open and all the engine smoke filtering through between all the bodies inside and outside it was suffocating.

When the rain was pouring down and all the windows were closed steam started to rise and it all became a question of survival. I have said I can "see" the Sahibs at the club drinking their John Collins, but I can still "smell" the carriages on the commuter trains between Kalyam and Bombay. They really were high.

The City of Bombay is situated on the island of Bombay. In India it is called the city to distinguish it from the province of Bombay. When I was there the city had a population of nearly two million and was the fifteenth largest in the world. I have checked and today it has a population of nearly nine million and is the sixth largest in the world. In 1945 the population of the province was twenty-one million. There are many provinces (states) nowadays in India and Bombay is not the largest. I mention all this to illustrate what was known as the "teeming millions" of people then and this must have increased many times over by now.

The huge city had many superb buildings of great architectural beauty and a hive of flourishing industries, also commerce, shipping and trading.

It was however the awful squalor that caught the eye. Beggars, children in tatters roaming the streets and obviously just surviving, people sleeping in shop doors off the main streets at night. Children following you asking for money. It was such an eye opener and difficult to comprehend. Crowds everywhere with scorching heat to contend with when it was dry and steam heat when it was raining.

In recent times I have watched television programmes about cities of India and noted that after forty-six years things had not changed. The human squalor was still there on the streets and a clip showed a train approaching a station with passengers still hanging on by their teeth outside.

During our visits I recall our routine was to do some sight-seeing until mid-day when it was either very hot or pouring with rain. We would then make for the British Forces Canteen in the main square run by the Indian NAAFI where we could have a drink and a meal. Come early afternoon it was always a visit to a large cinema near at hand. The main attraction was not the film it was the air conditioning which was just heaven. Like everyone else we stayed as long as we were allowed to do so. We would have another meal later and then the trauma of the train journey back to Kalyan.

Bombay was where I gained my first real impression of India and the peculiar fascination about the country was implanted in me. The feeling became stronger as I travelled on and saw the countryside visiting other cities of the great sub-continent. That same feeling remains with me to this day. I know it also does with others who have been there.

I had become used to the pleasant life at Kalyan but all good things come to an end. Suddenly on the 10th of July 1945 an order arrived from a most unexpected quarter which furrowed a few foreheads among the senior officers at the camp and especially that of the old man himself. It was from the 2nd Echelon Headquarters of the Supreme Allied Commander which happened to be at Jhansi in Northern India, the wording was all very official and something like: -

"7680868 Corporal Stark. J RAPC (RWAFFR) Field Cashier will report with utmost speed (translated to service jargon meaning - get your finger out!) to the Forward Base Pay Office of the Royal West African Field Force Regiment at Meerut."

At the time the order did not bother me much having got used to odd happenings, but it did later. The camp office certainly "got their fingers out." They were onto the Regimental Transport Officer at Bombay and had me booked on the first available train which departed on the 12th of July. Railway warrant, substance allowance, emergency rations and all the necessities were organised for me. Also included were a few drinks with the staff and a bottle of whisky for the journey presented to me by the Major the night before I left.

So having been exactly a month at the camp I was at Kalyan Station early on the morning of the 12th of July laden with full kit. Once again, I was all on my own a single unit prepared for a journey of nine hundred miles or so which would take me to my destination right across India going Northeast from Bombay. As always in such circumstances which were becoming familiar, I would be wondering to myself what lay in store for me this time?

CHAPTER SIXTEEN: 'WHERE THE HELL HAVE YOU BEEN STARK?"

I could cope by then with the train journey from Kalyam and our arrival at Bombay Central Terminus I reported to the Transport Officer who checked my documents and gave me clearance to travel. He had booked me on a train which departed early afternoon but gave me a shock when he said the journey would take three days! He explained that during wartime long distance trains in India had many stops as they had no catering facilities. They had to halt at least three times per day for lengthy periods to allow passengers obtain a meal either from the station restaurant or food bar.

I boarded a long and very busy train. The RTO had organised a corner seat for me with back to the engine in a second-class compartment reserved for British service personnel. It was reasonably comfortable rather like our own back home, taking eight passengers four each side but with all the gear included it was a crush. The corridor was always busy and noisy as the compartments had no doors or windows on the side. Depending on the weather the outside windows would be either fully open or tight shut. The first-class compartments were very good, but the third lowest class were awful. Heavy high-backed wooden seats for sitting back-to-back placed open plan in the long carriages. Every inch of space taken up with passengers with their luggage and gear and cases, bags and bundles all over the place. The toilet and washing facilities were very basic and it was most difficult to imagine what it was like during the night.

The monsoon was in action when we left Bombay City but by the following morning it had cleared. The sun was out in the blue sky and as each mile passed the hotter it became in the train. Windows were down to the full with usually smoky hot air coming in. We would pass through windy plains with a welcome breeze blowing until sometimes it would include part of a dust storm when all the windows would go up to avoid being blinded. However, it was not all bad and uncomfortable by any means. We would also pass through lovely countryside with valleys hills and mountains. Many of the towns were very interesting so we could see mosques, temples and sometimes places which could be magnificent. There was also many kinds of wildlife in the fields and the plains.

I was to discover how sacred and holy cows were to the Indian people. If the train came to a sudden jarring halt, as I have mentioned in previous chapters, it was certain to be because a cow was on the line. The engine driver would get out and gently shoo it off the line saying nice things to it and no matter how long the delay. They are allowed complete freedom to come and go anywhere and given utmost priority.

We stopped regularly at towns for passengers to come and go but it was usually of the larger ones we halted for food allowing about forty-five minutes. Most of them catered for servicemen having NAAFI canteens or the like. Officers were allowed out of the stations. I think from memory only three of us in the carriage were going all the way, which was to New Delhi, where I had to change for Meerut. Our numbers could vary from station to station, which was important during the two nights, as with more than four in the carriage it was most uncomfortable and making sleeping difficult. Stations are always noisy especially in the middle of the night. I have stretched my legs along a few Indian station platforms at two or three in the morning. It was often possible to catch some cool fresh air at such times.

At every stop we were pestered by beggars of all ages, some kids being no more than four or five years of age saying, "buckshee's sahib" and the grownups trying to sell you junk trinkets and all sorts of gear. Someone always had to stay in the compartment at a stop because if it was empty a little mite could be chucked in an open window by his elders and the place would be stripped in seconds. They were experts at thievery.

A lot of servicemen, Army, Navy and Air Force from many countries travelled by train in India and many could be on one like ours. It followed that service police were always active on the trains and at the stations. I certainly received some attention when asked to show my documents. My pass and service book were always studied carefully and many questions forth coming such as: -

"An RAPC Corporal on his own with a War Office Pass - most unusual. A field Cashier - I think I've heard of them. What does RWAFFR mean? Never heard of them!" It went on like that until I produced the order from HQ 2nd Echelon. "Oh, that's OK!" was the usual reply, because that is where they had come from.

Taking everything into account it was a great adventure for me. I was seeing a lot of India at first hand which helped me come to terms and be fascinated with that extraordinary country. Studying a map a few of the town names come back to me and I can therefore be confident of my route. On leaving Bombay we went north up the coastline close to the sea via Daman and Surat then inland to Baroda and onto the city of Ahmedabad. We continued to Palanpur then a long run across a lot of open desert and plains to Ajmer then on through the beautiful mountain scenery to New Delhi. The Regimental Transport Officer at Bombay was on target with his estimated time of arrival as we pulled in at noon on the third day, 15th July 1945.

Another two experiences awaited me. First, the heat which felt so powerful coming into contact with the real bone-dry stuff. When you looked some distance, everything really did shimmer. However, I was to discover intense dry heat was the easiest to cope with in most circumstances. Second, changing stations in a bicycle rickshaw. I was soon cold all over - with fear! Being pedaled along right in the middle of Delhi traffic surrounded by all sorts of ancient vehicles with impatient madcap drivers shouting and hooting their horns was definitely not the best place to be. Thankfully I reached the other station in one piece. On the way I had noticed, although full of traffic, wide streets and fine buildings and observed a capital city of quite some elegance. It was a lot different from Bombay but also had a good proportion of the teeming millions.

Somehow, I managed to be on the correct train to Meerut. The distance was about the same as from Bombay to Kalyan. The engine, carriages, people inside and outside, the heat, smells and general hullabaloo were the same, but, when the train stopped at Meerut and I stepped onto the platform the place had an unmistakable aura all its own. I knew immediately I was in a vast military environment.

Meerut was quite a large town with a population of about two hundred thousand and was a well-known cotton trade centre. It was however best known historically for its famous Cantonment i.e., quarters for troops which was really a town within a town. The Sepoy Mutiny which happened in 1857 and resulted in the great Indian Mutiny and siege of Lucknow started at Meerut. The famous church is there where the pews still have riffle marks. The Cantonment was built to accommodate thousands of troops and was very busy when I was there. The atmosphere was all military efficiency, precision and discipline.

I can remember being fascinated by the large buildings most of them stone built either side of long straight wide roads connected by large squares used for assembling and drilling. Many of the buildings were used for accommodation. The buildings were large bungalows, with high ceilings and very spacious. The outer ground floor area was surrounded by an ornate veranda. Each bungalow could take about forty men. They were excellent, being designed to attract every breath of air in the one-hundred-degree heat which would be normal at Meerut.

On arrival, the station being just outside the entrance of the Cantonment, I presented myself at the largest guard room I ever experienced. It had many offices and staff and my checking in took some time. There were comings and goings of officers and NCO's asking me questions. I got the impression they were not used to a single unit arriving all the way from the UK on his own. Maybe it was then I sensed something was wrong somewhere.

I was eventually accepted and then marched quite a long way to my quarters in one of the bungalows. A bed with fixed mosquito net (cage), table, chair, wardrobe and to my astonishment I was introduced to an Indian named Sukton who was to be my bearer but more of him later.

I was then directed to the Forward Base Pay Office of the Royal West African Field Force Regiment, which was in another part of the Cantonment. With no delay I found myself standing to attention in an office in front of Captain Brandes and Lieutenant Daniels trying to answer their question:

" Where the hell have you been Stark, as you should have reported here a month ago?"

I knew by the tone of their voices I was really in the doghouse and must have shown my complete surprise. My answer was to tell them the truth about myself from the day the Queen of Bermuda arrived at Bombay ready for disembarkation until I reported to the guard room that day, 15th July 1945. As my tale unfolded and giving answers to many questions along the way, suddenly the penny dropped, and I nearly dropped. The conniving old devil, Fairbrother had organised my delay at Kalyam to help him out. I had been "lost" after leaving the ship. When

I did not turn up after a week or so at Meerut enquiries were started but with no success. That was when the "big gun" HQ 2nd Echelon had to be informed. They "discovered" me at Kaylam and sent their urgent order to Fairbrother. They then kept tabs on me to Meerut hence the regular "pass please" on the train journey and the fussing around in the guard room when I turned up.

Fortunately, I was completely exonerated there and then by my new boss and by 2nd Echelon. At the time an official enquiry was mentioned and there is no doubt old Fairbrother would have been in the soup. It was agreed he was really asking for trouble delaying me especially when I was travelling on, of all orders, a War Office one! However, to my knowledge no more was heard about the incident and certainly not by me. I was glad as I liked the old boy. He had class.

The problem on my arrival was immediately forgotten and I was made very welcome by the FBPO which was a compact little unit responsible for the pay and allowances of all West African troops stationed in Southeast Asia. The vast majority of them were with the two West African divisions the 81st and 82nd which were a very important part of the 14th Army. At that particular time, they were helping to win terrific jungle battles pushing the Japanese back down through Burma and had captured Rangoon. It must be remembered that in those days British West Africa was made up of Gambia, Sierra Leone, Gold Coast and Nigeria. We had lads from all those countries on our books in the office.

The staff establishment of the Pay Office was Captain Brandes (paymaster) in Command, Lieutenant Daniels (paymaster) No2, also a Staff Sergeant and Sergeant. They were all RAPC and seconded to the RWAFF Regiment like myself but they were not Field Cashiers. Then there were twenty-eight West African clerks with their own NCO's the most senior being Command Sergeant Major Onumioi. Each division in Burma had with them a Field Cashier Unit, as usual an officer and two Sergeants who were a constant two-way contact and liaison with Pay Office at Meerut.

I was told by Captain Brandes on my arrival that I had to be with them for a six-week crash course about pay and allowances etc. for the West African Forces and also, do my best to learn what essential language was necessary. I was to be promoted to Field Sergeant and at the end of the period be posted as Active Field Cashier to the 81st Division taking over from the present member of the unit. It was all very exciting stuff for me to look forward to, but I am quite sure it was with some apprehension as the Burma campaign was certainly not the best or safest place to be.

I soon discovered the West Africans were great lads, so loyal to their British officers and NCO's and with a patriotic fervour for their mother country. Most had been tribesmen at home living off the land. To be chosen for military service was the greatest accolade they could receive. They were so proud to be in the army as being looked after, clothed, fed and paid was a new life for them. They had endured a very long period of training and had to come to terms with army discipline. Without realising it they were natural fitness fanatics and therefore developed into superb fighting men as war records will confirm. Some had never been away from their tribal districts until they were enlisted and to be sent overseas into an entirely new and so different environment was a tremendous experience.

The Africans in the Pay Office had received good education, were intelligent and good at their jobs and had a good commanded of the English language. They were amongst the smartest troops in the Containment and were rigid disciplinarians with themselves. Army law was army law, and an order was an order with no flexibility or compromise. This attitude caused trouble as they found it difficult to appreciate that very often some give and take was needed. If they thought anyone, no matter whom, from Private to General, was making disparaging remarks about them, their regiment, their superiors or King and Country, they would demand an apology there and then and would be sure to get it without hesitation. Their reactions could be a little frightening without being violent as their tribal instincts were surfacing. They were well known and respected for being full of fun, great sports and impeccable manners. If trouble was present, they were the chaps to have on your side.

I was very happy with my living quarters and of course had Sukron looking after me. He was over sixty and had been a lifetime in the Cantonment as a bearer and knew all the ropes and was a great help to me and spoke very good Urdu English. It was a rule that in the Cantonment every soldier had a leader. From memory I think the ratio was one bearer to ten men i.e., four per bungalow of forty. Each man paid him a few rupees per week. This may sound unbelievable in the army but as the Cantonment was a rather special place there was method and logic in what may have seemed madness to the powers at be.

The heat was such that two clothing changes per day were necessary. Short sleeve and trousers during the day and long sleeve and trousers in the evening. I had my two sets of clean outfits every day. Blancoed belts, polished boots and shoes etc. My bed made up and always a supply of ice-cold water handy. Everything including myself was smarter than smart and cleaner than clean. The result was that discipline and efficiency was outstanding. Inspecting officers visited all bungalows every day and kept an eagle eye on all ranks. We all knew the rules and there were no excuses for anyone who stepped out of line. The bearers were always on their toes as their job could be in jeopardy if there was a complaint about untidiness.

It really was a great system and accepted because in return we were well cared for having good quarters, excellent food in spotless and comfortable messes. There were plenty of sporting activities, late in the day if you could stand the heat even then and a day's leave often granted to visit New Delhi. The overall result was that the Cantonment was a happy place to be in.

I soon got my head down at the Pay Office as I had a lot to learn in six weeks. Pay and Allowances were not too difficult to understand as the system was the same as the British. It was only the case of becoming aware of the West African rates and currency equivalents. The real difficulty for me was the language. The African boys were very keen to help me. I had some sessions with them which always ended in uproarious laughter as they would fall about in hysterics at my efforts! I have mentioned British West Africa was made up of four countries and although there was a common dialogue of "army speak", I found it very difficult to understand. My pronunciations caused hilarity but I struggled on.

From the day I arrived in India the main topic of conversation by all service personnel was about how long the war with Japan would last and when would it end. I feel at this stage it is worth relating what I can what had happened in Southeast Asia.

By March 1944 having taken for starters Singapore in February 1942 the Japanese army had swept on crushing all before them. They had conquered Malaya and Burma including the Siam and Indo - China on the way. They had thoroughly beaten the British and Allied army at jungle warfare reaching and crossing the Chindwin River not many miles from the border of India where fortunately their advances were halted. Things looked bad for the Allies as the invasion of India was definitely on the cards.

Our defence line held as the Japs had to regroup and await reinforcements. In the meantime, Lord Mountbatten had been appointed Supreme Allied Commander Southeast Asia and he had chosen General William Slim to be in command of the 14th Army (they were the equivalent of Eisenhower and Montgomery of the European Campaign, great leaders of fighting men and winners). They made sure their troops were trained and prepared for jungle warfare. The defensive positions were held and at the end of May 1944 the British, Indian and African forces attacked the Japanese at Kohima and Imphal where a terrific jungle battle took place. The Japs were out fought and well beaten and that was the turning point from which they never recovered. It was the turn of the 14th Army to keep winning battles and advancing, pushing the Japs back continually until by the end of 1945, when I was at Meerut, they were closing in on Malaya and making for Singapore. A tremendous campaign had taken place fought in the worst possible conditions of jungle and searing heat against an enemy of great experience with troops who would rather die that give in.

The cost to the 14th Army in men killed and seriously wounded was terrific and they must never be forgotten. I remember at the time with the European war being over and won and all the celebrations having them take place, new arrivals like myself to SEAC were often asked if it was true the 14th had been forgotten about at home. We had to give very definitive assurances it was not and so had the Government and War Office as they had to answer to Lord Mountbatten who, like Montgomery, was God to all his men. It must also never be forgotten the part played by the Americans not only on land but also at sea and at tremendous cost in lives. They invaded and dug the Japs out of the Pacific, East Indies and China Sea Islands, having to win formidable naval battles to do so.

The combined Allied tactics were to squeeze the Japanese armies to death from both sides and at the appropriate time the Americans would invade Japan. That in my view was the overall position at the end of July beginning of August 1945 when I was struggling to come to terms with African pay, allowances and language at Meerut. The answer then to how long it would take to beat the Japanese and end the war taking into account what still had to be done, I am sure the consensus of opinion was six months to a year. That fair opinion was to be crushed by the devastating suddenness of two horrific incidents which were to reverberate around every country in the world.

CHAPTER SEVENTEEN:
JAPAN SURRENDERS.
OFFICER MATERIAL

On the 6th of August 1945 an American B29 Superfortress aircraft flew over Japan and dropped an atomic bomb on the city of Hiroshima. That single bomb killed 78,000 Japanese people. Three days later on the 9th of August a second B29 dropped another atomic bomb on Nagasaki, killing 39,000.

When news came through to Meerut the Containment went quiet and stayed that way for a couple of days. Very little work was done as everyone kept discussing the situation. There was confusion in all minds about the short term implications and worry about the future of us all including wives, families and friends. Would Japan surrender? Maybe they had an atomic bomb up their sleeves and use it? All the complex issues had been discussed a million times all over the World should such a catastrophe occur, but of course, it would never happen. But it jolly well had and for real. We listened to every word on Forces Radio, anxious for all the news and comments we could receive from home.

Army life gradually returned to normal routine after another few days but by then the grapevine was working overtime. Reports were coming in that many Jap units were showing white flags and their men had hands up in surrender. Sure enough, official confirmation was received on the

14th of August that the Japanese War Cabinet let it be known they had accepted the Allied terms of surrender. The war in the Far East was finally over. A vile and brutal enemy had been thoroughly beaten. The official surrender formalities were to take place later on the 12th of September when they were accepted from the Japanese most senior war chiefs by Lord Mountbatten on one of our warships in Singapore harbour.

WORLD WAR TWO HAD ENDED

Back to the 15th of August which was declared Victory in Japan Day and celebrated in countries, where it mattered, all over the world. In Meerut, as in all other parts of Southeast Asia, the celebrations went on and on. When we did return to reality and normality, we realised a new phase of service life was about to begin.

Southeast Asia Command stretched from India to Java, a huge, fragmented territory including island countries which an atlas will confirm. The situation as it stood was quite simple, everyone wanted to go home. That meant to Britain, Australia, New Zealand, South Africa, India, Africa, Europe, America plus the other countries whose men had been in SEAC helping win the war and included many who had been taken prisoner. All the prisoners would be freed from the awful prison camps. They would require immediate attention and given top priority for shipping home. They would include civilians from many of the countries I mentioned earlier. There were regiments of British and Empire troops situated all over the territory, some just out of fierce action. There were half a million Japanese prisoners of war to be looked after following the Geneva Convention - which they certainly had not followed. Thousands of civilians would be crying out for help as it had to be remembered that apart from India all the countries in SEAC had been more or less devastated towns, villages and countryside ruined by the ravages of war.

I mention a few of the problems and they were endless. The continual discovery of the terrible atrocities inflicted by the Japs on prisoners of war including civilians made it necessary for the little yellow scum to be isolated for their own good and safety. What I have been trying to say is that the conflict was over, the war was won. Some of the lads thought all they had to do was lie in the sun and wait for the boat to take them back to dear old Blighty! They had another think coming. The situation was that a monumental task of rehabilitation, repatriation and re-establishment of essentials, whatever they might be, had to be carried out.

It was a task the victor in war and in particular Britain, had to do as some of the territories belonged to us and others, for various reasons we wanted to help. The British soldier had no cause for being concerned as everything would be done in accordance with demobilisation procedures. We all had a demob number based on first in first out. In August 1945 I had been in the army nearly four and half years and with the war being over I could calculate from my demob number that it would be about a year 'before my number was up!"

We had a man ready and willing to organise what I called the monumental task ahead namely the "Supremo" himself. We all knew Lord Louis would do it with flair, precision, efficiency and not tolerate any delays. Following victory, he encouraged celebrations and let them go on to the full just long enough. Then suddenly he issued his orders. I may have mentioned previously that all three services had their own "Bibles" containing all the rules and for the army it was Kings Regulations. His order was quite simple and easy to follow. The appropriate rules for each service had to be strictly adhered to without question. We all realised immediately what he was telling us. The war was over and with it the necessary relaxed discipline. It is now peacetime, an order is an order, disobey it at your peril. The ordinary wartime routine becomes strict routine. Peacetime rules and regulations will apply from now on.

After all the traumatic happenings and the celebrations, how did the changes taking place affect me personally. I had cause to be excited as a letter arrived from Norah with the news, she was pregnant. We were both thrilled and very happy although so far apart. Then at the same time out of the blue an order arrived from HQ 2nd Echelon saying I was promoted Sergeant Field Cashier from 28 August 1945. More good news as it meant an increase in pay. My red book reveals that as a Corporal with over four years' service my gross pay was 10/8 (53p) Voluntary pay to Norah 6/6 (32p) leaving net pay 5/2 (26p). When promoted to Sergeant my gross pay increased to 14/4 (72p) Voluntary pay to Norah 6/6 (32p) Net pay 7/10 (39p). The increase helped our finances and our savings so carefully taken care of by Norah at home. She was helping all she could from her salary at the Scottish Insurance Corporation.

We were extremely busy at the Pay Office. When hostilities ended the two West African Divisions having battled all the way from the Indian border with the 14th Army had reached Malaya. They had fought with great bravery and distinction but paid a very high price in dead and wounded.

Although communications were still difficult there was a lot of activity between us and the Field Cashiers with the two divisions. Our own African boys were excited about the prospect of going back home because African forces were outside the British demob system - except those who were seconded to them - but they realised it would take some time for that to happen.

When made up to Sergeant I had to move into the NCO's quarters. The bungalow was similar to the one I had been in but not so many of us therefore there was more room and greater comfort. I think I was quite sorry to leave the old quarters and the pals I had made as they were good company. To me the most important factor was that I could keep Sukron as my bearer. The real plus of being a Sergeant was having the use of the NCO's mess facilities in the Cantonment with its bar, comfortable lounge and dining room with very good food. The mess rules were strict and traditional, it was quite an experience.

We all had to realise and keep in mind strict discipline was the permanent order of the day and you had to always act accordingly. The Cantonment was not quite as bad as the Black Watch barracks but in some ways similar. Never having been taught and Perth was long forgotten I had to think carefully what I was doing especially as a Sergeant. One thing was for certain my army outfit was always impeccable, Sukron saw to that. We British men in the Pay Office had to be on our toes as the Africans were superbly turned out and had discipline and courtesy.

Towards the end of September, I was ordered to attend a Medical Board and received a very thorough going over and my A1 grading was again confirmed. Regular medicals were routine overseas and I did not think there was any significance in getting it done. However, I realised there had been when a week or so later I was asked to attend a Selection Board to ascertain if I would be suitable for a commission and entry to an Officers Training Unit (OTU). Things were certainly happening.

That day came quite soon, and I found myself sitting on a chair quite a way back from one side of a long table. On the other side of the table were two Captains, two Majors and a Lieutenant Colonel as Chairman in between them. There are a few things I do remember. It was a long session. I knew immediately from their first few questions that my record file had followed me from the UK. Two questions stand out in my memory. Why, with the experience I had gained by then did I not apply for a Commission when I returned from Overlord or at any other time for that matter? I told the truth. I had made a promise to myself when I was called up never to volunteer or apply for anything in the army but take things as they come. Afterwards on reflection I felt stupid having said that and thought it would ruin my chances, if I ever had any. The other was to give an explanation how an RAPC Corporal had received very good reports from two Royal Engineers, Major Deputy Commanders, a

Lieutenant Colonel Commander and from the Chief Engineer Scottish Command a full Colonel! I explained the circumstances, but it was really surprise news to me. The Chief Engineer had taken the trouble to contact the CRE in Glasgow and DCRE's in Perth and Stirling and ask them to give him a report about me for my record file and included one himself. What a wonderful thing for him to do.

I was put to test on all the obvious Imprest Accounting problems, cash keeping routine, currency, pay and allowances all relating to Field Cashiering and told they would let me know their decision at a later date. It was mid-October when I was asked to attend the office of Lieutenant Colonel Jamieson who had been the Selection Board Chairman. I knew he was a Scot, but it was not until we met man to man, he told me he was from Edinburgh. His first comment was that he had been educated at the Edinburgh Academy and he was aware I had been at Daniel Stewarts College. Within minutes the "old school tie" was working and we discovered we had many mutual friends and acquaintances in golf, rugby and former pupil club circles so much, so it was quite some time before we got down to the business at hand. When we did, I could hardly believe what he was telling me.

I was to be commissioned without attending an Officer Training Unit. Experienced Field Cashiers were urgently required, and the Board was confident I could do the job without any further training. The Colonel was very forthcoming with me. His colleagues on the Board had been impressed with my record. As a Unit Accountant, then at Overlord on special field cashier duties which was a huge plus. Being seconded to the RWAFFR was another then he mentioned nothing I had known about. The War Office had included a note in my record suggesting I was "officer material!" My commissioning date as 2nd Lieutenant Field Cashier RAPC was to be the 1st of November 1945. He said I would know the Number11 Command Pay Office (83rd Battalion RAPC) was stationed in the Cantonment. They were leaving by troop train for Calcutta on the 5th of November then on by troopship to Singapore and I was going with them.

I would only be attached as I would retain my secondment to the RWAFFR. It was still possible but unlikely I would join the 81st Division who were at that time in Malaya, but a division would be made at Singapore. If the Division had departed Malaya for home my secondment would be cancelled, and I would join the Field Cashiers Section Number 11 Command Pay Office at Singapore. The Colonel then gave me a lot of most valuable advice. How to obtain my officers clothing and kit allowance. I must mention that quite separate Pay Offices in the UK handled officers pay only. They worked to a very different system which was done through the banks and with the use of cheque books etc with monthly calculations and payments, instead of the daily and weekly arrangements for NCO's and other ranks. Which reputable military tailors to visit in New Delhi. I had to be measured and fitted for a uniform, shirts, shorts, trousers, boots, shoes, peaked cap and obtain all the essential gear.

Not forgetting, camp bed, towels and so on. There were no quartermaster stores for an officer to go to as he had to provide and pay for all his own gear. I would be given an initial allowance but had to keep it as I had no spare cash.

I took leave of the Colonel that day saying to him very sincerely how much I appreciated his help and advice. I was aware he knew just how I felt when he wished me all the best of luck as an officer. He could feel and understand my depth of apprehension about my immediate future. I had gone from Corporal to Sergeant and then onto Commissioned Officer rank in only sixty-four days! I was going to be a Sergeant one day and an Officer the next with nothing in between. He knew I realised I was going to be in for a rough time and take some unpleasant stick from all and sundry which was understandable. When news got out life was certainly not going to be easy. It was just as well I would be on that train on the 5th of November.

I know my West African Pay Officer colleagues, officers, NCOs were great to me. They had sussed what was going on and said good luck take all that is going. None of them were Field Cashiers but had long pay office service including in the UK, West Africa and India. They had had enough, had low demob numbers and their main objective was to be on a boat home as soon as possible. My most difficult time was in the Sergeants Mess. It came from the regular soldiers, especially the senior Sergeants and Warrant Officers i.e., the Company and Regimental Sergeant Majors etc. and who could blame them. I certainly understood their feelings.

When the news broke, they started being facetious they called me "Sir" which I remember well, and they made me stand to attention. I am sure I expected something like that to happen and accepted it. I always reacted by saying "thank you" and there was maybe no answer to that because eventually the ice broke. On my last night as Sergeant, I laid on a party in the mess, they all turned up, drank many pints of my beer and I think we parted on good terms. I was lucky having Staff Sergeant Bill Phillipson and Sergeant Tony Quantill, my pals from the Pay Office who were quite long serving mess members and were very supportive to me.

Regarding Number 11 Command Pay Office of the 83rd Battalion I knew nothing about them. I had heard there were other Pay Corps lads in the Cantonment, but we had no connection with them. It was such a huge place and could be miles from us. They were in fact a Pay Corps Battalion based in the Meerut Cantonment for which it was famous, ready to move on - and I was about to join them. It was during that hectic time I visited New Delhi on two occasions each for a full day to have uniform fittings, collection and purchases of the basic necessities for being an officer. I shall never forget standing on Meerut Station quite early one morning waiting for a train. The platform had quite a lightweight roof and on one of the walls was fixed a huge barometer/thermometer which because of the roof was not in the direct glare of the sun. The thermometer registered one hundred- and seventeen-degrees

Fahrenheit. Some things stay permanently printed on one's mind and that certainly does on mine. I discovered the train journey was a repeat of the one from Kalyam to Bombay but more frightening. It seemed to me more people were hanging on outside than were inside of the speeding train because of the intense heat. It was very uncomfortable to say the least.

I managed to have a good look round the city which had a character all its own. As I noticed on my arrival from Bombay the teeming millions were there but had a much more spacious layout to contend with. I was also able to appreciate the architectural beauty of many of the buildings.

Unfortunately, there was a feeling of political tension against the British which we were all very sad about. India had loyally supported our cause during the war with more than a million of their soldiers many thousands of whom had been killed or wounded in action. Prior to the war starting in 1939 particularly the Muslims lead by Ali Jinnah were making vehement demands to the British Government for their own independence and self-government. Then in 1945 immediately the war was over, and peace declared the question of self-government was again reopened.

It was the start of a campaign which eventually following a great deal of political infighting between the Mohammedans and the Hindus with their complicated religious animosity of the Castle System, agreement was reached with Britain. It was to create the portion of India - as it was then - into two separate Dominions namely India and Pakistan. This eventually took place in 1947 when as we know the two countries became members of the British Commonwealth and still are today.

The surge to that end was just beginning when I was in New Delhi. A terrible outbreak of religious persecution between the Mohammedans and the Hindus was about to begin all over India. Pillaging and rioting took place and they started massacring each other. It was a bloodbath which was to last off and on for eighteen months.

I found New Delhi a lot more interesting than Bombay. The British influence was noticeable especially where shops were concerned. I remember many being very high class and going into one which sold only sarees. They had a tremendous stock some of them magnificent in design and colour. I was determined to bring one back for Norah and bartered with the assistant at the bottom end of their price range and eventually bought one I could afford. After all those years I can see the inside of that shop and all the beautiful colours of saree cloth.

CHAPTER EIGHTEEN:
CALCUTTA

The dark evening of the 30th of October 1945 was another special for me. On open ground near our office a bonfire was lit, and our West African boys started to drum and tribal dance round it as only they can. The only adequate word which I can think of is incredible because it was done in my honour! It was their way of saying to me goodbye and good luck. I was deeply touched and I was really full of emotion. What a wonderful send off with every member of the Pay Office, black and white together, all rank forgotten and having a happy evening together.

After the war British West Africa as it was then, gradually became nonexistent, as the Colonies were given self-government and led to a lot of strife, trouble and bloodshed. I wonder what happened to Company Sergeant Major Omena, Sergeant Akron and all the lads. They were wonderful people and I treasure the photograph of our super little unit in Meerut. At the time I was hoping so much I would join up with the 81st Division but from field reports coming in I knew it would be unlikely. It was a great honour for me to be associated with the Royal West African Field Force Regiment.

On the 31st of October 1945 I was a Sergeant and the following day a 2nd Lieutenant. My mind is blank how I carried out the changeover. I must have been moved into the Battalion Officers Quarters sometime on the 1st of November. I am sure I did not know anyone of any rank of the Number 11 Command Pay Office, and I was unknown to them. It is easy to remember how I felt that first day - petrified!

I imagined everyone was staring at me because every inch was covered in sparkling new gear. Being called Sir, receiving a salute instead of giving one. Remembering to return the salute. Concentrating hard and trying not to make a fool of myself. I do not recall my new quarters but can visualise the place which gave me palpitations, the Officers Mess. One of the beautiful old Cantonment buildings, very imposing. The entrance up some steps between large stone pillars and in through high wooden doors. Inside the atmosphere full of tradition, comfort, rank, discipline, beautiful silver, waited on hand and foot by Indian servants, excellent food and drink. I think it could be said I was thrown in at the deep end.

The Number 11 Command Pay Office was due to leave on the 5th of November. Every individual was involved preparing for the long journey. About one hundred and thirty officers and men had to be transported a few thousand miles by rail and sea from Meerut, Northern India, via Calcutta all the way to Singapore. I had therefore a few days to become acquainted before we departed. Any worries I had about being accepted were suddenly dismissed from my mind. Nobody bothered, I was part of the action, just another officer who had joined the Corps 83rd Battalion and was allocated to the Number 11 CPO. It happened I had RWAFFR tabs on my shoulder and was therefore sure to be a Field Cashier with a West African division. I was in the midst of people who knew about such appointments. It so happened I was a single unit and only attached to the CPO which was accepted. I knew that meant nobody would want to take any direct responsibility for me if they could avoid it.

Being an officer made no difference to single unit rules in my book as I had a great deal of experience in that respect. I made sure I was included in all the arrangements and planning for the trips. I was in the photograph of the Number 11 CPO taken a couple of days before departure seated with all the other officers. It is another photo I treasure because I was to become a full staff member and proud to be so as many in the picture, unknown to me then, were to become good friends and colleagues.

My promotion to the commissioned ranks made such a difference financially to me and Norah. I was paid monthly through a bank instead of weekly in my hand. My records show that as a Sergeant my gross pay amounted to £21.10s. 00d. (£21.50) per month. I allocated direct to Norah £9.15s.00d (£9.75p) leaving me with £11.15s.00d (£11.75p). As a new 2nd Lieutenant Field Cashier I received £46.00 and was able to give Norah £25.00 and I was left with £21.00 per month. It was all quite an increase. However, I had to keep a standard of living as befits an Officer and a Gentleman as the old manual said and that included paying mess fees and other extras. Fortunately, I kept within the initial clothing allowance which was important to get me started. The pay increase arrived just at the right time with a baby on the way and when Moira arrived Norah would receive family allowance. Norah continued to put money in the bank for us every month and I helped by saving what I could.

An advance party of thirty to forty headed by the Command Paymaster Lieutenant, Colonel Shaw-Hamilton had departed early September to set up and organise the Number11 Command Pay Office Headquarters in Singapore. It would cover the whole of the Southern half of the Southeast Asia Command and would be part of the Singapore Headquarters of Lord Mountbatten based also in Singapore. The remainder of the Number11 CPO about to leave was commanded by the Deputy Command Paymaster, a Major whose name escapes me! Unfortunately, he became ill on the journey and had to be sent home soon after arriving at Singapore.

So, the day of departure arrived, the 5th November 1945 and I was ready. I had been sixteen memorable weeks in Meerut. So much had happened in that short space of time, some of it history making:

- Being stationed in the famous Cantonment
- Being involved with the South Africans
- The dropping of the Atomic Bombs
- The Japanese surrender ending the Far East War
- Receiving news Norah was pregnant
- The suddenness of becoming an Officer

After a great deal of movement, activity and noise from early morning a long, long train packed with troops pulled by a massive engine moved gently out from Meerut Station in the very scorching afternoon heat. I was on my way and again officially a single unit, bound for a destination which on arrival would take me with the Army's guidance and pleasure near enough halfway round the World since leaving home. The outstanding difference from my previous train journey from Bombay to New Delhi was the comfort of travelling first class, four officers to a compartment. For sleeping, the two seats became beds and above were another two which pulled down from the compartment wall. As previously the train stopped for about an hour at stations for three mealtimes. The officers had a restaurant car on board and arrangements had been made for all other ranks to have their food at station restaurants reserved for them. We were allowed out at stops as I remember going to walk along streets near the stations of some towns. The Indian Railway system did things their own way and in their own time, hence the reason we took three days and nights for the journey of a thousand miles. Maybe it was slow, but it was fascinating and most interesting. Our route from Meerut was to New Delhi, then via Agra, Kampur, Allahabad, Varanasi, Gaya then along or near the great Hooghly and the mighty Ganges rivers arriving at one of the four terminus stations of Calcutta on the 8th of November.

Calcutta situated in West Bengal was the largest city in India. It was a very busy port but was in fact and I presume still is, nearly ninety miles from the sea on the wide Hooghly River, the western arm of the Ganges Delta. It was a much older city than either Bombay or Delhi and looked it. It had been the chief allied base for the Burma Campaign and was still very much war service orientated. We were given good accommodation in a large transit camp not far from the river and the dock area. There were a lot of service personnel about the city.

We were seven days in Calcutta, and I had complete freedom of movement and no duties. The first thing I did was contact Plummer Brothers who were Waddies agents in India. Before the war we exported crate loads of printing and die stamping every month from Edinburgh to our customers in India and Ceylon. I called at their very attractive offices in the centre of the city overlooking the Maidan which reminded me of Hyde Park in London but was not so nice. I was made very welcome and was invited to dinner. Jack Plummer and his wife had a mansion on one of the posh suburbs with servants galore. He was a wealthy merchant with many business interests. They were very kind and gave me a wonderful time because that evening it was arranged that the following day, I would be given a tour of the city including lunch at Jack's club, which was really something and dinner again with a few of their friends from the UK.

The next day was tremendous for me as what I do remember is being driven along a road which seemed to stretch for miles with ships of all sizes including naval, merchant navy, passenger liners and so they went on berthed one after the other line astern. My imagination is not running riot keeping in mind they were berthed on a river where docks can be in line. Calcutta was a great port for ocean traffic. The docks were always packed with merchant ships from all over the world, loading their holds with rice, cotton, tea etc.

I knew all about what was going on because as a young lad my Dad had told me. I was thrilled to be there seeing for myself. He had sailed the famous Indian trading routes back and forth from the UK dozens of times. The thought excites me now as I write because at my back on the wall is a painting of a large Ellerman Hall Line cargo vessel on which my father was Chief Engineer and about the house we have pieces of plate and ware that he brought home from his many voyages to the Indian continent.

I had been royally entertained by the Plummer's, and having been involved in many discussions with them and their friends I gained a lot of knowledge about India and what the future was likely to have in store for the British "jewel in the crown."

I had another interesting experience while in Calcutta. Just before the war it is safe to say the best-known footballer in Scotland was Tommy Walker who played for Herts. He was a great sportsman and gentleman and considered unique as the only professional footballer studying at university.

When I played for the Corps Battalion team in Edinburgh his brother Johnny also a professional footballer was our centre half. I promised him, if the opportunity arose when I was in SEAC, to contact Tom I would do so. Tom was a Captain and Sports Officer to no less than Supremo himself, Lord Mountbatten. With his backing Tom had organised teams of the finest international players to take part in matches when the war was on and for the sole purpose of entertaining and keeping up the troops morale. They often played not all that far from the action but usually at leave rest stations. The idea proved to be a terrific success and was continued for a while after the war was won. As luck would have it a match was on the week I was in Calcutta and Tommy was with the team. I contacted him and he invited me to the game as his guest. Both teams were full of famous names and the match was played to a packed stadium at Eden Gardens. The ground was well known then but more so nowadays for cricket where India plays Test Matches. It has increased in size since I was there as I keep an eye on the television when England play India at Calcutta.

Our sailing date was the 15th of November, and we were glad to embark as rioting had started. The shout for independence and self-government including " British out" had begun by Indian militants who were causing trouble and started the rioting. They were doing so much to the disgust of the ordinary Indian who also wanted independence but by peaceful and negotiated means having no wish to antagonise the British. The rioting was near the river and dock area and not far from the camp.

The day before we sailed a lot of rampaging went on, fires were started, and the police were having problems containing the trouble. During the late evening it became serious as gunfire started and bullets were whistling around close to the camp which was full of British troops. Then around midnight an amazing thing happened. In our camp were a detachment of rather special soldiers, the elite, who wore red berries, commandoes, who were also due to embark the following day, but to go home. The situation deteriorated until they just could not put up with it any longer so decided to take some action. Having been in the forefront and survived Burma and other campaigns no way did they want to take a stray bullet from a stupid excitable Indian militant in a back street in Calcutta. So off they went, officers and all, out the gates with Sten guns loaded and ready. They found the police officers in charge and told them to contact the rioters and tell them that if the shouting and rioting did not stop immediately, they would shoot the whole bloody lot of them in sight without any hesitation and they meant it, having nothing but home to Blighty on their minds! In no time at all quietness and peace prevailed and we lesser mortals felt safe for the rest of the night thanks to the superb and fearless men in the famous headgear.

The next day, 15th November 1945 we embarked on a troopship which I would call medium size. I am surprised to say I have no trace in my records of the name or line and cannot remember but I have a photograph taken aboard. So once again I was on my way, this time on a voyage of two thousand miles heading for Singapore and the Equator.

CHAPTER NINETEEN: SINGAPORE

All was quiet after the goings-on of the night before. We were all on board quite early in the morning and soon the ship was moving gently along the very busy Hooghly River. We eventually arrived at the wide expanse of delta where a network of rivers including the Ganges and Brahmaputra flow into the Bay of Bengal where we stopped, and a naval minesweeper came alongside. What they did caused us all just a little concern. They fitted the ship in no time with long mine sweeping outriggers from the bow on both port and starboard sides. We were told the Japanese had laid mines indiscriminately in the Indian Ocean and up into the Bay of Bengal and some ships had been seriously damaged.

During the voyage we had lectures warning us that although the hostilities had been over for about three months where we were going there were still many hidden dangers on land and sea. Mines were the real problem and although everything possible was being done, it could take months maybe a year or more to clear them all. They were not much of a problem at sea but more on land. On the beaches, in and around rivers and particularly in the jungle areas and sometimes in buildings where they could have been hidden or booby trapped. We were told how to cope and warned to take great care which we certainly did when later we could come face to face with causalities.

When we sailed from Calcutta, we were told our only stops on the way would be at the Chittagong which was a large port on the India-Burma border and that we would smell it out at sea. Hence the reason the "C" became an "S" to all who had been there. Sure, enough it was true and when we docked it was awful I think it had something to do with hides and tanning, although I could be wrong.

The inhabitants of Chittagong were held in the highest esteem by the allied commanders. Because of the ports natural deep water harbour, it had been "the" most important port during the Burma campaign. It was the main supply centre for the 14th Army and therefore had suffered furious ground and air attacks by the Japanese. The 14th Army of British, Indian African and all other Colonial forces had fought a tremendous defensive battle along the border, with huge casualties to save India and it did. The loyal people of Chittagong with their local knowledge and bravery had given outstanding help to the allied troops operating in a country so foreign to them.

We were not allowed ashore, but we could see, hear and "feel" the jungle which stretched all the way down through Burma. We could well imagine the hell it must have been for our troops fighting fearsome battles in such awful conditions against the Japanese.

We took on more troops. We got no sleep because of the heat, noise and stink. We were there twenty-four hours, and we were glad to be on our way out into the open sea again. During the remainder of the voyage, we had regular sessions from senior officers. They gave us information about work routine and other aspects of what to expect at a Far Eastern Command Pay Office Headquarters just after the end of a mighty bloody war. The circumstances were explained to us and that we would be involved in a complex and scattered area of Southeast Asia which included the East Indies Islands. We accepted the warning that a tremendous amount of hard work was ahead of us sometimes in very difficult conditions, but it would be very interesting.

The voyage continued and was really a very pleasant cruise in the sun in calm seas and without incident. We hugged the Burma coastline and I seem to remember we saw bright coastal lights one night which we thought might be Rangoon. We sailed close to the Southern tip of Siam (now Thailand) then down the Malaya (now Malaysia) coast into the Straits of Malacca where we made our way between dozens of tropical islands.

It was mid-morning with the sun full up on the 25th of November 1945 when I saw the most spectacular sight ahead, the fantastic harbour of Singapore in all its glory. Once again, I was thrilled because many times my Father had told me the finest harbour in the world was Singapore. Warships of all sizes from aircraft carriers, troopships, liners, merchant navy, tankers, masses of small boats and craft, Chinese junks and sampans. There were ships from all round the globe as Singapore was perhaps the largest and busiest shipping junction in the world at that particular time. What a sight to behold after almost twenty-seven weeks and twelve thousand five hundred miles from leaving the "tail of the bank" of the River Clyde at Glasgow on the 22nd of May. What had the future in store for me in that exciting part of the world.

The pilot guided our ship through the conglomeration of shipping to the dockside late afternoon. Disembarkation began immediately and standing on the quayside to greet us was the Command Paymaster and his senior staff of the advance party who had been in Singapore since the end of September. Officers were taken to their quarters. We were in what had been an exclusive area of Singapore with beautiful houses and gardens, as the photographs will show. Fortunately, the Japanese had left the house in quite good condition, but the gardens were four years overgrown.

All the rooms were used two or three to a room depending on size and each had a balcony. The photographs shows the house where I was quartered (I was in a room top floor at the back). Each room had a servant boy, Malayan Chinese, who did all our dhobying (washing) as we required two complete changes of clothing every day. They kept quarters clean and looked after us very well - which means they did everything for us. We were very comfortable. However, I doubt very much if I could have carried out my duties on very many occasions without knowing that Ching, our room boy, had everything under control as far as I was concerned. (I can sense obvious reactions to that statement! Just maybe, later on, as my story continues there might be some agreement to it.)

Not far away in what had been one of the very big houses was our own - the CPO - officers mess which had been made very nice indeed by the advance party. All mod cons with large dining room, very comfortable lounge bar plus a second lounge. The Malayan Chinese were very good cooks and food was always plentiful, so we certainly did not starve. Various fruits were grown outside and were there for the picking. A servant was always available for our needs. That first evening all officers of the CPO assembled in the mess in spit and polish order so that the new arrivals could meet all their new colleagues and be introduced personally to our Commanding Officer, the Command Paymaster Lieutenant Colonel Shaw-Hamilton.

He was a professional soldier from an army family background, having been in uniform since leaving college in his teens. He was then I would think in his fifties, six feet four inches tall at least, thin as a rake, ramrod straight, aristocratic, the old school upper crust. He "stood out a mile" in a room but did not want to as he was very approachable. Could be very tough but always fair and had a great sense of humour. Without doubt he was the finest soldier and leader of men I met during my army service. All ranks from top to bottom would work their guts out for "Squaw" as he was affectionately known.

A surprise awaited us during our first visit to the mess. The war being over we were told the routine had reverted to prewar regular army colonial system. It was the same in the messes of all ranks not only in Singapore but elsewhere. The order had been made by Lord Louis himself being one of the many disciplinary measures taken to keep everyone on their toes and remind them they were still in the army as a colossal job of rehabilitation had to be done. As far as the mess was concerned rules were there to be adhered to, procedures were traditional and strict and rank had to be observed at all times.

I do remember so well that a certain 2nd Lieutenant being the most junior and lowest rank present was feeling a bit of a strain and required all his wits about him every second he was in the mess that evening.

The following day 26th November my first duty was reporting at Mountbatten's Supreme HQ which was The Cathay Buildings not far from the CPO. I received the expected news. Both divisions of the RWAFFR were about to go home and therefore my services would not be required. My secondment had been cancelled and put through gazetted orders at the War Office which meant I was transferred back to the RAPC. I have always regretted missing out being a Field Cashier with one of the RWAFFR divisions even if it had only been for a short spell. The Command Pay Office was in what had been before the hostilities The Hong Kong and Shanghai Bank which was situated on a corner of Raffles Square. It was a large impressive Victorian style building and was still in good condition. The ground floor had a huge banking hall and many offices. The second and third floors were all office accommodation. The basement contained large safe vaults, which were to become very familiar to me. We required the whole building as the CPO staff there must have been maybe one hundred and fifty maybe more.

My first steps, after entering the marble hall with pillars along either side, was the office of the Colonel. I was not with him very long, but I know I came out full of enthusiasm and with the feeling his team could not do without me. He had the knack of inspiration and the charisma of all great leaders. He told me to report upstairs to the office of Captain Alexander who was the officer in charge of the Field Cashier Section.

I had met Bill Alexander just in passing the previous evening in the mess but within two minutes of being in his office I was back in Edinburgh. It was another amazing quirk of fate during my army travels. He was married and lived in Edinburgh. He had been educated at George Heriots and was a chartered accountant with Maxtone Graham and Lyme, well known accountants in Edinburgh and very good long-standing customers of Waddies. It turned out we had many mutual friends and acquaintances in business, golf and rugby circles. After quite a long question and answer session carefully exploring my Field Cashier experience, he said "you'll do."

Be all that as it may I very soon discovered that he was a brilliant accountant, a workaholic, only gave an order once and expected it to be carried out to the letter. He could use the language of a Black Watch Sergeant and be a real bastard at times. He was an expert at cutting through red tape and rank if it was necessary. He would back you all the way if he thought you were right, but God help you if you were wrong! Fortunately, he too had a great sense of humour and never held a grudge against anyone. He was very generous and would go out of his way to help anybody and everybody. He was such a mixture. I got no concessions from him - never - but very soon came to terms with his attitude and it transpired we really got on very well.

Harking back to that period with Bill Alexander in Singapore I doubt if I have ever worked harder both physically and mentally in my life, but I gained a tremendous amount of experience in the process. On the first-floor offices Alex had an inside staff of about forty made up of RAPC lads and also some local civilians who had suitable experience. Their job was to look after the administration of the Field Cashier Units out in the field and all their requirements. That was no easy task and could mean working at any given time in twenty-four hours.

When the fighting finished a monumental task had to be faced. Tens of thousands of British, Colonial and Allied troops were scattered all over Southeast Asia. Battalions, Companies, Divisions, including odd units of

Regiments and Corps. All those stationed in Siam (now Thailand) Malaya, Sumatra, Sarawak, Borneo (now Kalimantan), Java and some of the smaller East Indies islands came under the jurisdiction of the CPO. They all had to be financed. The men paid also the contractors, merchants and firms supplying food and everyday essentials. The Commanding Officers had to obtain hard cash in most cases as banks, if operating, were only doing so in large towns. Every penny had to be accounted for and to undertake all that responsibility was the Command Pay Office which was in effect a bank. That is why it was necessary for it to have a large, experienced military staff to provide this very important function. The Field Cashier Section was the vital link between the CPO and the COs of all the troops.

Bill Alexander had seven Cashier Units stationed permanently in the countries I have mentioned. He also had another three units at base always ready to take off on emergency journeys anywhere in the territory. They had often to fly with cash to keep Units supplied. A Field Cashier Unit was made up of the usual three, an Officer and two Sergeants. However, on field service duty there were two very important additions. A small military truck and a driver. The truck needed to be able to cope with the roughest possible mountain roads and jungle conditions. The driver had a real responsibility as it was his job to keep it maintained and running and never be without petrol as it could be the difference between life and death.

Cashiers could be carrying very large sums of money in their many large cash boxes to Units stationed at the back of beyond. Often travelling for days along rough jungle roads which had been bombed and mined. Tough small army trucks with heavy canvas backs did a great job. It could be an exhausting and nerve-racking experience as I was about to discover. So, Alex had a very active field staff under his command and keeping in communication with them was not easy. A look at a map will show the scattered territory from Siam to Borneo and Java. It was a huge awkward area to cover with a lot of sea and jungle land involved. He also had Embarkation Cashier Units under his control, more about that later.

It took me a week to settle in, getting to know the staff and colleagues of our section and the Pay Office in general. I became acquainted with the routine there and at our quarters and mess. I found my way around and discovered Singapore was an island on which was a city and port of the same name. The island was joined to the Malayan Peninsular by a causeway over the strait of Johor. That confirmed why the locals talked about Singapore Island and Singapore City. The Japanese had fought their way onto the island on 8th February 1942 and entered the city on the 12th. They occupied both until they surrendered on the 5th of September 1945. Except for the dock area the city was relatively undamaged during the war.

As it was the done thing to do, I joined the Tanglin Club which was for officers only and was very well known having been established as such for very many prewar years. It had been used by the Japanese but was still of prewar colonial vintage in every way. The rooms were cool and pleasant with large cooling fans circling silently. It was just right to sit out on the sheltered terrace or on the balcony above the swimming pool and call to one of the many servants for a John Collins or a G&T! My order was likely to be for a bottle of Australian beer. The Tanglin Club was really a great meeting place for officers of all services, British, Colonial and Allied. I got to know some Naval and Air Force pals who helped us a lot with our work and could pull strings in the right places. I was not much of a regular as it was only when I could find the time which was not very often. I preferred a quiet drink in the mess or in our quarters.

Mentioning Australian beer reminds me about one and there are many more, of the terrible atrocities discovered when the British and Allied forces recaptured Singapore. The Japanese had dumped hundreds of bodies of our prisoners of war including civilians into local reservoir not long before they surrendered. Everyone from Supremo down had seethed with rage. Repatriation was the order of the day, and it was certainly obeyed.

A very serious problem had been drinking water as the situation was desperate. Australia had answered the call by immediately dispatching an air lift of thousands of cases containing bottles of their famous beers. By the time we arrived the emergency was over, but the beer had become very popular and was cheap.

During my settling in week, I had chats with all the officers in charge of the various departments of the Pay Office who put me in the picture and of course with Alex himself. I soon realised the Command Pay Office at Singapore was different in many ways from the others I had known. It was in effect like an international bank not only for army purposes but also to provide help and advise to local businesses essential to the community getting back on their feet again after occupation. I found myself involved and working alongside office colleagues who had been in civilian life experienced bankers, accountants and money market experts. They were guided along army procedures by the few senior regular army officers of similar standing. We were all however under the expert control of our Command Paymaster for whom we had great affection. Squaw was just brilliant, and he had a very simple policy. He made certain every individual knew his job, including the relative army procedures and routine, then let him get on with it. He was always available to listen and help solve any problems and ready with a word of encouragement.

After about two weeks Alex suddenly informed me, I was to accompany him up country as there were quite a number of isolated units of troops of various regiments requiring our urgent financial help and attention. They were scattered about Malaya, and he had decided we would "blitz" them together. That definition was appropriate as it was to be my very first taste of his toughness of attitude, the driving force inside him and his outstanding ability.

He had an Indian Corporal driver, two hand-picked Sergeant Cashiers and all my requirements arranged and ready in no time. The Number10 Field Cashier Unit of the Number11 command Pay Office Southeast Asia under the command of 2nd Lieutenant J. Stark was ready for action. He had mustered his own unit which was always on standby ready for the road. He checked we all had our own necessary personal kit for up to twelve days away. The check was most important especially that we had the correct medical supplies.

Finally, early on the morning of departure day we visited the vaults and were subject to the most strict cash checking system and had our two trucks loaded with the special ammunition type cash boxes which were full to capacity. Then our two units in line astern, Alex in the lead, set off from Raffles Square full throttle out of town and on until we crossed the causeway out of the island. We were entering the Federal States of Malaya which in those days were nine in number.

I seem to remember the sweat was running down my back and my shirt was soaking. The cause was not only the torrid heat and high humidity but what is best described as adventure excitement coupled with a modicum of fear. Fear at the speed we were travelling, Alex having given our rather reckless driver strict orders to keep with him. I still had the departure warning ringing in my ears about very rough roads, avoid bomb craters and watch out for unexploded mines! Alex had heard it all before, paid no attention and belted on. No wonder I was hot!

We were on tour for ten days keeping to the lower part of the Malayan Peninsula which was in all seven hundred and fifty miles from top to tail. We visited many units some in quite isolated camps although often near the smaller inland towns. The big Companies and Battalions were encamped or barracked in or near the large towns down the west side near the coastline. The troops had a lot of work to do being involved with rehabilitation of the country. We were in one of the hottest and dampest climates in the world. Steam rising from the ground was not unusual and sometimes when walking we could not see our feet. Always a damp and sometimes dangerous experience.

The jungle of huge, tangled trees, trailing plants and dense undergrowth was never far away but it was a haven for beautiful birds of all colours and sizes. I did see some wild animals in the open spaces, deer and antelopes come to mind. There were very few about making a noise during the night. The locals explained that because of the jungle war many of them had made for the highland areas north and had not yet returned south. They told us about elephants, buffaloes, leopards and tigers and how great their country was with wildlife of all sorts.

The creepy-crawlies had not gone to the highlands, and they kept reminding us. Leeches, centipedes and all sorts of sting insects and flies were always ready to take a bite of us although we were plastered with anti-insect cream. Our real fear was always the dreaded scorpion as he could do serious damage.

In Malaya you were never far from a river as they intersected the whole peninsula. The troops could tell many stories about them as the fiercest fighting took place either attacking or defending them. Many of the natives lived along the swampy banks and so did the mosquitoes and because of them we took our yellow Mepacrine tablets every day to avoid catching malaria. Seldom a day passed without having your share of bites from the little devils.

The local people were very friendly and so clean. It was a serious ritual with them to bathe twice every day. They were so happy to see us having had a terrible time with the Japanese. We heard first-hand about the terrible atrocities committed by them on civilian women and prisoners of war in jungle camps that were situated in the southern area we were in. All the men had been sent to the north and into Siam and Burma to build roads, railways and bridges along with service prisoners.

We passed through many villages. They were usually a cluster of huts built of bamboo and palm leaves; the roof being thatched with them. Houses beside the river were built on piles, I think the reason being it kept the crocodiles at bay. There were many in the rivers and we certainly did not venture too close. We sometimes had to detour to find a bridge which was often the famous Royal Engineers - Bailey Bridge.

The village huts and houses were usually built in the shade of tall coconut palm trees and very often surrounded by fruit trees including the popular mango which was magnificent in blossom. It was not all jungle by any means as there were huge open areas, acre upon acres of them being rubber plantations. Rubber was Malaya's principal product along with, in those days, tin. Combined, their whole economy was based on them, and they produced great wealth for many.

The first couple of days of our travels I recall we had difficulty finding our destinations and found ourselves in some odd places. The trouble was none of us were any good at map reading. We wasted no time making certain each one of us could so as we had no desire whatsoever to be lost in that type of country. The Royal Engineers had done a terrific job making the main roads useable by filling in many bomb craters and clearing mines which kept traffic flowing. The going was very rough, but we got used to it. When we eventually arrived at Camp - "The cashiers are here" news immediately got around. We always received a great welcome from the CO's and staff. When we stayed overnight with them everything was laid on for us. Permanent armed guards for our cash boxes from the moment we arrived until we departed. The best washing facilities they could provide, plenty of food and drink in the mess and a good bed. We always carried our own for use if required along with emergency rations.

When we got on with our job on the first day, I immediately found myself back in the old routine. Helping with cash requirements, Malayan dollars, exchanging currencies, involved with the CO's, the troops pay and allowances and all the usual queries. Giving advice and assurance that any urgent financial worry they had at home would be attended to immediately when we got back to base. The main topic of course was always if we had any news and when they were likely to be going home.

I had the feeling after we had visited two or three camps that Alex realised, I had a lot of experience and knew what I was doing. He let me deal with a lot of things on my very own as he could carry on with other jobs saving time. He had chosen a really good team for me. My two Sergeants knew their stuff, were good workers and nice lads.

Our Indian friend at the wheel was a bit of a madman on the road - I soon discovered all Indian drivers were - but he was a star turn keeping us amused. Above all he looked after his truck and kept it in good condition. Alex of course had an excellent team; they had got used to him. He could be a bloody menace at times working us from dawn to dusk in days which were always in the nineties with humidity in the sixties as he kept chasing time. But we liked the so and so. He was good to work with, appreciated what we did and was always the same to everyone. Surely the ingredients of a good team leader, which he was.

The latter part of our tour was not so hazardous but very hectic. We spent three days covering Kuala Lumpur (always known as KL), Klang and Seremban. In those days KL was the seat of government of the Federation and was a large town, the other two being similar. When the fighting stopped the three towns had developed into a collecting area for troops from central and southern parts of the country and many who had been prisoners of war including civilians. When the CPO advance party arrived, Alex had immediately stationed a permanent Field Cashier and staff at KL to cover the three towns, the situation being a bit chaotic. He then arranged two or three cash runs per week by road from Singapore to KL nearly two hundred miles. My colleagues who were on it said it had been one hell of a journey, until fortunately one of the banks became organised at KL and helped us out. If there was a real emergency the RAF would fly cash in for us from Singapore, but it had to be escorted by a Field Cashier Unit.

When we arrived at KL things had settled down and there was order and organisation about the area although there was still a lot of troops and civilian movement. We got quite a surprise becoming involved with British and Allied troops and civilians, male and female, who seemed to come from most parts of the world. They had converged on the towns from all over the territory including Sumatra. They would be waiting patiently for transport either south to Singapore or north to Georgetown Penang, having only one thought on their mind - embarkation home. They all required help of some kind or another often the most important being hard cash and this is where we came into the picture. Imagine tough fighting men not long out of bloody battles against the Japanese in awful conditions all wanting cash and obtaining it without delay, thanks to the Field Cashiers. They would paint a town red and keep coating it in no time at all! The poor Cashiers at KL, my two Sergeants and the extra staff sent up from the CPO were defiantly feeling the strain and no wonder due to lack of sleep. Their book accounting, cash and currency balancing had got behind and many loose ends had to be tied up. Immediately on arrival Alex assessed the situation and gave his orders "We'll get stuck in and not leave until they are bang up to date". We were ready to leave in three days by working almost nonstop having only a minimum amount of sleep.

My memory is a bit vague about it all. I think our quarters and office were in the same building which had been a hotel. We maybe had our food there too. I was out and about in the towns having meetings with COs about their new accounts. I know I was fascinated to see the blood red soil caused by the tin mines. It must have been about then, those three days, that made me realise I was involved in a colossal process of rehabilitation organisation with all the complicated elements which had been under way since the day war against Japan ended.

We set off from KL early in the morning. Alex being determined we would travel the two hundred miles and make a call on the way and to be in Singapore before darkness. We belted down the Bukit Timah road. Fortunately, our trucks and ourselves stood the strain of a very bumpy ride although we did not keep to Alex's schedule. The latter part of the journey was in the dark which always had to be avoided if possible. Eventually we were glad to see the lights of Singapore in the distance as we crossed the causeway onto the island and then arrived safely outside our HQ late evening and very tired. Our cash boxes were put in the vaults for the night, then a shower, meal and off to bed.

Immediately on our arrival at the CPO the following morning we set about the task of "cashing up" and "balancing". It was my first experience of this very important procedure as an Officer and one which gave every Field Cashier some worry. The system was very strict at this point as the Paymaster, in our case Alex, was personally responsible for every penny. Notes and coins had to be counted, all the entries in our books and every transaction checked including documentation then balances struck. Then the lot would be handed over to the Command Cashiers Department for checking and only then would signed clearance documents be issued. The whole procedure could take from a couple of hours to well into a day. Large amounts of cash, as we had at the start, could pass through a cashier's hands with many different currencies being involved and accounted for. I had taken part in "cashing up" at Overlord, which was nothing compared to the complexities at Singapore, being in a different league all together.

It brought home to me the importance of having a good field team. Having complete trust in each other, being efficient, keeping to the system and not taking chances. Admitting mistakes immediately they were discovered. It could be easy to make a mistake with currency calculations when under a lot of pressure and why so much cross checking had to be done at the time of the transaction. It is worth keeping in mind, calculators as we know them today had not been invented, we only had our fingers!

On that occasion it would be well on in the day when Alex received clearance from the Command Cashier Major ("Dad") Grey. I have no precise memory of that particular occasion, but I am certain when we were finished and received the "all clear" Squaw would appear from nowhere as was his wont having received a report of our mission up country. He would speak to us all and say, "Well done lads take two days off and do not come near the office". Even Alex knew to keep away as the Colonel meant what he said. If you were caught on the premises when he had given the stay away order his wrath would land on you which was very unpleasant unless you had a most urgent or genuine reason for being there. It was just his way of doing things, leave entitlement would never come into his head. It applied to all ranks top to bottom. If it was his feeling, you required a rest he would say so, it was an order and you had to take it. God help you if you tried to pull a fast one - or work a "flanker" in army jargon - on him to get a rest. He had that "something" - he cared, and therefore all his staff had a great respect for him.

CHAPTER TWENTY:
NEW ARRIVAL AND MTB'S

No more than a week after my return from tour with Alex I was summoned to the Colonel's office and told by him the most unexpected and surprising news. I was being upgraded to Paymaster. The Pay Corps routine was when commissioned you would have the rank of 2nd Lieutenant, as was the route in all Regiments and Corps. If, however you were medical category A1, you would be automatically appointed to a Field Cashier Section of a Command Pay Officer within a Battalion. The stipulated programme was that you would spend the first six months becoming acquainted with all the Field Cashier duties working with an established Field Cashier Unit whose command had to be a Paymaster, as I had been, having been assisted by Alex. As it happened, he had given me his my very own unit, due to the circumstances and the number of urgent calls we had to make but effectively I was under supervision and only assisting.

At the end of six months, you would go before an Inspection Board of senior officers and if you made the grade with them you were upgraded to Paymaster with the rank of full Lieutenant i.e., Lieutenant and Paymaster. The tag meant you had the authority for all things financial and the carrying of cash etc. as laid down in the manual, similar to Sto and Alex and all the others. Paymaster was classified as a specialist ranking and with it went more pay which was very welcome. But, once again as in the past and on so many occasions since the day I joined the Army things just had to be different and often awkward where I was concerned!

I had only been commissioned 2nd Lieutenant Field Cashier eight weeks previously without going on an officers training course. I was now being upgraded to Paymaster without attending an inspection board and as a 2nd Lieutenant and Paymaster but there was no such rank in the rule book!

Alex was desperate for an additional unit as it had suddenly dawned on him, he was working his Singapore Cashiers and Sergeants into the ground due to a big increase in embarkation work. I was really just getting to know them all in our quarters and in the mess. They knew I was just a rookie officer with next to no service as such, but they made me very welcome. They were a very friendly lot and we all pulled together helping each other. Eyebrows were raised a bit when it was known I had been made a Paymaster so early, but their reaction was again a welcome one. They all required some breathing space and regular sleep and realised an extra unit would make all the difference.

Alex told me later that he had been surprised with my experience and confidence on tour. Also, with the reports in my file especially regarding Overlord and from the War Office. He had chanced his arm with the Colonel and to his surprise, convinced him I should be made up to Paymaster although only 2nd Lieutenant and Squaw decided to go out on a limb against all the rules.

I was just very lucky to be in the right place at that particular time. However, becoming classified as a Specialist was to come home to roost with me seven years later in the most amazing circumstances. More of that later.

That particular time I have mentioned was Christmas 1945. Celebrations were haphazard and had to coincide with our duties which continued as normal. There were at least a couple of Christmas dinners in the mess, and I managed to be at both. I was also at a Tanglin Club Christmas get together. I had something of great importance on my mind at the time as our baby was due mid-January. Letters were so precious and were a long time on the way, but Norah had kept me up to date as she wrote regularly. You could not lift the phone and speak thousands of miles in those days.

It was decided the best way my unit could help to relieve the pressure elsewhere was working up country in Malaya as many Commanding Officers of troops in isolated areas were crying out for help. There was continual troops disbursal going on due to the demobilisation procedure taking effect throughout Southeast Asia but there were still all sorts of different units scattered about the territory.

So, one of the last days of 1945 the Number10 Field Cashier Unit set off once again all on our own this time with JS suddenly feeling very much aware of his responsibilities. I had the same team as previously and once across the causeway my Indian driver whom I think we called "Smiler" put his foot down ready for the belt up the Bukit Timah Road. I immediately told our young racing driver to drive at a safe steady speed. "Yes Sahib" he would say with a big smile but within a couple of miles his foot would be down on the accelerator. I soon discovered they were all the same as I had a few different Corporal drivers with me on my travels and they were always Indian. I would sit beside the driver surrounded by small kit as space was always at a premium. The back of the truck was usually open when on the move with the heavy camouflaged tarpaulin cover rolled up high against the rear of the drivers' cabin. When the cover was down it could be stifling inside.

In the back would be my two Sergeants sitting on small canvas seats, who by our rules had to travel there to keep an eye on the cash boxes which they would never let out of their sight unless we had a proper armed guard on the vehicle. We were always armed. We could be carrying up to ten cash boxes plus all our necessary gear, kit and spares etc. making it all very cramped. We were continually bounced up and down over the bumpy roads with all sorts of holes and hidden damage lurking. We had some very hairy rides and moments. I can still easily recall the worry which was always in the background with me when I had the full responsibility for my own unit, until I got used to the situation. We might have an accident, require medical attention, get stuck, get lost, run out of petrol, be confronted by a wild animal and so on. It was a common worry and some of what I mention did happen but fortunately was never too serious. Anyway, so what, my problems are hardly worth a mention, only a few months previously on the territory we were in, there was a bloody war on and hundreds of men were killing each other every day.

The little trucks we used were tremendous vehicles and stood up to all the bashing they were given having wonderful engines. Very seldom did they break down. Most of the Company Units we visited had transport sections and we could usually obtain supplies of petrol. We always carried a few spare cans with us. It must be said that our Indian drivers had been well trained and were first class mechanics taking great pride in their vehicles.

I carried out quite a few consecutive tours of varying distances and days away. I think the longest was a week when visiting the Cameron Highlands and Ipoh, very rough country. We were over on the East Coast occasionally to Kuantan where it was very hot. I was up and down the Bukit Timah Road a lot as we had to return to the CPO for more cash, book balancing and updating all of what was going on. With luck I had a couple of days rest, then on my way again, often with a change of driver and Sergeants. I was becoming well accepted with Malaya and her inhabitants I was able to cope with the climate, prickly and blistering heat and insect bites. I was gaining a lot of experience as a Field Cashier, and also turning yellow from consuming the anti-malarial tablets.

Time went on and the weeks passed. Work up country became a lot easier for us as the disposal of troops continued. The stage was reached when, like any of my colleagues and their teams I could be sent anywhere in Southeast Asia. There was a lot of work for us to do in Singapore. However, by far the most important happening as far as I was concerned during that period of early 1946 did not occur in Singapore but in Edinburgh. A telegram arrived with the great news that Moira Elizabeth Mercer Stark had been born on the 20th of January 1946 and Norah and baby were both well. Suffice to say "Moira's" head was well and truly "wetted' in our mess, the Sergeants mess and the Tanglin Club! Great happenings for Norah and myself although so far apart and also an amazing family coincidence. When I was born at Carron in 1920 my Father was at the other side of the world with his ship going through the Panama Canal.

When I completed my up-country tours which must have been sometime in March 1946, Alex said he wanted me to do embarkation cashiering. I was very happy to do so, being connected to ships as I had often talked to my colleagues who were on that particular duty and thought it would be very interesting. The magnificent natural harbour of Singapore could take a great number of ships no matter how big they were. It was always bustling and busy being for me a great sight to behold. Since entering the harbour on the day of arrival I had been fascinated by the continually changing panorama. A look at a map will confirm the strategic position of Singapore and how important it was in wartime. When hostilities ended in August 1945 it became in effect a shipping junction. When Colonel Shaw-Hamilton and his advance party arrived and set up the Command Pay Office he had realised this would happen and knew his Field Cashiers would have an important part to play and prepared accordingly.

Thousands of prisoners of war of many nationalities both service and civilian were being released from captivity and had to be given top priority for repatriation home after medical checks and hospitalisation. It would be a mighty operation which would continue for many months.

Ships began to arrive at Singapore carrying servicemen and civilians from the Far East, East Indies, Hong Kong etc. They would take more on board and sail for Britain and Europe, Australia and New Zealand, the Americas and all countries on the way. The same movements would be happening in the opposite directions. Large ships and liners of all flags would converge on the famous harbour many of them being for troops only. Trading was under way again and many merchant Navy vessels were loading and unloading goods. It was an amazing sight as the harbour and dock areas could be like Piccadilly Circus at times!

Our Embarkation Cashiers were involved with all the ships carrying army personnel. This makes me mention that the Navy and the Air Force had cashiers just like us to look after their own wherever they may be, home or abroad. Our paths often crossed, and we would help each other out. There was a camaraderie among the three service pay branches. We would always be ready and willing to take care of the civilian and public side of our duties under our own banners.

All the men with around five years' service at that time could not contain their excitement knowing they would be on their way home any day as the demobilisation procedure was under way. The system was very fair and simply based on the first in first out principle. Every soldier had been given a demob number in numerical order therefore as time went on you could assess when your demob date would be due.

I knew about the time I left India that subject to no unforeseen circumstances my number would come in approximately nine to ten months' time which proved correct. Demob added to the huge shipping movement taking place as it had to be done at the home base of every serviceman and therefore, he linked up at each end i.e., home and overseas. We were only one port of many involved.

Time and tide wait for no man. I was to discover that saying was very appropriately related to embarkation cashiering which I can best describe as a "hectic hell for leather" type of duty but very interesting. The arrival and departure of ships were as always controlled by tide times which could also control our daily lives on that duty as we could be on at any time of the day or night. The routine for me and my two Sergeants was to collect our loaded cash boxes from the vaults - which were often open for us during the night - stack them in the truck and take them under guard down to the docks. Our destination would be a ship actually docked, or "lying off" out in the harbour. The harbour was always busy, and the docks could only take a limited number of vessels. It all depended on various circumstances. If our ship was docked, we just got our boxes on board and started work. If, however the ship awaiting our attention was out in the bay and often the big liners were, we would take our cash boxes to the naval dockyard as we had an arrangement with the Navy to get us there. That was always an exciting prospect.

We would be put with our goods on board the duty Motor Torpedo Boat (MTB). They were small, all engine craft. They had two torpedo tubes, one on either side, a small bridge and tiny accommodation for four. They were usually captained by young Naval Lieutenants who had been in the real action and were madcaps! The MTB had terrific power capable of slicing through the water at nearly forty knots. The young skipper would have fun zig-zagging his way full throttle between the ships in the harbour, and were usually loud, hollered, cursed and shouted at by every captain and crew who saw them coming. It is just as well they were brilliant helmsmen which was very necessary in their type of warfare action. An eye closing experience for us at times and always a spray soaking! They really were super chaps. We got to know them quite well and often had a drink together.

Our boxes would be winched aboard and there would usually be a side gangway for us. Sometimes it was a rope ladder which I never liked very much if the weather was bad, or when it was dark. Upon arrival on board, I would report to the Captain, then the OC Troops. I received a list of all passengers, service and civilian, who wanted to see us starting where had they come from, where they were going and how many. We could then organise ourselves ensuring we had enough of the currencies required, prepare a timetable and set up shop. In no time a queue would be forming. Our first mugs of tea would be at hand an order having been given that we must have a regular fresh supply which was essential. Being static for long periods our bodies required a regular liquid intake as it was a very hot and sweaty job.

We immediately got into our routine. My number two Sergeant would receive the money, count and enter in our cash book. He would pass it to number one who would calculate the exchange rate for Stirling or whatever was required and count out the new money, pass the lot over to me for checking, handing over and receiving receipt signature. All teams had become quite expert at handling money and could do so at some speed and we had our own system for double checking. We could sense if something was wrong, especially if someone was trying to "con" us, as often the "wide boy' fraternity would come through our hands, and they could be very sharp. We had various ways of dealing with them not least using the authority I had as Cashier, of not allowing them to sail with the ships and reporting them to the OC Troops or the Captain.

It was very demanding work. We were often on board eight to ten hours and sometimes we would be one of two units going hard at it. As always, we were well looked after with plenty of good food and sometimes before leaving and waiting for our transport would be invited for a quiet drink with the OC Troops and the Captain or ships officers.

If out in the bay the MTB's would arrive, and off we would go on the fast and furious return to the naval dockyard. I have just remembered those MTB's could be very scary in the dark. We would then have our truck journey to the CPO and no matter when that would be we had to set about cashing up and balancing which could take a long time as many currencies could be involved. We were exhausted at times always working to sailing deadlines and with Alex pushing us to our limit. But I liked that duty. I loved being on board ships, especially the larger ones, the liner troopships with their special atmosphere. There was no doubt about shipping being in my blood. I must also admit - I loved the excitement of the MTB's!

The outflow of homeward bound troops and other personnel developed into a steady movement as the repatriation and demob systems became effective. Our job became easier although we still had plenty to do but not in such frantic haste. Our Field Units in the West Indies Islands of Java, Borneo, Sarawak etc. were called into Singapore as they were no longer required.

It gave me the opportunity of meeting other colleagues for the first time as they had been with the advance party and sent out before we arrived. They had some stories to tell and so have I about one of them. He had been our man in Borneo who had a very posh sounding name - Bill Werrey- Easterbrook and I am not likely to forget him.

He arrived late at night and was put in our quarters. I did not know he was there until very early the following morning when I had to get up from bed and go to the toilet. When I opened the bathroom door to come out, a big black and white snake was coming straight towards me only a few feet away. I nearly died on the spot but jumped back, crash and closed the bathroom door and locked it. After a little while the palpitations stopped, and my senses returned caused by one of our lot yelling blue murder from the shock he had received stepping on the snake with his bare feet going to the same toilet! The whole house became alive with everyone upstairs wondering what the hell was going on. Bill eventually appeared on the scene picked up the snake and it gently curled itself around his arm and shoulder. He calmed us all down and apologised saying it had escaped from a box under his bed, which took some believing. He assured us it was harmless, and really quite tame and convinced us that in civvy street he was a zoologist, and his speciality was snakes. He had brought with him a box of them which he knew would be of interest to London Zoo!

He was a character and a most interesting bloke. Within a few days he had started a menagerie being in his element in jungle country. He was always finding small wildlife, creepy crawlies, lizards and all sorts of peculiar specimens and telling us all about them. He was soon isolated to a room of his own in one of the other quarters which had a hut outside for his pets. I have a photograph of Bill he is the one at the end of the back row with the bush hat.

It was about this time Alex received his "crown" and became Major Alexander. We were all delighted in the section as he deserved that senior promotion. A hard taskmaster he was but his number one priority at all times was his staff, and he was an excellent boss.

Singapore had been occupied by the enemy for three and a half years, therefore returning to their normal way of life was not easy. The essential services such as food, medical and communications etc. had to be given priority and the business community required financial help. It was so important to have the town and Islands economy on a sound footing as soon as possible. A Command Pay Office had the organisation to cope, being in effect like a bank, having the experienced officers to deal with the situation. We certainly had in Singapore and Alex was one of them.

As usual we got stuck in with great enthusiasm. I spent many hours with him in the company of Malayan and Chinese businessmen and with Pay Office colleagues, discussing financial deals which would enable them to start up again. It was often way above my head and financial brain, but I could listen and learn. The whole experience was to be of great value to me later, when I left the army and rejoined Waddies. Our help was very much appreciated, and I recall being invited to their homes for a meal on a couple of occasions. A Malayan/Chinese family dinner of about twelve courses with a small glass of gin downed neat between each course, lasting at least three hours, takes some doing!

I took part in another most unusual special duty which was very interesting and required much organisation and made us realise the Japanese were thieves and robbers just like the Germans had been.

The finding of stolen loot was being reported from many parts of Malaya including paintings, works of art, gold, silver, precious stones, jewellery etc. The Japanese had stolen everything of real value they could find. We presumed a lot must have been shipped home but they had left considerable loads behind, and their hiding places were being discovered by the Intelligence Corps. Supreme HQ had decided the CPO should arrange collection and listing of all items and decide the best way of ensuring they were returned to their owners, some task it was going to be.

I remember the first thing we did was put out a call throughout Southeast Asia Command for qualified auctioneers and antique experts. We set up collecting teams made up of our own units, preparation of an armoured convoy with one of the regiments and coordinated collection points at suitable strategic locations in Malaya. I may say it was easier said than done causing many a headache as armed guards had to be in attendance.

Eventually one day the convoy, a few large trucks and an armoured vehicle pulled up outside the CPO and tea crate after tea crate was unloaded along with many other boxes and cartons and put in the vaults. They were all sealed but I had a look into one. It was a large tea crate containing jewellery, silver plate and cutlery not quite half full but so heavy it took four of us to move it a few feet along the floor.

I had to go to the Sultan of Johor's Palace at Johor, Bahru. What a magnificent place which fortunately had escaped heavy damage during the war. I had a meeting with some of his staff as he had priceless contents stolen. I obtained details in the hope they could be identified. There was little more we could do, and it was decided the antique experts should take over. They moved with all their stuff to another safe place. I do not know what the outcome was as we had completed our task and went onto another duty.

CHAPTER TWENTY ONE: OVER THE EQUATOR AND NEAR TO DEATH

I have not the date recorded but it was towards the end of April 1946. I know it was the last journey order I received from Alex as he was due to sail for home and demob during the first few days of May. He had received a very urgent message from Alfie Knowles our Field Cashier in Sumatra, requesting a load of cash and it was needed tomorrow. Political troubles causing rioting had blown up on the Island and as was usual in such circumstances in those days a lot of our troops had been dispatched to keep the peace.

I was called very late at night and told to be at the airfield with my unit early the following morning. Our destination would be Padang on the mid-west coast of Sumatra, but we would call in at Kuala Lumpur, then at Medan in the north east of Sumatra. We had to be armed as we were visiting an arms carrying area. I did not have a good night's sleep knowing that in the morning I was going to fly in an aeroplane for the very first time in my life! I was up at the crack of dawn and after breakfast collected my Sergeants then we visited the armoury for revolver and Sten Guns. Then to the vaults for a load of full cash boxes.

A camouflaged Dakota aircraft awaited us at RAF Seletar. We were introduced to the pilot and navigator, the only crew. Our boxes were loaded into a goods cage in the rear section, and we were accompanied by a few passengers, service and civilian. We took off soaring up into a clear blue sky of glorious morning sunshine. The interior of the plane was very basic, and you got the impression it had seen much service. We were seated in bucket seats situated along either side of the fuselage facing inwards. We were strapped in with thick webbing safety belts which were over each shoulder and round the waist. The centre gangway was wide enough to take another line of troops standing and then discovered the rails above were for the parachute regiment lads, confirming our aircraft had been in action over Burma and elsewhere.

We had a very smooth flight to KL and as we were landing could see, from the air this time, the blood red soil from the tin and pewter mines. Some passengers went off and others came on and after a short stay we were on our way again. At KL we were briefed by an officer about the situation in Sumatra and advised to be careful what we did and said and to keep a low profile as there was a communist element developing. There had been some shooting with British troops involved.

We flew across the Straits of Malacca looking down on the dozens of tropical Islands below set in a brilliant blue sea. The reason for the wonderful view from the sky became apparent when we touched down at Medan. Alighting from the plane the heat just took our breath away. I can recall the feeling and have never experienced to this day sun so bright and scorching. I have mentioned about Meerut Station when I could confirm the temperature was 117 degrees. It must have been a lot higher that day in Medan.

An armed guard of the RAF Regiment was stationed round the plane when we landed. We did not waste any time at Medan as all we wanted was a long cold drink, a bite to eat and be on our way as it was so hot. We could also feel real tension about the place. There was a change of passengers again, but I remember exactly who were on the Dakota when we took off for Padang. The RAF pilot and navigator, myself and my two Sergeants, five army and four civilians, fourteen in all. The plane had been standing in the midday sun and was suffocatingly hot inside. We were desperate to be "up, up and away into the deep blue yonder" having about two and half hours flying time to Padang. We had been going along very smoothly for about an hour and had noticed the sky becoming dull and the ride a bit bumpy. The pilots voice came over the intercom saying he had received a storm warning and to tighten our seat harness.

The sky became a very dirty looking colour and the ride very bumpy and quite frightening for a newcomer to flying like me and I was not alone in that respect. The pilot was on the intercom again informing us to reach Padang we had to fly over the high Barisan Mountains which ran along the west side of the island and if the weather worsened, he was doubtful if he could make it. It became as black as night outside, the clouds seemed to be pushing us down, which in fact they were, and we realised the whole atmosphere outside had suddenly changed and we were in a terrific wind and rainstorm.

Our sweat began to flow a bit when the pilot told us, with a sense of urgency in his voice, that he was aborting the flight to Padang and changed course back to Singapore as a gale of wind would be right up our backsides - although I am sure that is not the word he used! It was then the flight turned into a nightmare. We were told to tighten our seat harness to maximum which pinned us from the waist up to the back of our seats. That was just as well because the plane developed frightening movements as it started to weave and bank from side to side.

The best way I can describe it is as a pendulum motion. We would go banking up to near the horizontal on the port side, shudder, then come weaving down through the arc and up we would go to near horizontal on the starboard side, a horrible sensation as we could feel the plane being hurtled along at a terrific speed.

I had a small window at my left ear. With some difficulty, being strapped in so tight, straining neck and eye I could just see out of and will never forget what I saw when at the bottom of one of the arcs I have described and through the eerie grey light the Sumatra jungle and bush was bending over with the force of the storm, and we were that close to the ground. The awful motion of the plane continued and got worse until the time when we went up on our side and I blacked out. It was only a short time, and I eventually came to my senses, hearing yelling and shouting. The pilot and navigator were doing so from the cockpit and also into the very crackly intercom. I soon discovered they were encouraging us all to do the same. They had been trained for such an emergency being a form of concentration therapy to make our brains work and do what we were told. We were all shouting our heads off, the air being blue with some choice language. It did the trick as we became very much aware of the dangerous situation we were in, and it certainly made us concentrate because we were all scared stiff.

The blacking out, fortunately only by some of us, had been caused by the plane very nearly tipping over. In other words, going beyond the ninety degrees towards the one hundred and eighty degree - which would be upside down. But, by the grace of the Good Lord and two brilliant RAF saviours in the cockpit and the toughest plane in the world, the old Dakota, righted itself. More in detail about that later.

What chaos it was inside that Dakota. I had the feeling my stomach was being squeezed from my body. My head, shoulders, neck and both sides ached all over and the front of my bush jacket was covered in blood which was coming from my nose. The twelve of us inside the fuselage soon realised we all had the same internal and body aches and pains, because in each case our seat harness belts had held us tight against all the strains endured. However, a lot of external injuries had been caused by loose flying objects, kit bags, small gear and equipment etc. We all had cuts and bruises, some quite bad. But the most important factor of all, was that the goods case at the head had held firm. It was bolted down but many of the metal rods were bent. Had it broken up the consequences did not bear thinking about.

The awful pendulum motion subsided but we continued to rock and dive up and down being storm assisted from behind. The shouting had stopped, real fear can keep you alert and wide awake. The pilots pleaded with us to keep our harness on to avoid being catapulted from one end of the plane to the other. We were allowed to slacken them a little as we could hardly bear the webbing touching us.

Under the difficult circumstances we did our best to help each other. We took chances hanging on and got to the first aid kit. There was a lot of blood and some sickness about. One of my Sergeants was in a bad way having received a bad gash to the head.

We did not realise it at the time, but our pilot and navigator were in a hell of a state. They would never admit it but must have been suffering the agonies of the dammed. They both had broken wrists and torn muscles in their arms neck and shoulders also severe bruising all over their bodies. Their troubles were due to the titanic struggle they were having with the controls coupled with their outstanding flying skills to keep the Dakota flying. There is no doubt about it, they saved our lives.

I remember later on, in what would nowadays be called a laid-back attitude, they apologised to us for allowing the Dakota "to flop over a bit!" That must be the greatest understatement I have ever heard in my life. It was of course typical of all RAF pilots who always minimised their problems and bravery in the air.

At last, the news we were waiting for, the pilots voice saying Singapore was near but with a warning landing was going to be difficult. A very high level of turbulence was expected. We had to grit our teeth and strap up as tight as we could bear it. Suddenly the Dakota was weaving about on a downward path and appeared to be flying sideways at times and then righting itself. Without warning we hit the ground with a hell of a bump. The engines roared full throttle and we were on vertical ascent straight up followed by a very steep bank going left to port. I know for certain at that particular moment, we all thought our end had come as the feeling inside was that we were going down. Eventually we could feel a levelling out and the pilots voice bellowing from the cockpit and through the intercom, crackling badly but still working - "Sorry chaps keep holding on, we'll have another go!" or words to that effect which could only come from an RAF officer!

By then some of the "chaps" had passed out in their harness, others including me had been forced to loosen it up or be throttled. I was tangled up in mine, half of me on the seat the other half on the floor, hanging on to the straps with all the energy and determination I had left when the Dakota's nose went down again. It was an eyes shut and pray job. Then we hit the ground solidly but stayed there, ran on and eventually stopped. There was silence. Then suddenly we all shouted, cheered and cried. A mixture of tears and blood running down our faces.

The RAF station at Seletar was on emergency procedure when we landed. We were immediately surrounded by fire tenders and ambulances then some doctors, nurses and station staff came on board. I remember the Dakota was shaking on the runway as the weather was still determined to bother us. It was blowing a gale and lashing with rain outside making the ambulances reverse close to the plane. The doctors gave each of us a check over while the nurses did temporary clean-up job on us. It transpired we all had difficulty working our legs and our coordination seemed out of control which was alarming. We could not have walked off the plane. However, the doctors put our minds at rest explaining we had shock reaction and body disorientation caused by the flying conditions we had endured. They assured us we would be ok after a good rest. We were all stretcher cases, and it was not long before the exodus began.

One of the first on board when we landed was the Station Commander and Group Captain. He spoke to us saying he had been a bit worried until we touched down safely. He paid generous tributes to the pilot, navigator and ourselves and also the Dakota. He asked if we would like to know just briefly what had caused our discomfort or would we prefer to wait. As one voice we replied "Yes Sir, now!" He confirmed our pilot had made the correct decision aborting the flight to Padang and making for home as Singapore was the only airfield which was safe to open in the whole area due to the storm conditions. It would have been suicidal to attempt flying over the high Barisan Mountains. The pilot had also anticipated the problems with very sudden weather changes caused in that area. He then explained how unlucky we had been as we were caught in an equatorial cyclone one of the fiercest and most dangerous storms in the world.

The pilot had been forced when the cyclone was at its worst to fly near ground level as he was being pushed down by the low cloud base. They were dangerous clouds because of the powerful vertical air pressures up and down and inside, which could suck in a plane and at worst turn it over. We had been very, very close to such a happening.

He said fortunately such an occurrence very seldom took place as it could only happen on the Equator and for part of our flight the pilot had been forced by the cyclone to fly along the zero line. Any world map will confirm that the town of Padang is just a fraction below the Equator and Singapore a fraction above.

It is a well-known tradition when anyone "crossing the line" for the first time all sorts of fooling around and celebrations take place, especially if at sea when "Father Neptune" takes over. We were certainly not celebrating. I wonder how many people have actually weaved and zig-zagged their way crisscrossing the line as we did? I doubt if there are many members of that club!

The comments from the Station Commander made us appreciate to the utmost the bravery and flying skills of our pilot and navigator. They were taken off just ahead of me very slowly and carefully as just a tiny bump on the stretchers could cause them agony. Their bodies had taken so many strains and as I have mentioned, they had the most painful injuries.

The previous pages referring to the flight have been the most difficult to relate since my story began. Over the years when the occasion demanded I have mentioned to Norah and the family, about my war time experiences, and this particular one but in a general way not in any detail. This is the only time I have given serious concentrated thoughts to what actually happened. Thanks to my Red Book detailing my service movement dates in sequence I am continually surprised how my memory slips into gear and at any given time allowing me to recall so much information. Often minor incidents push their way to the front giving a lead in to more important facts.

I have tried hard to live through the flight again from start to finish also to portray my feelings and emotions. I have taken care not to over dramatise what took place and not to get carried away but keep to what the authentic facts. Having said that, for me and my colleagues on that Dakota, every minute became dramatic as at times we really did think our end was coming. Be that as it may there is a very important point I must say at this stage. What occurred to us along the Zero Line that day put in proper context could only be termed an incident. It must be remembered real war was not long over. The horrors and anxieties were still very much in the minds of the soldiers, sailors and airmen, male and female and civilians who had been involved. Our planes had been shot down or crash landed, the occupants killed or maimed, airfields bombed, fighting and slaughter taking place in jungles not many miles away. The point I am making, is that we had received a bit of a fright, survived ok, had excellent attention with no fuss or bother. Using an Americanism of the time and still in use today our adventure was really "no big deal" and should be treated as such.

There is no doubt my first flight in an aeroplane from Singapore via Kuala Lumpur and Medan to just short of the Barisan Mountains in Sumatra then along the Equator and back to Singapore left its mark on me. I was a long time in coming to terms with flying again, in fact over thirty-five years.

The next time I set foot in an aircraft was on the 4th of September 1981 at Gatwick Airport, London, on a Laker Airways DC 10 Skytrain with three hundred and seventy-seven other passengers on board. We travelled at an average speed of five hundred and fifty miles per hour at thirty-five thousand feet to New York Kennedy Airport. I loved every minute of the flight and the experience. It was a far cry from the old Dakota. I have flown on several occasions since, and enjoyed all the flights.

When I reached the Services Hospital, I was immediately taken to a ward and gently lifted from the stretcher and placed onto a bed. What happened next must have made me think I was dreaming because again the most amazing quirk of fate took place. It was a "Hello Jim, fancy meeting you here," situation! Looking down at me was Bert Rutherford. We had been pals since our short trousers' days. Been in the same gang at Larbert, played golf and shared sporting interests. He went to Stirling High School with the Taylor boys and our families were friends. We had lost touch after moving to Edinburgh. He had not long been qualified as a Doctor, joined the RAF and was posted to Singapore. He checked me over inch by inch. I had no broken bones but severe bruising round my rib cage, stomach, neck and shoulders caused by the belting of the seat harness. Also cuts and bumps all over including face and head. I was really very, very lucky especially not to require any stitches. Many of my companions had broken bones, noses, wrists etc. also bad cuts and bruises, caused by flying objects and being bashed about inside the plane. Some of them required a lot of stitching up. I was worried about my Sergeant who was in a bad way with many injuries including a large gash on his head.

Bert did find something wrong with me which at the time seemed so incongruous as it had nothing whatsoever to do with the flight. His eagle eye had spotted the early symptoms of toe rot in one of my feet. He explained it was a campaign ailment caused by wearing socks for too long at a time in the sweaty heat and swampy damp of the jungle. I had obviously picked it up on my travels in a shower or bathroom and walking about in my bare feet which was always risky. It was not serious but had to be given attention. The cure was painless but just awful. Both feet plastered from ankle to toe with Gentian Violet ointment of the most brilliant blue in colour. A sticky mess which dyed everything it touched and could change the colour of khaki socks to its own bloom in seconds!

I had my feet checked regularly for the next three weeks during which time the ointment caused the old skin to peel off and new skin arrived in its place. I have never had any further trouble with my toes, but I can still feel the sensation of walking about in that dreadful stuff. When wearing shorts, a "toe rotter" stood out a mile! The lack of news about our saviours, the pilot and navigator, caused us all concern until days later we were all assured they were ok. The truth was they had been about half dead when taken off the plane and both were rushed to the intensive care unit.

I was in hospital for a week. By then my cuts, bumps and bruises were on the mend, although I was to be black and blue in places, and rib cage very tender for a long time afterwards. Bert explained that following the experience I and the others had been through a real danger could be delayed shock. The effect could be most unpleasant in all sorts of different ways depending on the makeup of each individual. About a week later he had a chat with me saying he was pleased with my progress and had decided to discharge me from hospital. However, under no circumstances would he allow me to take part in any duties until he was satisfied I was fit to do so. My only duty would be rest and relaxation. I knew he was deadly serious as he gave me a PND (Positively No Duties) medical certificate, and I was to report to him every second day. When I returned to my quarters and the mess, I had to take some stick from my colleagues.

The first night I was set up being told to meet the Colonel at a specific time for a pre-dinner drink in the mess. I duly arrived on time, entered the lounge and found it had a full attendance. I approached the Colonel who was sitting, and he immediately stood up to greet me which meant that everyone present had to stand up. He then said something like this -

"Gentlemen, welcome back to a battered and bruised Starkey and to prove it he has got himself a PND certificate from the MO. So, we must all take care of the poor bugger. Be sure to take his arm, help him upstairs and crossing the road and (other things which I am not going to put in writing!) A PND must be worth him buying his fellow officers their wine at dinner tonight, do you all agree?" A loud chorus of "Yes!" followed. I sat beside him at dinner, and he made me feel he and the company were really pleased to see me.

Being in possession of such a medical certificate I knew Squaw, as Commanding Officer would have received a full report about me from Bert Rutherford. I also knew to be careful as he would be keeping an eye on me just making sure I did as I was told. The next ten days easily come to mind as my activities included early to bed, late to rise, lazing in the sun either outside the bungalow or beside the pool after a gentle swim at the Tanglin Club. It was all part of the wonderful recuperation routine, however there was a snag. All PND's like myself and others were under supervision by the Medical Corps and RAF medical lads who would visit without warning each day.

I was transported down to hospital every second day for a check-up by Bert or another Doctor. Those visits gave me the opportunity to see my injured Sergeant, the two RAF heroes and other flight companions who were still detained. I kept in touch and am glad to say they all recovered, some taking longer than others. Bert signed me off fit for duty, following a thorough medical examination and it was endorsed with the all-important Grade A1. He said my physical and mental fitness had helped me through the ordeal. There is no doubt the wonderful attention and therapy I received both inside and outside the hospital was the reason why I did not feel any reaction. Maybe deep down the fear of flying was lurking somewhere for a time but no harm in that respect was done.

Looking back, I was twenty five then and I am sure at the highest peak of fitness in my life. I had trained hard, just had to, especially when playing football for the battalion. I managed to find the time to play both football and rugby while in Singapore.

CHAPTER TWENTY TWO:
OPERATION COUNT AND THE
JAPANESE SCOTSMAN

From early 1946, the uppermost thought in the mind of every man in uniform was demobilisation. I have mentioned we had been given a demob number based on length of service i.e., first in first out. It therefore became possible with reasonable accuracy to calculate when you would be out of uniform and into civvy street. I knew by my number and my sailing date would be sometime in July to obtain my demob in the UK during August.

Many changes therefore were taking place at the Command Pay Office in Singapore. Familiar faces had gone including Bill Alexander and others were waiting on a troopship. Whole divisions had been cleared out of Southeast Asia for home therefore there was very little work for Field Cashiers. My colleagues had been arriving almost nonstop from all over that vast area in time for their troopship back to the UK. The farewell parties were almost nonstop too!

As the work of the Cashiers diminished so did the work and staff at the CPO, which became much more compact. What was in fact taking place, was the gradual return to the old peace time colonial army system. We now know that was not going to work as ahead were many self-government requests and subsequent problems all over Southeast Asia with our troops involved. Lots of blood was spilt and lives lost - but that is another story explained in our modern history books.

Captain Ted Blackwell a regular soldier took over from Alex. We were on the same wavelength from the start as he retained me as personal assistant. He was a "regulations" man, the very opposite of Alex and could quote "the book" from cover to cover. However, my past experience and even admiration for such types stood me in good stead. He admitted to being an "inside man" and left me to get on with things "in the field". Anyway, the most important regular soldier around, Lieutenant Shaw-Hamilton thought we were a good team and that was what mattered as it was essential to have Squaw on your side. I was becoming a real "old soldier!"

I am going to relate another quite amazing situation I found myself in in Singapore. It actually got me publicity and my photograph in the local press, a fuss I did not want. Alex was involved so it was sometime before the Sumatra flight. I was told to report to the Colonel's office and on arrival found Alex and Major Gray the Command Cashier with him. Squaw opened by saying in effect "Stark we have a good job for you. How would you like to command a squad of Japanese soldiers?"

I have just no memory or idea how I replied but can imagine, knowing the three senior officers well enough to say, "Sir, you are kidding me?" To my astonishment, amid some joking and laughter, I realised they were serious! I have mentioned on previous pages about the stolen loot the Japanese had hidden. A discovery was made that they had also stashed away in Southeast Asia vast amounts of cash, real money, in just about every currency possible. The job of collecting, then counting, had landed with a firm hand on the plate of the Command Paymaster by order from Supreme HQ SEA Command up the road at Cathay Buildings. The Colonel estimated the whole operation would take at least three months to complete.

Someone had come up with a brilliant idea. There were still thousands of Japanese prisoners of all ranks and grades on some of the large Islands at the southern end of the Straits of Malacca. When the fighting was over the armistice signed, they had been put there by Mountbatten given starter supplies and necessary requirements to look after themselves until their own ships arrived from Japan. It was then up to them to become self-sufficient and obtain everything they required and use their own shipping to return to Japan. It would take a long time but not to be a drain on their visitors' resources in any way. Surely there would be managers, tellers and bank officials among them. Let them do the counting!

Enquiries were made and sure enough they had what we wanted including a high-ranking paymaster. He was being collected and brought over to Singapore for a meeting. Alex was to organise the collection which was another armoured convoy effort. Meeting points would be established at suitable places in Southeast Asia and the money crated. Eventually it would arrive at the CPO, and I would then take over the counting. Alex certainly had a major operation on his hands. "You'll have a free hand to get on with it Stark, any problems see me." I am sure that would be the typical order I would receive from Squaw. A few days later following the meeting at Singapore HQ it was confirmed that twenty-four bank experienced Japanese soldiers would be available, so Operation Count was on.

I found myself up at Supreme HQ with my two Sergeants for briefing with I think Major Gray (he was a grand old regular Number 2 to the Colonel - known to us all as Dad!). I recall we were confronted by two senior Staff Officers. I was unhappy at that meeting and said so, as to my surprise it had been decided the counting would take place in the main hall of our Command Pay Office which, as I have mentioned, had been the Hong Kong and Shanghai Bank, a large and impressive building at a corner of Raffles Avenue.

My reaction was that we would continually be surrounded by the coming and goings of our staff, a lot of whom were civilians. We also had a continual flow of visiting military and civilian personnel of all ranks as we were a bank to them. The ordinary public would also see the Japanese as the huge doors would be open. Everybody hated them, having every right to do so and I dreaded what could happen. However, my orders from the Staff Officers were made quite clear. I was told exactly how I should approach the duty ahead of me. Everything had been done by the book, no deviation.

They pointed out thousands of Japanese were seen daily by the public doing the filthiest, dirtiest and unpleasant jobs in and around Singapore. It was unlikely any trouble would take place. I soon reached the conclusion I was involved in some sort of psychological set up and knew "keep quiet and do what you are told signals" when I heard them.

The morning arrived when twenty-four Japanese soldiers unloaded themselves from trucks outside the Command Pay Office. I was standing outside the large main entrance with a Sergeant on each side of me. The Japanese lined up in two ranks in the street an officer in front facing me standing to attention. They were small, all appeared to look alike, surprisingly smart considering they were from crowded damp conditions. Each was dressed all over in khaki, shirt, shorts, rubber boots and the small, peaked caps. I think the officer wore a bush jacket. At my signal to follow they bowed, fell in behind the three of us and we all marched inside.

A long line of wooden tables had been positioned down the centre of the banking hall, two tables being placed across the top making a "T" shape for me to sit in the centre with a Sergeant on either side. The Japanese officer's place was at the front of the "T" leg. They went to their places on each side, stood behind their chair, waited for me to sit then bowed again and did likewise.

I am describing what happened in some detail on purpose because that ritual was to go on morning and evening (in reverse) until Operation Count was concluded. It became a local event at 8.30 a.m. and 5.30 pm each day. Traffic was held in the square outside, crowds gathered to watch then rushed to the door to see what happened inside! That was the reason why Lieutenant and Paymaster J. Stark got his name, photo and headlines in the local press. Why his face became familiar and why he took a lot of stick from all and sundry including colleagues. "The Japanese Scotsman - so you've joined the Japanese Army", to name but two comments which come to mind but all in good enthusiastic fun I am glad to say as my position could be a bit awkward at times. The Staff Officers were right as we had no real trouble, nothing worse than some insults shouted at the Japanese from the crowd. I think they were very, very happy to see them bowing and scraping, therefore accepting they were a beaten race - or so it was thought at the time!

During the operation guards were on duty inside the building twenty-four hours per day. A tremendous amount of money was continuously coming and going with loads lying about on tables. It caused me some worry as I was responsible for inside the hall. We were only a part of Operation Count and at the end of the line. It was a huge operation throughout Southeast Asia and a great number of people were involved.

Reverting back to that first day. My urgent objective was, hopefully, to find a member of my squad who could speak English. Some could manage with a struggle, including the officer but fortunately one of them had an excellent command of our language. I remember we called him Sam, presumably because his Christian name sounded like that. I sat him close to our table. It must be kept in mind, I was dealing with well educated, upper class and intelligent people with impeccable manners. Maybe they were from the other side but the upside of the Japanese character being in such a stark contrast to their downside, of disregarding and inhumane qualities relating to fellow human beings in times of war. I know at the time I could not quite come to terms in my own mind with the contrast and come up with an adequate answer. My squad was a hot talking point. Due to my position at the time, I just could not escape discussions about Japanese every day. In my quarters, in the mess at the Tanglin Club. I was often stopped in the street and had to be very careful what I said.

When they got their hands on the money and the counting started the three of us just looked on in amazement. They would take a large bundle of notes in one hand and flick them through their fingers at high speed. They counted coins by running them through their fingers from one hand to the other, again at high speed. They were experts, totals always being correct. We had many civvy street bankers in the CPO and they soon kept coming to watch and eventually were being taught by the Japanese their techniques. In a couple of days, the ice was broken, and we were all settled into a routine of complete cooperation, understanding and above all confidence which had to be my aim from the start. I think we all suddenly realised that we all had families waiting for us at home and that day could not come soon enough. The dogeared photos gradually appeared for us all to see. A room had been set aside at the rear of the bank which had toilet facilities. They had their mid-day meal there which they brought with them. I gave them an hour for lunch and also, a short break mid-morning and afternoon.

The duty for them was manna from heaven as they kept telling us, they were the luckiest of all the camp islands. The conditions were obviously very basic. They had to look after themselves and rely on everything coming from Japan. After a few days we noticed at every opportunity they would pick up fag ends lying about and pocket them. They told us cigarettes were very difficult to obtain in the camps and they were always desperate for a smoke. Their plight soon became known and typical of the British, pity was taken. Ash trays from all offices in the building were emptied each day and sent down. The contents were put into a large tin for the Japanese to take to the camps. Cigarette papers appeared from nowhere and I am sure news reached my deaf ears as tobacco barons were operating in the Japanese confinement areas!

I would not allow them to smoke when working but they could do so during the lunch break in the room. I recall the officer asked if two of his men could be excused counting duties for about an hour each day before "closing time" and I agreed. The room, including toilets, was washed, scrubbed and polished every day ready for his inspection before they marched at 5.30pm We were very lucky having Sam who could speak English better than some of us, so anything we had to say was conveyed correctly to his officers and the team which made things go very smoothly. The Sergeants and I had many a chat with him, often "off the record". He had been to one of the universities and I think he was in commercial banking before the war and in quite a high position. Operation Count was completed in about two weeks. We had become quite a "show piece" inside as well as outside, having many onlookers every day including top brass from all services. I had to repeat the story of how it all happened many times and kept being told I must be in the most unique position in the whole of the British Army, having command of a squad of Japanese!

When the day arrived for them to leave, they were sad. Their officer asked for permission to parade in the hall. Sam on his behalf and all the squad made a speech of great sincerity to a crowded gathering. He finished off by giving me a most unexpected and tremendous surprise as he asked me to accept a Parker pen. What made it quite touching for me was when he explained it had belonged to one of them, had been used by the donor throughout the war and was a treasured possession. I was not to ask to whom it belonged, as with respect I would not be told. It was their way of saying thank you as a team for our kindness and understanding of the difficult circumstances both sides had found themselves involved in. I accepted the pen being sure they would have been deeply insulted had I not done so. I said a few appropriate words of thanks and wished them good luck for the future. Later, I was told from on high I had done and said all the right things and told to keep the pen as a memento. As I write these words with my right hand, I am holding the Parker pen in my left hand. It is still in good working order. When I hold it up to the light I can see the owners initials roughly engraved in Japanese on the stem and on the nib the wording "Parker Duofold 14ct". It is a treasured possession.

The usual formal parade took place out in the square for the last time with most of the staff and many of the public looking on. Bowing and salutes were exchanged, and they climbed into the trucks and drove off.

CHAPTER TWENTY THREE: MEMORIES AND TIME TO HEAD FOR HOME...

I have said my time in Singapore is related as events come to mind, and are not always in the correct sequence as my Red Book is limited to movement dates and only a few other important ones. One date I have noted is the 22nd of April 1946 when I was promoted full Lieutenant and Paymaster. I am sure it coincided with the time I went on the flight as I remember Alex left for home just after that event. The promotion increased my pay to the equivalent of £65.00 per month. I was able to give Norah a good monthly payment. Her allowances from the Government increased and plus that she had family allowance for Moira. Our finances began to look a whole lot better.

I may have been giving the impression that in Singapore it was all duty and no relaxation. I certainly worked very hard often all hours of the day and night, but I did manage time off. I repeat the Colonel was very strict about fitness and health and made sure time was given and taken by his officers to lead accordingly by example. I had routine medical check-ups including vaccinations and inoculations for all the known tropical diseases, fevers and illness. All games and sporting activities took place between 5.30pm and 6.45pm when the temperature dropped to a reasonable level - around the high 75-degree mark! Then darkness came down suddenly, like slowly pulling down a black blind, about 7.00pm

We were lucky to have a badminton court outside our quarters, a game was played every day and I played when I could. It was not all that long after my arrival when I knew what it was like to be involved in (Singapore) top level sport. They knew at the CPO from my records I had played football for the Battalion at Edinburgh. Alex however had opened his mouth saying I played rugby for the school! As it happened a trial match was being arranged, to check out players who could be chosen to play for Singapore Services against Malayan Services, in an upcoming rugby match being arranged by the Staff Officer (sports) at Singapore HQ. In army parlance I was "dragooned" - a nice way of being ordered - by the Colonel to let my name go forward. It was Squaw's way of letting everyone know that Pay Corps chaps were not just pen pushers but could play rugby, soccer, cricket and other sports with the best of them! Hence the reason he was a stickler for health care and physical fitness. There were two trial matches, I played in both, and to my astonishment was chosen to play for the Singapore Services team as right wing three quarter. That is how I came to run out with the rest of the team at the well-known Jalan Besar Stadium on a very hot evening in front of a very big noisy enthusiastic crowd anxious to see a good old, fast no holds barred rugby game ahead.

The reason for the large crowd was that it had become known "Buzz" Leyland was playing for the Malayan Services side. In rugby circles in the UK, he was a household name being a famous English International player with many Caps - not only before the war but after and for some years. He was a Lieutenant Colonel and CO of the Parachute Regiment stationed in Malaya and we reached the conclusion a lot of his men had also been rugby players. Not only that the Parachute lads along with the Commandoes were recognised as the fittest in the British Army. We tried hard but they beat us easily. Our game plan was to try to keep the ball away from Leyland at stand-off but when he got it, he just "buggered off straight through us".

I was chosen again for a similar game which we won, but Buzz and his boys had departed from Malaya. We were then two evenly matched teams and we scraped home. We were gluttons for punishment. The pitch was always bone hard and after each match we were black and blue and covered in nasty grass burns which could be very painful. But we were young and fit, and it was good clean fun. Buzz (Roy) Leyland died a few years ago (1984) and I was interested to read a lengthy tribute to him in the Daily Telegraph. He had an excellent war service and it mentioned about him being a Lieutenant Colonel in the Parachute Regiment. He also had an outstanding international and club rugby career. I am now sorry I did not cut out the piece about him for my records. I also played a few football matches for the Corps. Looking back it was all go. We must have been a very active lot considering the heat. My fitness then may well have stood me in good stead later on. I think it made me aware of the importance of exercise and looking after yourself.

The elegance and old colonial atmosphere of the Raffles Hotel had fortunately remained although it had been occupied by the Japanese for three and half years. I watched at one of the many punishments given to the Japanese that was to make them realise they were well and truly defeated. A column of more than one thousand of them, marching to attention through all the main streets of Singapore with only an Indian Lance Corporal in command at the head of the column and another of the same rank at the rear.

Making them paint all the kerb stones white right up to the main door of Supreme HQ and when doing so each one of them bow to all ranks in uniform who came within their sight. Those were psychological punishments which really hurt and there were many more. Keep in mind Mountbatten, his Generals, and men of all ranks were livid and outraged when they discovered what the Japanese had been up to when occupying Malaya and Singapore.

I recall the hustle, bustle and food smells of the Chinatown district. All the little narrow streets and the peculiar high-sounding chatter of the language. At every opportunity admiring and being fascinated by the magnificence of the harbour. Watching ships and craft of all sizes from all nations lying off or slowly moving in or out. When on Embarkation Cashiering duty a few of us were invited by our Navy chums to join them for a day inspecting one of the many tiny uninhabited islands in the South Malacca Straits. We knew a hair-raising trip would be in store for us all as we would be travelling on a MTB (Motor Torpedo Boat). The island was many nautical miles away, but we got there in no time at all - or so it seemed. The approach to the island lives in my memory. It was exactly like the illustrations in magazines when you think they must be over the top just too magnificent to be true. Our first sighting was like that but turned out to be true! Brilliant blue calm sea lapping gently onto a golden sandy beach with palm trees, or similar, in the background, the sun blazing down from a clear blue sky. We anchored close in. It must have been close because it was near enough for me to swim ashore having jumped off the bow of the MTB.

We split up into two sections, one to check the interior the other, to which I was allotted, to go round the perimeter including the beach. Our hosts insisted we plastered ourselves with anti-mosquito and insect cream and sure enough a regiment of them awaited us but kept their distance. I think it took us three quarters of an hour to go round. Very hot and we had to take a few rests but what a fascinating place as I do remember it well. Exploring a little island on its own with no one anywhere near at hand. A jungle type interior surrounded by a perfect beach, uninhabited by human beings. It was a great one-time experience. The Navy boys had come well prepared with food and drink. After a swim we were ready for it. We sat on the beach close to the water under a canvas canopy from the boat which they erected. The time came when we just had to leave, and we all got back on board. The throttle was opened up to maximum, we hung on for dear life being frightened half to death. We were almost drowned by the force of the heavy spray caused by the speed we were travelling at. We "buzzed" all the ships on the way back into the harbour then eventually, smoothly and silently glided into the naval base, in ship shape order as if we had been for a gentle cruise around the harbour. It was the end of an eventful day with the Navy. They were mad, but great company and good friends.

By contrast the next day I was walking in the semi-jungle of what had been the beautiful Singapore Golf Course. Trying to locate where the tees and greens had been situated and trying to visualise the holes was an almost impossible job. Similarly walking in a jungle of colour, an amazing sight for what had been the Botanical Gardens. While in Singapore my one huge disappointment was dealing with the Australians. I had a spell of dealing with them and took an immediate dislike to their attitude of being rough tongued, uncouth and arrogant. They got up my nose as they did with most people I knew. One of the very few occasions I had to seriously pull rank, was caused by them. I threatened to have a few of them taken off a troopship when I was Cashiering on board and make sure they would miss the sailing home and must wait for the next ship. They got a hell of a fright as the OC Troops on board backed me up. They were on their bended knees about half an hour before the ship sailed and we then let them go.

Relating my memories of Singapore, I must not forget those who were to me most important of all - my Sergeants. I would have been nothing without them. The system was they were allocated to us from a special pool of them at the CPO. They had all been specially trained for the job and were most efficient at it. We all got to know each other very well as out in the field we had to be a perfect team each sharing equal responsibilities and keeping to a strict accountancy routine. It was essential to have complete faith and trust in one another. I have only been able to remember the odd name so on purpose I have not mentioned any by name, not even the two who were on the plane with me. It is just my way of paying tribute to them all being equally outstanding as Sergeant Field Cashiers. I also just want to mention how very lucky I was to have served my apprenticeship as one at Overlord, which helped me a lot when in Southeast Asia.

I knew my embarkation date was near when I was asked to report for my release medical. It was very important as the army did not want any liability or responsibilities in the future regarding your health. I was delighted when A1 went on my record following a thorough check up. Our section was always advised when a troopship was due. We would receive in advance the name, estimated time of arrival, number on board etc., so we could make our arrangements for arrival. After my medical I made enquiries through our shipping grapevine and received the wonderful news the "Mauretania" was on its way and sure enough my name was on the return voyage list and the ETA was seven days.

I was really excited about the prospect of travelling home on her as she was one of the most famous ships in the world. Cunard White Star Line, 36,000 tons, launched in 1938 and could travel at thirty-five knots. She was surpassed for size and speed only by her two big sisters the renowned 'Queens", Mary and Elizabeth. Without doubt the two most famous ships in the world, pre-war and post-war. When the war began, the three great liners were refitted into troopships, each to carry thousands of men. When the war ended, they had the most outstanding record. They had carried thousands upon thousands of men to all theatres of war and, established a ferry service across the Atlantic loaded with American forces to help our cause and to win. They came through it all unscathed because they were so fast no German naval vessel or U Boat submarine could catch them.

I had a week to clear up and obtain all necessary clearance certificates from the Command Cashier "Dad" Gray and also Ted Blackwell. The Sergeants Mess gave me a farewell "do". There was a get together at the Tanglin Club and of course "quite a night before departure" in our own Mess. It had become routine procedure as for the previous few months hardly a week passed without someone being on their way home. It was always a good excuse for a few drinks to be taken and reminiscences discussed.

When I arrived, I was the rookie, the newest and youngest officer at the CPO and when I departed after eight months, I was considered an old hand at field cashiering. So much had happened in that short space of time and for me every day was an adventure. Looking at the photograph taken outside the Officers Mess a few days after my arrival when all the Field Cashiers throughout Southeast Asia were present for a conference. When I left only the Colonel (Squaw) his three staff officers and Ted Blackwell all regular soldiers remained. New officers had been arriving from the UK and elsewhere but not in such numbers as preparations were well under way for the return of the old peacetime colonial style routine.

Gradually the vast majority of troops throughout the whole of Southeast Asia both British and Allied had gone home for demob. All their essential and necessary requirements were no longer required. It was therefore taken for granted the old pre-war establishment of Field Cashiers and their CPO backups would be able to cope. If another similar photograph had been taken only twelve officers would be in it instead of twenty-one. Everything would soon settle down and be back to the old normal routine in no time. For some, with very short memories, peacetime was great in Malaya and Singapore! Little did they know what was ahead in just a few short years' time.

The whole of Southeast Asia would be in turmoil. Self-government was the demand. Out with the British was the shout. Ships full of British troops arrived again at the famous harbour and all the well-known war time ports. They were piled into Southeast Asia to keep the peace, fierce actions and killings took place. Three years would pass by before the various countries were capable of looking after themselves. Many not very good at it to this day. I would have hated to be a Field Cashier under those circumstances but that is another story well documented in the history books.

During the early morning of the 17th of July 1946, the Mauretania had arrived in the harbour and then berthed in the biggest dock which was quite a way from the town. By daylight it seemed the whole population of Singapore Island and town were down at the dockside, the place was choked with people. The famous lady towering above all the buildings was causing a sensation. The news was that she would be turning round very quickly and be on her return journey that evening as she was attempting to beat the record of Liverpool to Singapore and back which stood at thirty-two days. All the stops were pulled out that day. I think she was carrying two thousand troops and other personnel who had to be disembarked then approximately the same number embarked for the homeward journey.

I was the only officer from CPO embarking but there were also nine Non-Commissioned Officers and other ranks with me. We were all transported down to the docks and found a large crowd of well-wishers whom we knew, from all over the island, some have come from the mainland, Malaya. They had realised it was a sure way of having a close view of the famous ship.

To me however there was above all Lieutenant Colonel Shaw Hamilton doing what came naturally to him with great dignity, charm and sincerity. Saluting each one of us in turn, shaking hands and thanking us for all we had done and wishing us well for the future. I was so fortunate to have served under his command.

I was among the last to go on board and found myself in a four-berth cabin on one of the upper decks with four other officers. Between 9 and 10pm the tugs pulled us very gently away from the quayside out into the harbour. We must have been a magnificent sight as we were floodlit and 'dressed all over" (pendants of all colours strung masthead to masthead and on all the yardarms). There was absolute bedlam in the harbour as all ships including the Navy heavies were blowing and hooting everything at their disposal. What a wonderful never to be forgotten send off.

It was a beautiful night and like many others on board I stayed up on deck until the lights of Singapore and the wonderful harbour I had got to know so well faded into the darkness. The sea was calm and full steam ahead had been rung from the bridge to the engine room. There was a feeling of excitement on board as just out of the harbour the Captain had been on the tannoy confirming we were taking part in what he hoped would be a record run. He intended being at the mouth of the River Mersey on the 3rd of August, which would break the record by two days and so far he was on schedule to do just that.

ACKNOWLEDGEMENTS

The Stark Clan. Celebrating my 47th birthday in 2002.
L to R – Daughter Sarah, wife Christine, son Richard, my mother Norah, me, son
James and my father James

I am indebted to my cousin Sheila Brunies, who lives near Montreal Canada, for meticulously going over all of my typed text and checking, via many emails, for any punctuation and grammatical errors I may have made.

To my wife Christine for her love and loyal support.

To my sister Moira, who due to ill health, never had the opportunity to read our Father's amazing story.

Dear friends Carol & John Graham. Carol published her third book in 2020 and this inspired me to take my Father's memoire to its conclusion and have it published.

To my daughter Sarah and son in law Paul and their two children Ella and Rosie.

My two sons James and Richard who have been so supportive in helping me finally publish their grandfathers book.

.......................This book is for you.

JS Original Binders - Handwritten 90,000 words

Mount Carron, Falkirk, Scotland - Where JS was born 5th September 1920

JS with Father James Stark

WADDIE & CO., LTD.,

EMBOSSING SPECIALISTS

TELEPHONES:
EDINBURGH 30155-6-7
LONDON HOLBORN 8200
SOUTHPORT 1870
CALCUTTA N° CAL 572

GRAMS & CABLES:
"EMBOS, EDINBURGH"
"EMBOSSURS, WESTCENT, LONDON"
CODES A.B.C. 5TH EDITION
BENTLEY'S & PRIVATE

ST. STEPHEN'S WORKS
EDINBURGH

Our Ref.	Your Ref.	Phone Extension	Date
PLB/JMcD	2	2	16th April, 1942.

SECRETARY'S OFFICE

TO WHOM IT MAY CONCERN.

This is to certify that Mr James Stark has been employed by us from the 13th January, 1936 to 22nd April, 1941 when he was called up for Military Service.

During that period he completed a five year's Apprenticeship as stationer and works Estimating Accountant, the major portion of which was spent in estimating and costing. At the outbreak of war our senior Estimating Accountant was called up and Mr James Stark, although only in the middle of his Apprenticeship at the time, took over his work and carried on with the utmost efficiency until called up himself for military service. He has had an excellent training and practical experience in estimating not usually found in so young a man.

In all ways we have found him to be most honest and trustworthy, intelligent and keen on his work, and we can thoroughly recommend him, and look forward to the time when he will return to our employ.

For WADDIE & CO., LIMITED.

M Donald

SECRETARY.

PLUMMER HOUSE
5 & 6 FANCY LANE
CALCUTTA

OFFICES & AGENCIES:—
BANGKOK   COLOMBO   PALESTINE   SHANGHAI
BATAVIA   HONGKONG   RANGOON   SINGAPORE
BOMBAY   KENYA   RHODESIA   SOUTH AFRICA
BRITISH AND DUTCH WEST INDIES AND CENTRAL AMERICA

EXCHANGE BUILDING
4A DES VOEUX ROAD
HONGKONG

April 1942. Letter from Waddies - To Whom It May Concern

JS Home Guard from January 1940 - March 1941. (JS Back row third in from right)

Unit Accountant to Deputy Commander Royal Engineers at Perth and Stirling

JS in uniform with Norah, ready to go to war

JS and Norah's Wedding 17 June 1943

JS seconded to the Royal West African Field Force
Regiment (RWAFFR) services overseas 1945

RWAFFR forward base - Meerut, India, July 1945. (JS seated end left second row)

Command Pay Office - Meerut, India, November 1945. (JS seated end left)

Officers' quarters in Singapore. (JS room top floor rear)

Officers of The Command Pay Office - Singapore. Taken outside officer's mess March 1946. Colonel Shaw-Hamilton Command Paymaster (centre right seated) (JS back row 4th left)

It was hot playing Badminton! (JS Four in form left hand side)

Singapore swimming pool. JS about to dive in

Malayan village on the Buketima Road between Kula Lumpur and Johore

SINGAPORE

Historic Raffles Hotel first opened its doors in 1887

Historic Raffles Hotel Singapore

Top - Japanese Ten Dollar note

The Mauretania. Home in one of the largest fastest troop ships. Singapore to Liverpool in 15 days via Ceylon, Suez Canal, Med, Gibraltar. Very rough at times (3 days in monsoon) and very hot!

Troopship. Having just sailed from Chittagong on the way to Singapore.
(JS on board not in picture)

Singapore harbour. Said to be the finest natural harbour in the world

JS at officers' quarters Singapore

JS Soldiers Service and Pay book (Front)

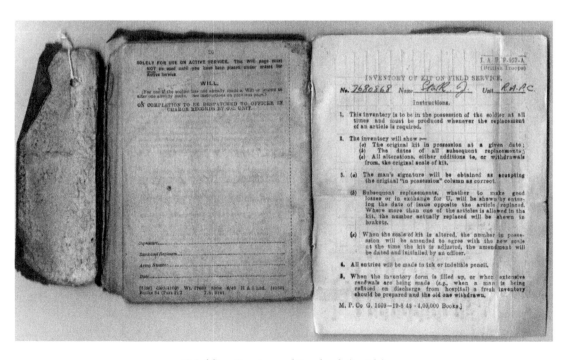

JS Soldiers Service and Pay book (Inside)

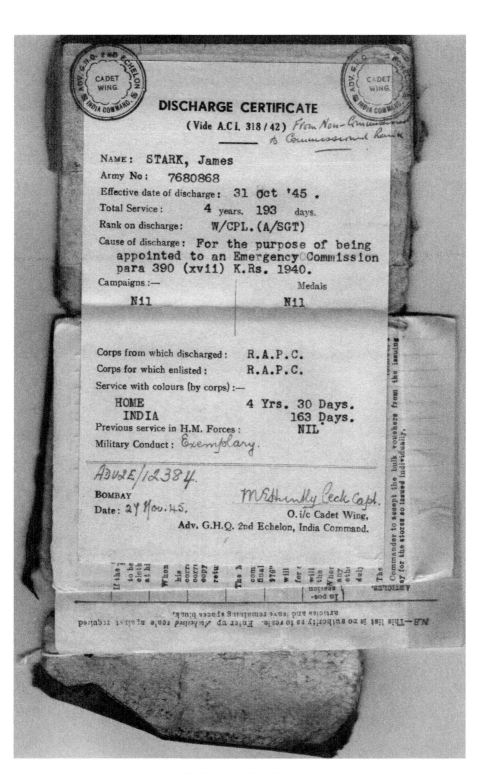

JS Discharge Certificate

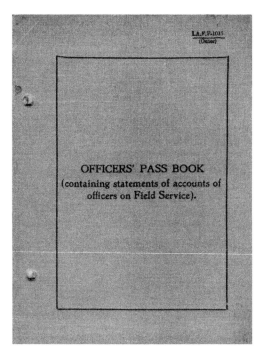

JS Officers Passbook

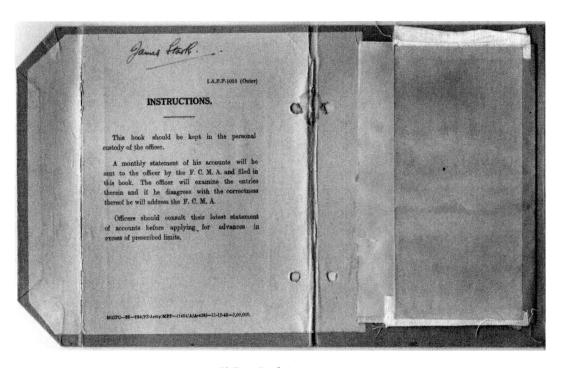

JS Pass Book inner page

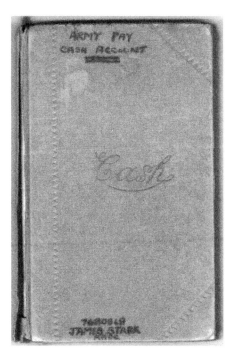

JS Red Book

JS Red Book inner page

<u>Lieut. J. STARK</u>

The above-named is authorised on my behalf to enter the Dock Area of Singapore on Embarkation Cash Duties.

Singapore,
19th June, 1946.

Chapple Lieut.,
for Command Paymaster,
Malaya.

JS Embarkation cash duties slip

23rd August, 1946.

Sir,

Now that the time has come for your release from active military duty, I am commanded by the Army Council to express to you their thanks for the valuable services which you have rendered in the service of your country at a time of grave national emergency.

At the end of the emergency you will relinquish your commission, and at that time a notification will appear in the London Gazette (Supplement), granting you also the honorary rank of **Lieut.** Meanwhile, you have permission to use that rank with effect from the date of your release.

I am, Sir,

Your obedient Servant,

Lieut. J. Stark.

JS Honorary Lieutenant - Release document

Army Form X212
(Original)

RELEASE CERTIFICATE

EMERGENCY COMMISSIONED OFFICERS—REGULAR ARMY

(CLASS "A" RELEASE IN U.K.)

W.S/Lieut. J STARK.
(359408) ROYAL ARMY PAY CORPS

The above-named has been granted *70* days' leave commencing *4·8·46* and is, with effect from *13·10·46*, released from military duty under Regulations for Release from the Army, 1945.

S.E.S. 3
Office Stamp

The War Office
F. 9
13 AUG 1946

Initials RP

NOTICE.

This certificate is not valid unless it bears the official War Office stamp, showing date of issue.

This document is Government property. Any person being in possession of it without authority or excuse is liable under Section 156 (9) of the Army Act to a fine of £20 (twenty pounds), or imprisonment for six months, or to both fine and imprisonment.

IF FOUND, please enclose this certificate in an unstamped envelope and address it to the Under Secretary of State, The War Office, London, S.W.1.

(8617) P.T.O.

JS Release Certificate

Army Form D 407 (W.O.)

DETACH THIS PAGE AND KEEP IT
NOTICE TO RESERVIST WARNING HIM THAT HE WILL BE REQUIRED TO ATTEND FOR TRAINING
(To reproduce the particulars of the Reservist and his training on to page 3, insert carbon)

To (Name and Initials)	STARK. J.		
No. P/359408		Rank (Subs or W/Subs)	LIEUT.
Regt/Corps	R.A.P.C	Class of Reserve	V/LIST.

1. His Majesty's Government has decided that a limited number of reservists should be given training during this year.

2. You have been selected for training under the scheme and will be required to train with :—

(Unit) RP Yamston
from (Date) 12 July 52 to (Date) 26 July 52
at (Provisional Place of Training)

and about two months before you are required, you will be sent a "NOTICE TO JOIN FOR TRAINING" (Army Form D 461).

3. WHAT YOU MUST DO ON RECEIPT OF THIS NOTICE

(a) Detach this page from the remainder of the form.
(b) Acknowledge the receipt of this form by signing on page 3.
(c) Read carefully the instructions and information on the back of this page and comply with the instructions when necessary.
(d) Fold the remainder of the form as indicated and post.
(e) Warn your employer (if any) that you will be recalled for training for the period stated above.

Office Stamp

-1 JAN 1952

Date

Page 1

Reservist Call Up form – 1st January 1952

RESERVE AND AUXILIARY FORCES (TRAINING) ACT, 1951

MINISTRY OF LABOUR AND NATIONAL SERVICE

Local Office................ ACTON LANE

HARLESDEN, N.W.10

Service No. *359408*

2 5 APR 1952 ....(Date)

Mr *J Stark*
39 Hunters Grove
Kenton
Middx

DEAR SIR,

I have been directed by the *Army Council / *Air Council to inform you that in accordance with the Reserve and Auxiliary Forces (Training) Act, 1951, you are required to submit yourself for medical examination by a medical board at *1.0* a.m. / p.m. on *Fri* day, 9 MAY 1952 19......, at the Medical Board Centre,

BLOCK 1., SPUR. 9., GOVERNMENT BUILDINGS

WATFORD ROAD, HARROW, MIDDLESEX

When you attend for medical examination you will be required to furnish details of your family and personal medical history.

If you wear glasses, and in particular if you have any of Service issue Mark III steel-framed or "gas mask" type, you should bring them with you to the Medical Board. On reporting for medical examination you should present this form and your Service Warning Notice, together with your Service Release papers and your National Registration Identity Card, to the clerk in charge of the waiting room.

*A Travelling Warrant for your return journey is enclosed. Before starting your journey you must exchange the warrant for a ticket at the booking office named on the warrant. You should take special care of the return half of the ticket as in the event of loss you will be required to obtain a fresh ticket at normal fare at your own expense.

*If you reside more than six miles from the Medical Board Centre and travel by omnibus or tram your fare will be paid at the Centre. (N.B. Reimbursement of fares is restricted to the cost of the cheapest means of travel.)

Any subsistence allowances which may become payable to you in accordance with the scale overleaf will be paid to you on application when you attend at the Medical Board Centre.

Immediately on receipt of this notice, you should inform your employer of the date and time at which you are required to attend for medical examination.

Your attention is directed to the Note printed on the back of this Notice.

Yours faithfully, ...

Manager.

*Delete if not applicable.

Z.R.6. (Revised)

[P.T.O.

Reservist Training Form – 25th April 1952

War Medals

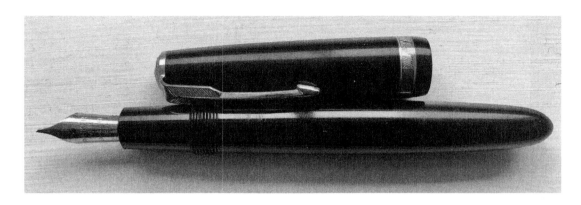

Parker Duofold 14ct Nib Fountain Pen. Awarded to JS by his Japanese prisoners!

10 Sedberge Road, Wallasey. The home of JS parents photographed shortly after the war

*JS returns to what was CRE Headquarters Edinburgh,
during the war. (Return visit 2nd May 1991)*

Daniel Stewarts College, Edinburgh. JS attended from 1930 - 1936

Waddie & Co, Edinburgh. (For many years Scotland's largest printers) JS went from apprentice, starting in 1936, to Board Director in 1959. Retiring after forty five years' service in 1980

Printed in Great Britain
by Amazon

83179635R00160